# VISUAL QUICKSTART GUIDE

# Eudora

## FOR WINDOWS & MACINTOSH

Adam C. Engst

Peachpit Press

Visual QuickStart Guide
# Eudora for Windows & Macintosh
Adam C. Engst

## Peachpit Press
1249 Eighth Street
Berkeley, CA 94710
(510) 548-4393
(510) 548-5991 (fax)

Find us on the World Wide Web at: http://www.peachpit.com/

Peachpit Press is a division of Addison Wesley Longman

Copyright © 1997 by Adam C. Engst

Cover design: The Visual Group

### Notice of rights
All rights reserved. No part of this book may be reproduced or transmitted in any form or by any means, electronic, mechanical, photocopying, recording, or otherwise, without prior written permission of the publisher. For more information on getting permission for reprints and excerpts, contact Trish Booth at Peachpit Press.

### Notice of liability
The information in this book is distributed on an "As is" basis, without warranty. While every precaution has been taken in the preparation of this book, neither the author nor Peachpit Press shall have any liability to any person or entity with respect to any loss or damage caused or alleged to be caused directly or indirectly by the instructions contained in this book or by the computer software and hardware products described herein.

### Trademarks
Eudora is a registered trademark and Eudora Pro and Eudora Light are trademarks of QUALCOMM Incorporated.

Throughout this book trademarked names are used. Rather than put a trademark symbol in every occurrence of a trademarked name, we state we are using the names only in an editorial fashion and to the benefit of the trademark owner with no intention of infringement of the copyright.

ISBN: 0-201-69663-0

0 9 8 7 6 5 4 3 2 1

Printed and bound in the United States of America

Printed on recycled paper

## Dedication

To my grandparents, Bernard and Estelle Deutsch, for whom I set up an elderly Macintosh SE/30 with Eudora Light when I was starting this book. Since then, they've become email aficionados, communicating regularly via email with the rest of our family.

## About the author

Adam Engst is the editor and publisher of *TidBITS*, one of the oldest and largest Internet-based newsletters, distributed every week to hundreds of thousands of readers. He has written and co-authored numerous Internet books and magazine articles, including the best-selling *Internet Starter Kit* series. In addition, he has collaborated on several Internet educational videos and has appeared on a variety of nationally broadcast television and radio programs. He has yet to be turned into an action figure.

Adam graduated from Cornell University with a double major in Hypertextual Fiction and Classics. He lives on a mountain in the Pacific Northwest with his wife Tonya and a dedicated Internet connection.

Please send any comments regarding this book to Adam at: *eudora-vqs@tidbits.com*

## Other books by Adam Engst

The Official AT&T WorldNet Web Discovery Guide

Internet Starter Kit for Macintosh, 4th Edition

Internet Starter Kit for Windows 95

Simply Amazing Internet for Macintosh

Internet Starter Kit for Windows, 2nd Edition

Internet Explorer Kit for Macintosh

## Acknowledgements

No computer book is the work of a single person these days, and I had able assistance from numerous people while working on this book. Some of the most helpful were:

Tonya Engst, who is not only my wonderful wife, but also a great copy editor.

Nancy Davis, my editor at Peachpit, who made great comments and was utterly relaxed.

David Rogelberg of Studio B, my agent, who made this book a reality.

Steve Dorner, for writing Eudora.

Pete Resnick, Gary Nash, John Noerenberg, and everyone else at Qualcomm for answering questions about current and future versions of Eudora.

## Colophon

I wrote this book using the following pieces of software:

- The Macintosh and Windows versions of Eudora Light and Eudora Pro (of course!)
- QuarkXPress 3.32 (the page layout beast)
- Snapz Pro 1.0.1 and SnagIt/32 4.0 (for Mac and Windows screenshots)
- clip2gif 0.7.2 (for screenshot conversions)

In terms of hardware, I rely on:

- A Power Macintosh 8500/150 with a pair of 20-inch color monitors (he who dies with the most pixels wins)
- A no-name Pentium 150 running Windows 95 (it works)
- A dedicated 56K frame relay connection to the Internet (watch out, they're addictive)

## People

Book Design: Adam Engst

Editor: Nancy Davis

Copy Editor: Tonya Engst

Index: Rebecca Plunkett

# Table of Contents

| | | |
|---|---|---:|
| | **Introduction** | **xi** |
| **Chapter 1:** | **Eudora Basics** | **1** |
| | Hardware and software requirements . . . . . . . . . . . | 2 |
| | Getting Eudora . . . . . . . . . . . . . . . . . . . . . . . . . . . . . | 3 |
| | Installing Eudora . . . . . . . . . . . . . . . . . . . . . . . . . . . . | 4 |
| | Launching and quitting Eudora . . . . . . . . . . . . . . . . | 6 |
| | Configuring Eudora . . . . . . . . . . . . . . . . . . . . . . . . . | 7 |
| | Configuring Eudora for multiple people . . . . . . . . . | 8 |
| | Configuring Eudora Pro for multiple accounts . . . | 10 |
| | RAM requirements . . . . . . . . . . . . . . . . . . . . . . . . . | 11 |
| | Official help resources . . . . . . . . . . . . . . . . . . . . . . | 12 |
| | Unofficial help resources . . . . . . . . . . . . . . . . . . . . | 13 |
| | Email glossary . . . . . . . . . . . . . . . . . . . . . . . . . . . . . | 14 |
| **Chapter 2:** | **Creating Messages** | **17** |
| | Creating a new message . . . . . . . . . . . . . . . . . . . . . | 18 |
| | Replying to a message . . . . . . . . . . . . . . . . . . . . . . | 19 |
| | Replying to part of a message . . . . . . . . . . . . . . . . | 20 |
| | Replying to all recipients . . . . . . . . . . . . . . . . . . . . | 21 |
| | Forwarding a message . . . . . . . . . . . . . . . . . . . . . . | 22 |
| | Redirecting a message . . . . . . . . . . . . . . . . . . . . . . | 23 |
| | Sending a message again . . . . . . . . . . . . . . . . . . . . | 24 |
| | Using the recipient list . . . . . . . . . . . . . . . . . . . . . . | 25 |
| | Turbo redirecting a message . . . . . . . . . . . . . . . . . | 26 |
| | Creating a stationery message . . . . . . . . . . . . . . . . | 27 |
| | Creating a new message using stationery . . . . . . . | 28 |
| | Replying to a message using stationery . . . . . . . . . | 29 |
| **Chapter 3:** | **Writing Messages** | **31** |
| | Addressing messages . . . . . . . . . . . . . . . . . . . . . . . | 32 |
| | Choosing a personality . . . . . . . . . . . . . . . . . . . . . | 33 |
| | Entering a subject . . . . . . . . . . . . . . . . . . . . . . . . . . | 34 |
| | Text selection and navigation . . . . . . . . . . . . . . . . | 35 |
| | Entering text . . . . . . . . . . . . . . . . . . . . . . . . . . . . . . | 36 |
| | Editing text . . . . . . . . . . . . . . . . . . . . . . . . . . . . . . . | 37 |
| | About message plug-ins . . . . . . . . . . . . . . . . . . . . . | 38 |
| | Spell checking . . . . . . . . . . . . . . . . . . . . . . . . . . . . . | 39 |
| | Spell checking options . . . . . . . . . . . . . . . . . . . . . . | 41 |

Formatting text . . . . . . . . . . . . . . . . . . . . . . . . . . . 42
Changing the font . . . . . . . . . . . . . . . . . . . . . . . . . 43
Changing font styles . . . . . . . . . . . . . . . . . . . . . . . 44
Changing font colors . . . . . . . . . . . . . . . . . . . . . . . 45
Changing font sizes . . . . . . . . . . . . . . . . . . . . . . . . 46
Changing justification . . . . . . . . . . . . . . . . . . . . . . 47
Changing indents . . . . . . . . . . . . . . . . . . . . . . . . . 48
About signatures . . . . . . . . . . . . . . . . . . . . . . . . . . 49
Creating and using signatures . . . . . . . . . . . . . . . . 50
Custom signatures . . . . . . . . . . . . . . . . . . . . . . . . . 51
Editing signatures . . . . . . . . . . . . . . . . . . . . . . . . . 52
About attachments . . . . . . . . . . . . . . . . . . . . . . . . 53
Attaching files via dialog box . . . . . . . . . . . . . . . . 54
Attaching files via drag-and-drop . . . . . . . . . . . . . 55
Attachment formats . . . . . . . . . . . . . . . . . . . . . . . 56
Outgoing message toolbar menus . . . . . . . . . . . . . 57
Outgoing message toolbar buttons . . . . . . . . . . . . 58
PureVoice plug-in . . . . . . . . . . . . . . . . . . . . . . . . . 59
PGP plug-in . . . . . . . . . . . . . . . . . . . . . . . . . . . . . 60

## Chapter 4: Sending and Receiving Messages  61
Sending queued messages . . . . . . . . . . . . . . . . . . . 62
Sending messages immediately . . . . . . . . . . . . . . . 63
Sending messages at a later date or time . . . . . . . . 64
Preventing a message from being sent . . . . . . . . . 65
Checking for incoming messages . . . . . . . . . . . . . 66
Checking for incoming messages periodically . . . 67
About messages left on the server . . . . . . . . . . . . . 68
Leaving mail on the server . . . . . . . . . . . . . . . . . . 69
Retrieving only small messages . . . . . . . . . . . . . . . 70
Special mail transfer options . . . . . . . . . . . . . . . . . 71

## Chapter 5: Working with Messages  73
Selecting messages . . . . . . . . . . . . . . . . . . . . . . . . 74
Opening messages . . . . . . . . . . . . . . . . . . . . . . . . . 75
Changing message priority . . . . . . . . . . . . . . . . . . 76
Changing message labels . . . . . . . . . . . . . . . . . . . . 77
Changing message status . . . . . . . . . . . . . . . . . . . . 78
Changing message personality . . . . . . . . . . . . . . . 79
Changing message text . . . . . . . . . . . . . . . . . . . . . 80
Revealing boring headers . . . . . . . . . . . . . . . . . . . 81
Navigating within messages . . . . . . . . . . . . . . . . . 82
Navigating between messages . . . . . . . . . . . . . . . . 83
Visiting URLs . . . . . . . . . . . . . . . . . . . . . . . . . . . . 84
Deleting messages . . . . . . . . . . . . . . . . . . . . . . . . . 85

Transferring messages to mailboxes . . . . . . . . . . . 86
Opening attachments . . . . . . . . . . . . . . . . . . . . . . 87
Moving attachments . . . . . . . . . . . . . . . . . . . . . . . 88
Deleting attachments. . . . . . . . . . . . . . . . . . . . . . . 89
Saving messages . . . . . . . . . . . . . . . . . . . . . . . . . 90
Printing messages . . . . . . . . . . . . . . . . . . . . . . . . 91

## Chapter 6: Working with Mailboxes    93
Opening mailboxes. . . . . . . . . . . . . . . . . . . . . . . . 94
Sorting messages in a mailbox . . . . . . . . . . . . . . 95
Different types of sorts . . . . . . . . . . . . . . . . . . . . 96
Creating mailboxes . . . . . . . . . . . . . . . . . . . . . . . 97
Transferring messages into mailboxes. . . . . . . . . 98
Creating a mailbox during a message transfer. . . . 99
Creating mailbox folders using menus . . . . . . . . 100
Creating mailbox folders in
 the Mailboxes window . . . . . . . . . . . . . . . . 101
Opening and closing mailbox folders. . . . . . . . . 102
Renaming mailboxes and mailbox folders . . . . . 103
Reorganizing mailboxes and folders. . . . . . . . . . 104
Deleting mailboxes and mailbox folders. . . . . . . 105
Compacting mailboxes . . . . . . . . . . . . . . . . . . . 106
Eudora and aliases. . . . . . . . . . . . . . . . . . . . . . . 107
Being a pack rat. . . . . . . . . . . . . . . . . . . . . . . . . 108
Taking out the trash . . . . . . . . . . . . . . . . . . . . . 109

## Chapter 7: Working with Filters    111
Creating filters . . . . . . . . . . . . . . . . . . . . . . . . . 112
Selecting messages to filter . . . . . . . . . . . . . . . . 113
Header lines . . . . . . . . . . . . . . . . . . . . . . . . . . . 114
Contains menu . . . . . . . . . . . . . . . . . . . . . . . . . 115
Filter actions . . . . . . . . . . . . . . . . . . . . . . . . . . . 116
Activating filters . . . . . . . . . . . . . . . . . . . . . . . . 117
Filter ideas . . . . . . . . . . . . . . . . . . . . . . . . . . . . 118
Finding filters . . . . . . . . . . . . . . . . . . . . . . . . . . 119
Modifying filters. . . . . . . . . . . . . . . . . . . . . . . . 120
Reordering filters . . . . . . . . . . . . . . . . . . . . . . . 121
Deleting filters . . . . . . . . . . . . . . . . . . . . . . . . . 122

## Chapter 8: Finding and Searching    123
Finding text in a message . . . . . . . . . . . . . . . . . 124
Searching for text in a mailbox. . . . . . . . . . . . . 126
Searching for text in a mailbox folder. . . . . . . . 127
Searching in multiple mailboxes. . . . . . . . . . . . 128
Searching for text in message summaries . . . . . 130
Searching tips and tricks. . . . . . . . . . . . . . . . . . 131

# Table of Contents

### Chapter 9: Working with the Address Book — 133
Creating nicknames for individuals. . . . . . . . . . 134
Creating group nicknames . . . . . . . . . . . . . . . 135
Nickname tips. . . . . . . . . . . . . . . . . . . . . . . . 136
Using the Address Book window . . . . . . . . . . 137
Adding nicknames to messages. . . . . . . . . . . . 138
Multiple nicknames files . . . . . . . . . . . . . . . . . 139
Finding nicknames . . . . . . . . . . . . . . . . . . . . . 140
Modifying nicknames. . . . . . . . . . . . . . . . . . . 141
Managing your recipient list . . . . . . . . . . . . . . 142
Deleting nicknames . . . . . . . . . . . . . . . . . . . . 143

### Chapter 10: Working with the Toolbar — 145
Turning the toolbar on and off . . . . . . . . . . . . 146
Toolbar settings. . . . . . . . . . . . . . . . . . . . . . . . 147
Default toolbar functions . . . . . . . . . . . . . . . . 148
Adding a button to the toolbar . . . . . . . . . . . . 149
Button ideas . . . . . . . . . . . . . . . . . . . . . . . . . . 151
Moving toolbar buttons . . . . . . . . . . . . . . . . . 152
Deleting toolbar buttons . . . . . . . . . . . . . . . . . 153
Changing button functions. . . . . . . . . . . . . . . 154

### Chapter 11: Using Directory Services — 155
Setting up Ph and Finger. . . . . . . . . . . . . . . . . 156
Selecting another Ph server . . . . . . . . . . . . . . . 157
Searching a Ph server . . . . . . . . . . . . . . . . . . . 158
Using the results of a Ph search . . . . . . . . . . . . 159
Searching a Finger server . . . . . . . . . . . . . . . . 160
Online directories on the Web . . . . . . . . . . . . 161

### Chapter 12: Working with Settings/Options — 163
Getting Started . . . . . . . . . . . . . . . . . . . . . . . . 164
Personal Information . . . . . . . . . . . . . . . . . . . 165
Hosts. . . . . . . . . . . . . . . . . . . . . . . . . . . . . . . . 166
Checking Mail. . . . . . . . . . . . . . . . . . . . . . . . . 167
Sending Mail. . . . . . . . . . . . . . . . . . . . . . . . . . 168
Attachments . . . . . . . . . . . . . . . . . . . . . . . . . . 169
Fonts & Display . . . . . . . . . . . . . . . . . . . . . . . . 170
Toolbar . . . . . . . . . . . . . . . . . . . . . . . . . . . . . . 171
Eudora Labels/Labels . . . . . . . . . . . . . . . . . . . 172
Getting Attention . . . . . . . . . . . . . . . . . . . . . . 173
Extra Warnings . . . . . . . . . . . . . . . . . . . . . . . . 174
Replying . . . . . . . . . . . . . . . . . . . . . . . . . . . . . 175
OT/PPP and MacSLIP / Advanced Network . . . . 176
Moving Around. . . . . . . . . . . . . . . . . . . . . . . . 177

Miscellaneous . . . . . . . . . . . . . . . . . . . . . . . . . . . 178
Settings Icons . . . . . . . . . . . . . . . . . . . . . . . . . . 179
Mailbox Columns . . . . . . . . . . . . . . . . . . . . . . . 180
Styled Text . . . . . . . . . . . . . . . . . . . . . . . . . . . . . 181
Personalities and Personality Extras. . . . . . . . . . 182
Spell Checking . . . . . . . . . . . . . . . . . . . . . . . . . 183

# Index 185

# Keyboard Shortcuts

# INTRODUCTION

Welcome to the Visual QuickStart Guide for Eudora, one of the most popular and powerful Internet email programs. Some eighteen million Internet users, myself included, rely on Eudora every day.

If you're getting started with Eudora, this book will provide you with the information you need to become a fluent Eudora user.

Or, perhaps you're a Eudora fan already and want to make the most of Eudora. If so, you won't be disappointed. Eudora has a lot of power under the hood, and this book brings it to the surface.

## What is Eudora?

Eudora is an email client program. It enables you to write and send email, and to receive and read email. Eudora has numerous other features that enhance these basic capabilities.

More important, Eudora uses standard Internet methods of transferring mail, called SMTP and POP (check the email glossary in Chapter 1, "Eudora Basics," for definitions). As a user, you need not care about specific protocols; what you should realize is that you can use Eudora with almost any Internet service provider and many corporate networks.

Introduction

# About Eudora...

Eudora was the brainchild of a programmer named Steve Dorner, then working at the University of Illinois at Urbana-Champaign. Early versions of Eudora were free from the University of Illinois, but in 1992, Steve joined Qualcomm, a large company primarily focused on wireless communications. At Qualcomm, Steve continued to enhance Eudora. Qualcomm soon created two versions, Eudora Light and Eudora Pro.

Eudora Light is essentially a stripped-down version of Eudora Pro, but for many people, Eudora Light offers sufficient power and flexibility. The other significant difference is that Eudora Light is completely free, whereas Qualcomm sells Eudora Pro for prices ranging from $50 to $90, depending on the vendor.

Most people start with Eudora Light because it's good and it's free. After a while, if you receive a lot of email, you start to think that the additional features in Eudora Pro would be handy, which is how Qualcomm entices people to upgrade to the commercial version.

The current versions of Eudora are 3.1 on the Mac and 3.0 on Windows (see **Figure 1** through **Figure 4** for the About Eudora dialog boxes), and those are the versions I cover in this book. However, Steve and the other programmers working on Eudora are sensitive about making changes to a program that so many people use regularly, so I'm confident that the information in this book will apply to future versions of Eudora as well.

## ✔ Tip

- Steve Dorner named Eudora after the writer Eudora Welty, specifically because of her story "Why I Live at the P.O." It's on the Web at http://www.torget.se/artbin/art/or_weltypostoff.html.

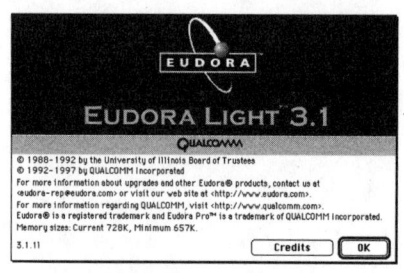

**Figure 1** The About Eudora dialog box for the Mac version of Eudora Light.

**Figure 2** The About Eudora dialog box for the Windows version of Eudora Light.

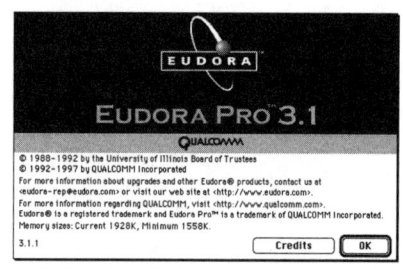

**Figure 3** The About Eudora dialog box for the Mac version of Eudora Pro.

**Figure 4** The About Eudora dialog box for the Windows version of Eudora Pro.

## Macintosh and Windows differences

Eudora is one of the best of today's breed of programs that provide extremely similar interfaces and features in the Macintosh and Windows versions of the program.

Unfortunately, human interface requirements on the Mac and Windows differ, so, in a few places, Eudora's programmers were forced to trade consistency between the platforms for following the appropriate human interface guidelines for each platform.

### Dealing with differences

- If there is no difference between the Mac and Windows versions of Eudora for a specific feature, I make no explicit comment either way.

- If a dialog box, window, or settings panel simply has a different name on the different platforms, I separate the names with a slash, putting the Mac name first, as in "Open the Settings/Options dialog box."

- If a difference is minor, I build it into the discussion, as in "Choose Filters from the Special menu (Mac) or Tools menu (Windows)."

- If a difference is major, I either write separate steps for that task or devote separate pages to each platform, clearly marking each page with a "Macintosh Only!" or "Windows Only!" graphic.

- I alternate between Mac and Windows screen shots throughout the book to illustrate features appropriately. For brevity's sake, I don't label them explicitly—I assume Mac users can recognize a Mac screen shot and Windows users can recognize a Windows screen shot.

# Eudora Light and Eudora Pro differences

As I noted before, Eudora Light is essentially a stripped-down version of Eudora Pro. Many of the high-end features in Eudora Pro don't exist in Eudora Light or are present in a limited fashion.

## Dealing with differences

- When I refer to the program generically, I just call it Eudora. However, when I wish to distinguish between Eudora Light and Eudora Pro, I use the full specific name.

- If there is no difference between Eudora Light and Eudora Pro for a specific feature, I make no explicit comment either way.

- If Eudora Pro has some minor additional feature, such as a menu with an additional item or a unique shortcut, I either include a parenthetical, as in "(Pro only)," or write a separate tip or comment discussing that feature.

- When Eudora Pro offers a major feature that's not in Eudora Light, I devote a separate page to that feature, clearly marking the page with a "Eudora Pro Only!" graphic.

- I use Eudora Pro, so all the screen shots in the book come from Eudora Pro. I believe it's better for Eudora Light users to see what they're missing than to confuse Eudora Pro users with shorter menus and other missing interface items.

**EUDORA PRO ONLY!**

## How to use this book

If you've never used a Visual QuickStart Guide from Peachpit Press (there are dozens of them, covering most major software packages and numerous other topics), I think you'll enjoy this book.

Unlike more traditional computer books, Visual QuickStart Guides focus on specific tasks, with screen shots parallel to the tasks being explained so you can easily follow along. Most tasks are simple and take only a few steps and a single page.

When a topic doesn't lend itself to step-by-step instructions, a Visual QuickStart Guide includes a clearly written list of possibilities rather than paragraph upon paragraph of explanatory text.

You may want to read the book from front to back. This method is probably the best for beginners. I've organized both the chapters in the book and the topics within each chapter in the order you're likely to experience them. So, for instance, in the chapter about Eudora's Filters, I work through creating filters, activating filters, ideas on using the filters you've created, finding filters, modifying filters, and deleting filters.

Alternately, if you're more of an experienced Eudora user, open to the Table of Contents and look for the task you're interested in performing. Once you've used the book for a while, you can probably just flip through the pages of the appropriate chapter—I've found myself doing that with other Visual QuickStart Guides.

### The unnecessary details

This book covers all the features of Eudora that you're likely to use in normal situations. It does not delve into the truly geeky ways in which you can customize Eudora using AppleScript (Mac), editing your Eudora Settings file using Apple's ResEdit (Mac) or by editing your eudora.ini file (Windows).

That additional flexibility can be useful, but few Eudora users ever need it. If you do, more information is available from the unofficial help resources listed in Chapter 1, "Eudora Basics."

Introduction

# Why I wrote this book

I was thrilled when Peachpit Press approached me about writing this book. I've written numerous books about the Internet before, but none about a specific program. The Internet is a huge topic to cover, whereas delving into the inner workings of a single program is rather a different task.

And what a program! We all have our favorite programs, and Eudora ranks right up there for me. Eudora launches at startup on both my Mac and my PC, and it's always available, sending and receiving mail automatically throughout every working day. I receive between 100 and 200 messages each day, and I send about 50 messages a day. In addition, I save a fair amount of my incoming mail and all outgoing messages, so I have over 200 megabytes of stored messages covering the last few years of my life.

In short, I rely heavily on Eudora. I've looked at numerous other email programs over the years, and nothing has come close to providing Eudora's power and ease-of-use when dealing with that amount of mail.

I hope my enthusiasm for Eudora comes through in this book, and even more important, I hope that you find this book an enjoyable and useful adjunct to Eudora itself. Let's start exploring!

# Eudora Basics

In this chapter, I introduce some of the basics of Eudora and email that will help you make the best use of the rest of the book.

We'll look at the hardware and software requirements for using Eudora to ensure that you can run Eudora on your computer. In case you don't have the latest version of Eudora, I'll also explain how to get a copy.

Once you have Eudora installed, we'll take a quick look at how you set up Eudora for basic use. The rest of the book explains how you use the program in much more depth, of course, but just in case, I'll show you where to find even more help on the Internet.

Finally, so you don't become overwhelmed with the terminology, this chapter includes a short email glossary as well.

Come then, and let's start exploring Eudora. Once you've read this chapter, feel free to flip around in the book for the specific pieces of information that you need.

# Hardware and software requirements

Eudora has fairly minimal hardware and software requirements.

## Macintosh requirements

- A Macintosh Plus or later model, with a high-density disk drive if you purchase Eudora Pro on floppy disk.

- Macintosh System 7.0 or later.

- An email account with an Internet service provider or one that's accessible via an Internet-capable network connection.

- Some non-essential features of Eudora rely on additional software called Macintosh Drag and Drop. It was included in System 7 Pro and all versions of the system software after System 7.5, but not in earlier versions of System 7. The easiest way to get drag-and-drop capabilities is to upgrade to the latest version of Apple's system software that's appropriate for your Mac. Consult your Apple dealer, but note that Mac OS 8 is appropriate for 68040- and PowerPC-based Macs.

## Windows requirements

- IBM-compatible PC.

- Microsoft Windows 95 or Windows NT 3.51 or later for the 32-bit version of Eudora. You can use Microsoft Windows 3.1 with the 16-bit version of Eudora, but it will look and act slightly differently from the 32-bit version covered here.

- Winsock 1.1 networking package (the Microsoft TCP/IP networking included in Windows 95 is ideal).

- An email account with an Internet service provider or one that's accessible via an Internet-capable network connection.

### Macintosh System 6

Older Macintosh computers might be running System 6. If that's true, and if upgrading to System 7 isn't feasible (it requires at least 4 MB of RAM), you can download and use Eudora 1.3.1 for free. It's not nearly as capable as current versions of Eudora Light or Eudora Pro, but Eudora 1.3.1 works fine on those older machines, assuming that they can connect to the Internet. If you do use Eudora 1.3.1, be aware that many features discussed in this book won't be available.

# Getting Eudora

If you don't have the latest version of Eudora Light, or if you want to purchase Eudora Pro, there are several ways to get a copy.

## Methods of getting Eudora Light

- Using a Web browser, go to http://www.eudora.com/ (**Figure 1**), follow the links to the Eudora Light page, and then download a copy.

- Using a Web browser or an FTP program, go to ftp://ftp.eudora.com/eudora/eudoralight/ and navigate to the proper Mac or Windows folder, where you can download a copy.

## Methods of getting Eudora Pro

- Using a Web browser, go to http://www.eudora.com/ and download a demo copy that works for 30 days.

- Using a Web browser or an FTP program, go to ftp://ftp.eudora.com/eudora/eudorapro/ and navigate to the proper Mac or Windows folder, where you can download a demo copy that works for 30 days.

- If you have Eudora Light, you can request an ordering program that you can use to fill out an order.

    In the Mac version, choose Purchasing Information (**Figure 2**) from the Guide menu (it looks like a question mark).

    In the Windows version, choose Request Ordering Program (**Figure 3**) from the Eudora Pro menu.

- Visit a software store that carries Eudora Pro (it might be hard to find in most general computer stores) or an online software vendor like Cyberian Outpost at http://www.cybout.com/ and buy a copy.

**Figure 1** You can download a copy of Eudora Light or a demo of Eudora Pro from the Eudora Web site.

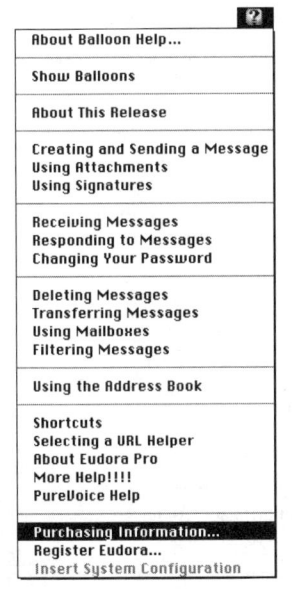

**Figure 2** To request a copy of the Eudora Pro ordering program in the Mac version of Eudora Light, choose Purchasing Information from the Guide menu.

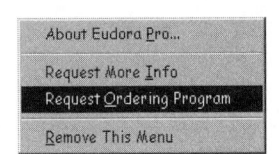

**Figure 3** To request a copy of the Eudora Pro ordering program in the Windows version of Eudora Light, choose Request Ordering Program from the Eudora Pro menu.

Chapter 1

# Installing Eudora

Once you've downloaded or purchased a copy of Eudora, you must install it on your computer. For the most part, the installation process is self-documenting, so I won't discuss every possible step here.

## To install Eudora

1. Double-click the Eudora installer.

   The installer displays a splash screen, then a ReadMe screen, and finally the installation window (**Figure 4**).

2. Select Full Eudora Pro or Full Eudora Light, and click the Install button.

   The installer first warns you that you'll need to restart, then asks if you want to install a 680x0, PowerPC, or Universal version of Eudora (**Figure 5**).

3. If you use a Power Mac, I recommend you click either PowerPC or Universal. If you use a 68000-based Macintosh, click either 680x0 or Universal. If you think you'll switch between a 68000-based Mac and a Power Mac, click Universal.

   The installer presents you with a dialog box asking you where you want to store the program (**Figure 6**).

4. Select a location for Eudora and click the Install button.

   The installer copies all the necessary files to your hard disk, then displays a dialog box asking you to restart.

5. Click Restart to restart your Mac.

   When the Mac restarts, you're ready to use Eudora.

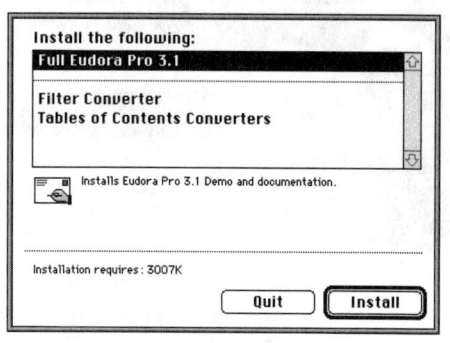

**Figure 4** To install Eudora, click Full Eudora Pro 3.1 (this line may look different for you—I'm installing the demo of Eudora Pro 3.1 here) and then click Install.

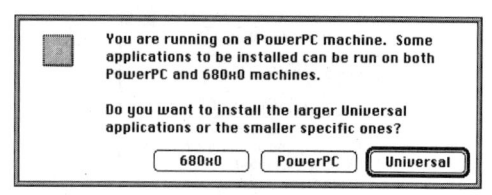

**Figure 5** The installer asks which version you want to install. Click the button that corresponds to your desired version.

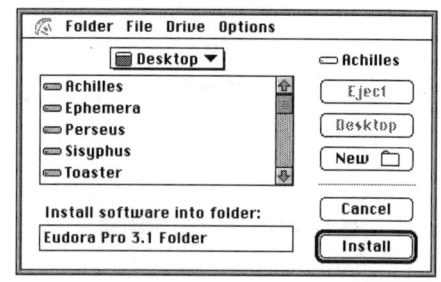

**Figure 6** The installer then asks where you want to store the Eudora program. Navigate to the desired location, then click the Install button.

## Installing Eudora

Once you've downloaded or purchased a copy of Eudora, you must install it on your computer. For the most part, the installation process is self-documenting, so I won't discuss every possible step here.

### To install Eudora

1. Double-click the Eudora installer.

   The installer displays a welcome screen, then a license screen, and finally the installation window, where it asks you to select a location for the Eudora program (**Figure 7**).

2. If you don't want to store Eudora in the default location, click Browse, and select a location. Then click the Next button.

   The installer asks which version of Eudora you want to install (**Figure 8**).

3. If you use Windows 95 or Windows NT, select the 32-bit version of Eudora and click Next. If you use Windows 3.1, select the 16-bit version of Eudora and click the Next button.

   The installer summarizes what you've asked it to do (**Figure 9**).

4. Click the Next button.

   The installer copies all necessary files to your hard disk, then displays a dialog box asking if you want to read the README file.

5. Click Yes if you want to read the README file or No if you don't. Either way, the installation process is finished at that point.

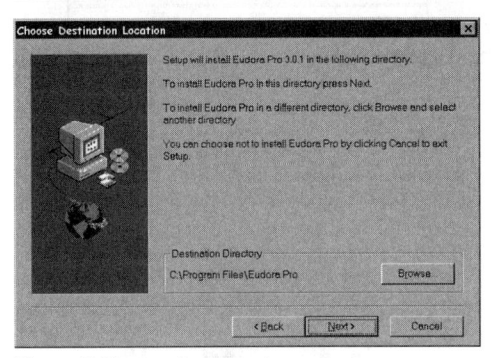

**Figure 7** The installer asks where you want to store the Eudora program. Either choose the default, or click the Browse button and navigate to the desired location. When you're done, click the Next button.

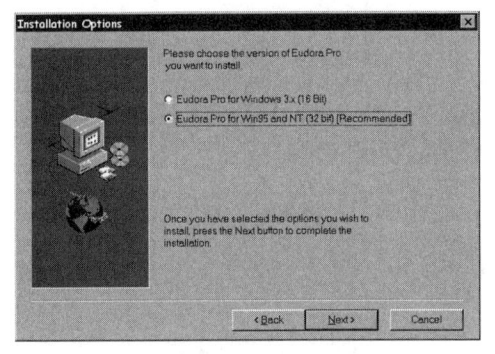

**Figure 8** The installer then asks which version of Eudora you want to install. If you use Windows 95 or Windows NT, select the 32-bit version. If you use Windows 3.1, select the 16-bit version. Then click the Next button.

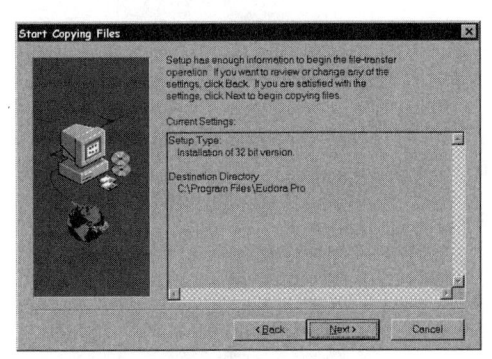

**Figure 9** Then, the installer presents a summary of what it will do. Click the Next button to start copying files to your hard disk.

Chapter 1

# Launching and quitting Eudora

After you've installed Eudora, the next step is to launch the program.

### Launching Eudora (I)

1. In the Macintosh Finder or the Windows desktop, find the Eudora icon (**Figure 10** and **Figure 11**).

2. Double-click the Eudora icon to launch Eudora.

### Launching Eudora (II-Windows)

1. From the hierarchical Programs menu in the Start menu, choose Eudora (**Figure 12**).

### Quitting Eudora

1. From the File menu, choose Quit (Mac) or Exit (Windows).

   Eudora quits, prompting you to send queued messages first if you have any waiting to go out.

### ✔ Tips

- If you use a Macintosh, I encourage you to make an alias to Eudora and place it either in your Apple Menu Items folder (so it appears in your Apple menu) or on your desktop for easy access.

- If you use Windows, I encourage you to make a shortcut to Eudora and place it on your desktop for easy access.

- If you plan to use Eudora all the time, as I do, consider putting an alias (Mac) or a shortcut (Windows) to Eudora in your Startup Items folder (Mac) or your Start menu (Windows). That way, Eudora will launch whenever you turn on your computer.

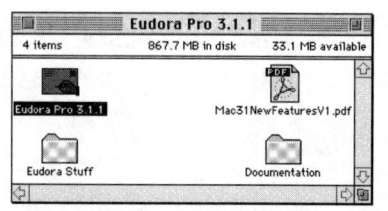

**Figure 10** To launch the Mac version of Eudora, double-click the Eudora icon in the Finder.

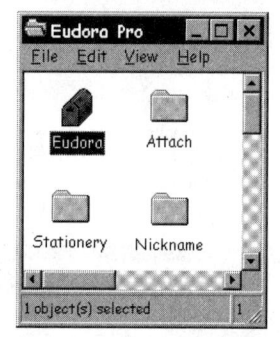

**Figure 11** To launch the Windows version of Eudora, double-click the Eudora icon in the Windows desktop.

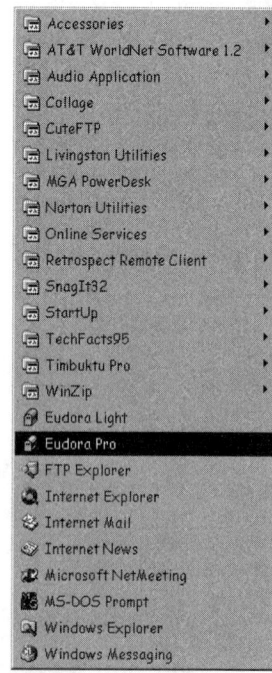

**Figure 12** Alternately, to launch Eudora in Windows, choose Eudora from the hierarchical Programs menu in the Start menu.

# Configuring Eudora

Now you must enter the minimal information required to send and receive mail. Eudora has many other settings; here I cover the essential ones for getting started. (*See Chapter 12, "Working with Settings/Options"*)

## To configure Eudora

1. From the Special menu (Mac) or Tools menu (Windows), choose Settings (Mac) or Options (Windows).

    Eudora opens the Settings/Options dialog box with the Getting Started settings panel selected (**Figure 13**).

2. In the Getting Started settings panel, enter your real name in the Real name field, then enter your POP account in the POP account field, and finally, enter your return address in the Return address field. Make sure that the TCP/IP button (Mac) or Winsock button (Windows) is selected.

    Your Internet service provider or network administrator must provide you with your POP account and return address.

3. If your Internet service provider or network administrator has directed you to enter an SMTP server, switch to the Hosts panel and enter the SMTP server in the SMTP server field.

4. Switch to the Checking Mail panel and check the "Send on check" and Save password checkboxes (**Figure 14**).

5. Switch to the Sending Mail panel, and uncheck the Immediate send checkbox (**Figure 15**).

6. Click the OK button to save your changes.

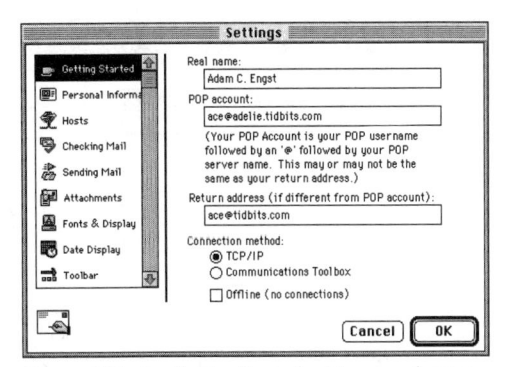

**Figure 13** In the Getting Started settings panel, enter your real name, POP account, and return address in the appropriate fields.

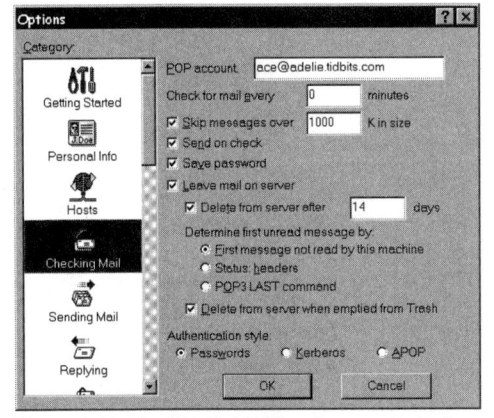

**Figure 14** In the Checking Mail settings panel, check the "Send on check" and Save password checkboxes.

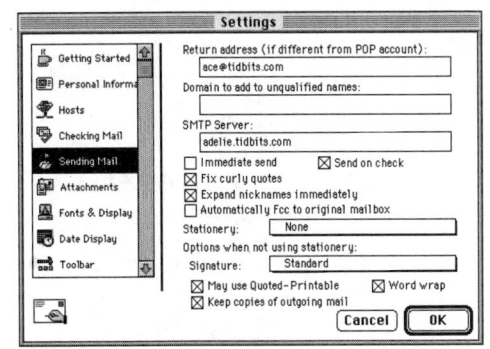

**Figure 15** In the Sending Mail settings panel, uncheck the Immediate send checkbox.

Chapter 1

## Configuring Eudora for multiple people

What if you and your sweetie share a computer but don't want to share an email address? You can each create a personal Eudora Folder with its own settings.

### To configure Eudora for two people

1. Quit Eudora if it's running. Then, in the Finder, open the System Folder and select the Eudora Folder.

2. From the File menu, choose Duplicate.

   The Finder makes a duplicate of the Eudora Folder, called Eudora Folder copy.

3. Rename the copy to start with your first name, as in **Adam's Eudora Folder**.

4. Open the original Eudora Folder. Inside it is a file called Eudora Settings. Select that file, and from the File menu, choose Make Alias to make an alias, called Eudora Settings alias.

5. Rename the alias with your sweetie's name, as in **Tonya's Email**, and move it to the desktop.

6. Repeat steps 4 and 5 with the second Eudora Folder. Rename the second Eudora Settings file with your name, as in **Adam's Email** (**Figure 16**).

7. Double-click the first alias you created to launch Eudora.

8. Configure Eudora with your sweetie's email account and settings as discussed on the previous page.

9. Double-click the second alias you created to launch Eudora, and repeat step 8 with your email account and settings.

**MACINTOSH ONLY!**

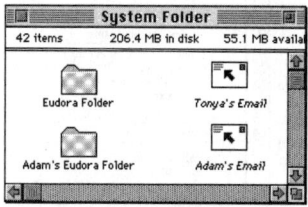

**Figure 16** The eventual goal in setting up Eudora for two people is to end up with two Eudora Folders, and differently named aliases to the Eudora Settings files within those Eudora Folders. Note that here I haven't yet moved the aliases to the desktop, and if you don't want them on the desktop they can go anywhere else that's easily accessed.

### Multiple people using Eudora

These steps walk you through creating two Eudora Folders, each with its own Eudora Settings file. You must launch Eudora by double-clicking the aliases to those Eudora Settings files. If you launch Eudora by double-clicking the program, it loads the Eudora Settings file in the folder called Eudora Folder in the System Folder.

Think of those Eudora Settings files as Eudora documents. When you double-click the alias to one, you're launching Eudora and loading those settings. It's just like double-clicking a spreadsheet document to launch the spreadsheet program and open the document.

## WINDOWS ONLY!

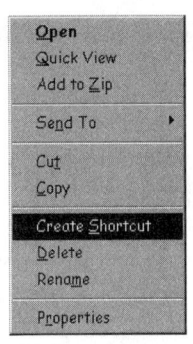

**Figure 17** First, create two shortcuts to the Eudora application, one for each person.

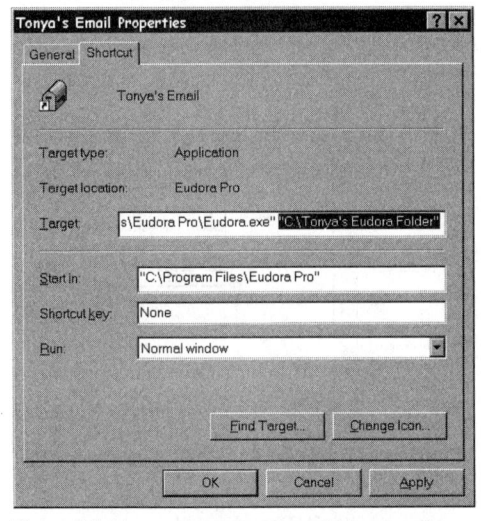

**Figure 18** After you've created two folders, one for each person, edit the Target field in the Shortcut properties to point at the new folders you've created.

### Multiple people using Eudora

These steps walk you through creating two Eudora Folders, each with completely separate settings and mailboxes. You *must* launch Eudora by double-clicking the shortcuts, or else Eudora won't load the proper settings.

## Configuring Eudora for multiple people

What if you and your sweetie share a computer but don't want to share an email address? You can each create a personal Eudora Folder with its own settings.

### To configure Eudora for two people

1. In the Windows 95 desktop, right-click the Eudora program, and from the pop-up menu, choose Create Shortcut to create a shortcut to Eudora (**Figure 17**).

2. Move the shortcut to the desktop and rename it with your sweetie's first name, as in **Tonya's Email**.

3. Repeat steps 1 and 2, but rename the second shortcut with your first name, as in **Adam's Email**.

4. In the C: window, create two folders with your first names, as in **Tonya's Eudora Folder** and **Adam's Eudora Folder**.

5. Right-click your sweetie's shortcut, and choose Properties from the pop-up menu.

6. Click the Shortcut tab, and in the Target field, type a space, and then the path to your sweetie's folder, as in **C:\Tonya's Eudora Folder** (**Figure 18**).

7. Repeat steps 5 and 6 with your shortcut and folder.

8. Double-click your sweetie's shortcut to launch Eudora.

9. Configure Eudora with your sweetie's email account as discussed previously.

10. Quit Eudora.

11. Double-click the second shortcut, and repeat step 9 with your email account and settings.

**EUDORA FOR MULTIPLE PEOPLE (WINDOWS)**

9

# Configuring Eudora Pro for multiple accounts

If you have multiple email accounts, you can configure Eudora Pro to work with all of them using personalities.

## To configure Eudora Pro for multiple accounts

1. From the Special menu (Mac) or Tools menu (Windows), choose Settings (Mac) or Options (Windows) to open the Settings/Options dialog box.

2. Click Personalities to display the Personalities settings panel (**Figure 19**).

3. Click the New button to create a new personality.

4. Enter a name for the personality in the Pers. Name (Mac) or Personality (Windows) field.

5. Enter the personality's POP account, real name, and return address in the appropriate fields.

6. Check the "Check mail on manual checks" (Mac) or "Check mail" (Windows) checkbox.

7. If necessary, in the Windows version, enter the SMTP server in the SMTP server field.

   In the Mac version, switch to the Personality Extras panel and then enter the SMTP server in the SMTP server field (**Figure 20**).

8. Make any other necessary configuration changes in the Personalities and Personality Extras (Mac) settings panels.

9. Click OK to save your configuration for that personality.

**Figure 19** To create a new personality, click the New button, then enter the necessary information in the various fields in the Personalities settings panel.

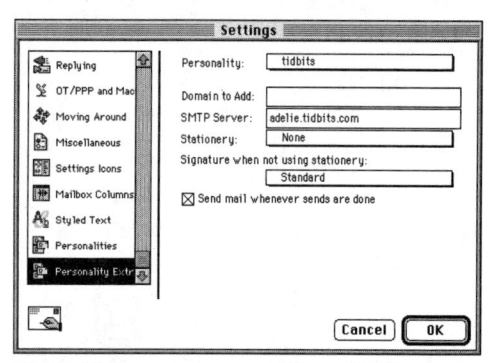

**Figure 20** If you need to set a different SMTP server in the Mac version of Eudora Pro, click Personality Extras and enter it in the SMTP server field.

# Eudora Basics

## MACINTOSH ONLY!

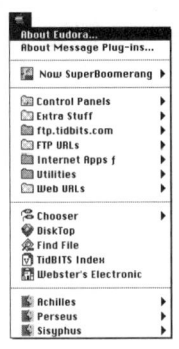

**Figure 21** To determine Eudora's proper RAM allocation, choose About Eudora from the Apple menu.

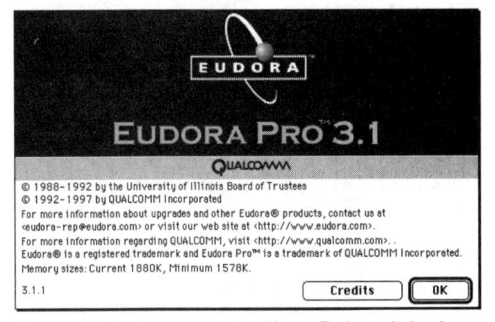

**Figure 22** Eudora opens the About Eudora dialog box. Notice that the last line tells you the current and minimum memory (RAM) sizes.

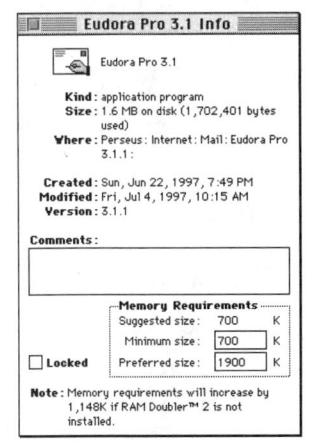

**Figure 23** Bring up the Get Info window by selecting the Eudora icon and choosing Get Info from the File menu in the Finder. Then, enter the desired RAM allocation in the Preferred size field.

## RAM requirements

The Macintosh versions of Eudora come set to require a mere 700K of RAM by default. That's not very much, but it is enough for most situations. However, if you store a lot of messages in your In, Out, and Trash mailboxes, Eudora's RAM requirements will increase.

### To determine RAM settings

1. With Eudora as the frontmost program, from the Apple menu, choose About Eudora (**Figure 21**).

   Eudora opens the About Eudora dialog box. At the bottom, Eudora displays the current memory setting and the minimum that's required (**Figure 22**).

2. If the two numbers are close (within 100K), you should increase Eudora's RAM allocation.

### To increase Eudora's RAM allocation

1. If necessary, quit Eudora, then, in the Finder, click the Eudora icon once to select it.

2. From the File menu, choose Get Info ([Cmd]-I).

   The Finder opens the Get Info window (**Figure 23**).

3. Enter a new number in the Preferred Size field (in System 7.0 or 7.0.1, the field is called Current Size). The number should be several hundred kilobytes larger than what was there before. So, if Eudora was set to 1700K, change it to 1900K.

4. Close the Get Info window by choosing Close Window ([Cmd]-W) from the File menu or by clicking the Get Info window's close box.

11

# Official help resources

Although this book provides all the information you need to use Eudora normally, special circumstances may send you looking for help further afield.

## Official resources for additional assistance

- Eudora has good online help, accessible from the question mark-like Guide menu (Mac) or the Help window (**Figure 24**) available from the Help menu (Windows).

- Even better, Eudora has great balloon help (Mac) and contextual help (Windows).

  To use balloon help in the Mac versions, choose Show Balloons from the Guide menu, then point at the item in question (**Figure 25**).

  To access contextual help in the Windows versions of Eudora, click the Contextual Help button at the right end of the toolbar, then click the item about which you want more information. If you're in a dialog box, click the question mark button in the right hand corner of the dialog, then click the item in question, or just right-click the item in question (**Figure 26**).

- Eudora comes with a good manual, although Eudora Light users must download it separately from the program. The manual should always be your first resource (after this book, of course).

- Qualcomm provides technical support information and answers to frequently asked questions on the Web at *http://www.eudora.com/techsupport/*.

## ✔ Tip

- In the Mac version of Eudora Pro, press the Help key to toggle balloon help on and off.

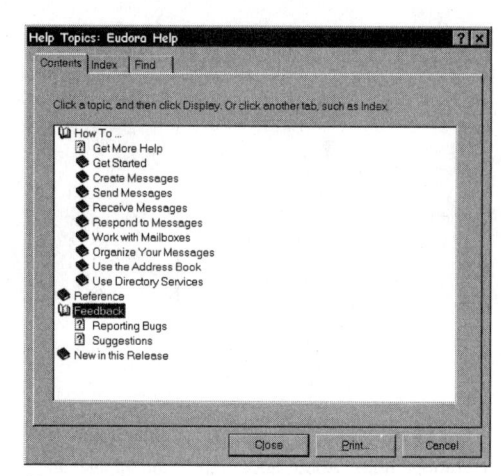

**Figure 24** To open the Help window in the Windows versions of Eudora, choose Topics from the Help menu.

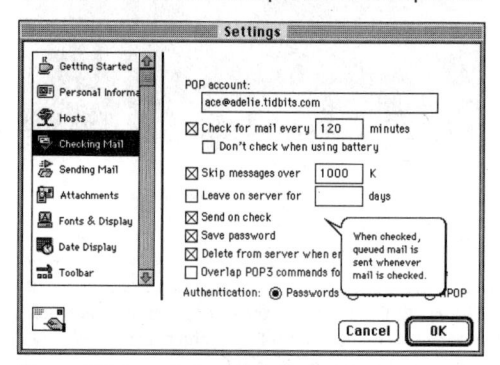

**Figure 25** To use balloon help in the Mac versions of Eudora, choose Show Balloons from the Guide menu, then point at the item in question.

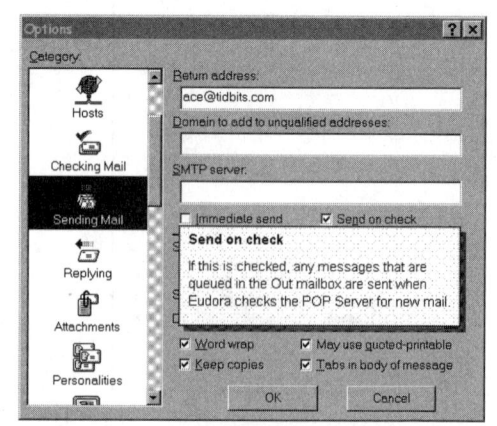

**Figure 26** To use contextual help, either click the Contextual Help button, then the item in question, or, if you're in a dialog box, right-click the item in question.

# Unofficial help resources

As good as Qualcomm's official support is, it may not suffice for all questions. And at times, you may simply need to ask another Eudora user a question. Luckily, there are a number of unofficial sources of information about Eudora as well.

## Unofficial resources for additional assistance

- Two newsgroups, *comp.mail.eudora.mac* and *comp.mail.eudora.ms-windows*, carry discussions about the Mac and Windows versions of Eudora, respectively. Both are excellent places to ask specific questions. You need a Usenet newsreader to access these newsgroups.

- Williams Students Online runs mailing lists for discussions of both the Mac and Windows versions of Eudora.
  To subscribe to the Mac mailing list, send email to *majordomo@wso.williams.edu* and put **subscribe eudora-mac** in the message body.
  To subscribe to the Windows mailing list, send email to *majordomo@wso.williams.edu* and enter **subscribe eudora-win** in the message body.

- Andrew Starr's Unofficial Eudora Site (**Figure 27**) offers numerous tips, tricks, and pieces of Eudora-related information, along with links to Eudora resources.
  *http://www.amherst.edu/~atstarr/eudora/*

- Pete Beim's Unofficial Eudora FAQs & Links site (**Figure 28**) contains a vast amount of information about the Windows versions of Eudora.
  *http://www.cs.nwu.edu/~beim/eudora/*

- I've created a Web page containing additional Eudora information useful to readers of this book.
  *http://www.tidbits.com/eudora/*

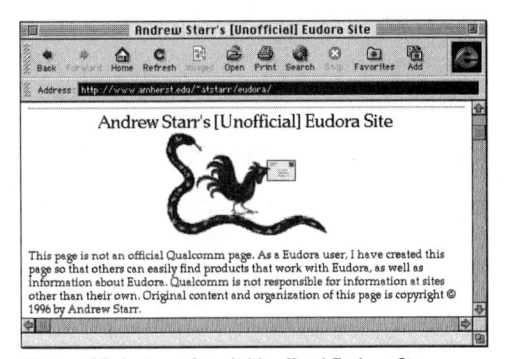

**Figure 27** Andrew Starr's Unofficial Eudora Site contains numerous tips, tricks, and pieces of Eudora-related information.

**Figure 28** Pete Beim's Unofficial Eudora FAQs & Links site contains a vast amount of information about the Windows versions of Eudora.

# Email glossary

I can't avoid the jargon inherent in talking about email—these words are the only ones we have. But, I can provide definitions so you can read this book knowing that information.

**AppleDouble**: AppleDouble is the best method of encoding file attachments in the Mac versions of Eudora such that they can be transferred via email. Always try AppleDouble first. *(See Chapter 3, "Writing Messages")*

**AppleSingle**: AppleSingle is a less commonly used method of encoding file attachments in the Mac versions of Eudora such that they can be transferred via email. Use AppleSingle for sending Mac-specific files to other Mac users. *(See Chapter 3, "Writing Messages")*

**attachment**: An attachment is a file that you send with a message, much as you might attach a newspaper clipping to a letter with a paperclip. *(See Chapter 3, "Writing Messages")*

**BinHex**: BinHex is an older method of encoding file attachments such that they can be transferred via email. Use BinHex when sending files to Mac users who have old email programs. *(See Chapter 3, "Writing Messages")*

**body**: The body of a message contains the primary content of the message. *(See Chapter 3, "Writing Messages")*

**bounce**: A message bounces when it is returned because it could not be delivered as addressed. *(See Chapter 2, "Creating Messages")*

**dial-up connection**: A dial-up connection is an Internet connection that you make using a modem to connect to an Internet service provider. *(See Chapter 12, "Working with Settings/Options")*

**domain name**: A domain name is the part of the email address after the @ character. In my address, ace@tidbits.com, tidbits.com is the domain name. *(See Chapter 3, "Writing Messages")*

**email address**: An email address is the unique address that identifies each Internet user. Email addresses are composed of a username, the @ character, and a domain name. *(See Chapter 3, "Writing Messages")*

**encoding**: Encoding is the process of converting attachments in such a way that they can travel through email without being damaged, much as you put letters in envelopes to protect them. *(See Chapter 3, "Writing Messages")*

**filter**: A filter is a set of rules and related actions that Eudora applies to messages. *(See Chapter 7, "Working with Filters")*

**finding**: In Eudora's parlance, finding is the process of searching for text in a single message. *(See Chapter 8, "Finding and Searching")*

**Finger**: Finger is an Internet service like Ph that enables you to look up information about people. *(See Chapter 11, "Using Directory Services")*

**forward**: You forward incoming messages when you wish to send them to someone else but have them come from you. Forwarding is like taking a letter from one person, putting it in another envelope, and sending it to another person. *(See Chapter 2, "Creating Messages")*

**hanging indent**: A paragraph of text with a hanging indent has the first line at the left and all following lines indented to the right. *(See Chapter 3, "Writing Messages")*

**header**: The header of an email message contains the information necessary to deliver the message. Think of the message header as the outside of an envelope, containing an address, a return address, and the postmark. *(See Chapter 4, "Sending and Receiving Messages")*

**helper application**: A helper application is a program Eudora relies on for tasks, like viewing a Web page, that Eudora can't do itself. *(See Chapter 5, "Working with Messages")*

# Eudora Basics

**Internet Config**: Internet Config is a free program for the Macintosh that helps centralize Internet preferences. Eudora can optionally work with Internet Config. *(See Chapter 5, "Working with Messages")*

**kilobyte**: A kilobyte is a unit of measurement equal to 1,024 bytes or characters. *(See Chapter 4, "Sending and Receiving Messages")*

**match string**: In the context of filters, a match string is the text you want the filter to look for in message headers. *(See Chapter 7, "Working with Filters")*

**message plug-ins**: A message plug-in is a file that extends Eudora's text-editing functionality. *(See Chapter 3, "Writing Messages")*

**message summary**: A message summary is a line in a Eudora mailbox that includes the sender's name, the message date, and the message subject, with other information. *(See Chapter 5, "Working with Messages")*

**MIME**: MIME stands for Multi-purpose Internet Mail Extension and in the Windows versions of Eudora is the best method of encoding file attachments for transfer via email. *(See Chapter 3, "Writing Messages")*

**nickname**: A nickname is an easily typed and remembered name that replaces one or more email addresses. A nickname for me might be "Adam", which would replace ace@tidbits.com. The Windows versions of Eudora call nicknames "address book entries." *(See Chapter 9, "Working with the Address Book")*

**nicknames files**: A nicknames file is a file that contains nicknames in Eudora Pro. *(See Chapter 9, "Working with the Address Book")*

**personality**: A personality is a group of settings in Eudora Pro. Personalities are useful for working with multiple email accounts. *(See Chapter 1, "Eudora Basics," Chapter 2, "Creating Messages," and Chapter 12, "Working with Settings/Options")*

**Ph**: Ph is an Internet service like Finger that enables you to look up information about people. *(See Chapter 11, "Using Directory Services")*

**POP**: POP stands for Post Office Protocol and is the primary method that email programs like Eudora use to retrieve incoming Internet email messages. *(See Chapter 4, "Sending and Receiving Messages")*

**POP account**: A POP account is essentially the electronic mailbox where your incoming email sits until you retrieve it with Eudora. The POP account is composed of a username, an @ character, and the domain name of your POP server. POP accounts look like email addresses. *(See Chapter 1, "Eudora Basics" and Chapter 12, "Working with Settings/Options")*

**POP server**: A POP server is a program that runs on an Internet computer and sends your incoming messages when you check mail. *(See Chapter 4, "Sending and Receiving Messages")*

**queue**: When you queue a message, you set it to send at a later time. *(See Chapter 4, "Sending and Receiving Messages")*

**quote**: When replying to a message, Eudora automatically quotes the original text by putting a > character before each line. *(See Chapter 2, "Creating Messages")*

**recipient list**: The recipient list is a list of nicknames that appears in the hierarchical Insert Recipient, New Message To, Forward To, and Redirect To menus. *(See Chapter 2, "Creating Messages" and Chapter 9, "Working with the Address Book")*

**redirect**: You redirect incoming messages when you want to send them to someone else but have them appear to come from the original sender. Redirecting is like putting a letter back in its original envelope, affixing a sticker with someone else's address over your address, and sending it again. *(See Chapter 2, "Creating Messages")*

**EMAIL GLOSSARY**

15

**reply**: You reply to a message when you want to respond to it. (See Chapter 2, "Creating Messages")

**return address**: The return address is the address that everyone sees on mail from you. It's also the address to which their replies will be sent. (See Chapter 1, "Eudora Basics" and Chapter 12, "Working with Settings/Options")

**Rot13**: Rot13 is a simple method of encoding text to prevent prying eyes from reading it. (See Chapter 3, "Writing Messages")

**search term**: The search term is the text that you want to find when finding or searching. (See Chapter 8, "Finding and Searching")

**searching**: In Eudora's parlance, searching is the process of searching for text in multiple messages. (See Chapter 8, "Finding and Searching")

**signature**: The signature contains personal information that appears at the bottom of every message you send. (See Chapter 3, "Writing Messages")

**SMTP**: SMTP stands for Simple Mail Transfer Protocol and is the primary method that email programs like Eudora use to send messages. (See Chapter 4, "Sending and Receiving Messages")

**SMTP server**: An SMTP server is a program that runs on an Internet computer and accepts your outgoing messages when you send mail. SMTP servers also transfer mail between one another on the Internet to move messages to their eventual destinations. (See Chapter 1, "Eudora Basics," Chapter 4, "Sending and Receiving Messages," and Chapter 12, "Working with Settings/Options")

**spam**: Spam, also known as unsolicited commercial email, is email messages from people you don't know, advertising products or services you don't want, often in a fraudulent manner. Spam is a blight on Internet email. (See Chapter 5, "Working with Messages")

**spammer**: A spammer is someone who sends spam messages to tens or hundreds of thousands of recipients. (See Chapter 5, "Working with Messages")

**starting point**: The starting point for a search is the message with which Eudora starts searching. (See Chapter 8, "Finding and Searching")

**stationery**: Stationery is previously composed outgoing messages you can use when creating messages. (See Chapter 2, "Creating Messages")

**URL**: URL stands for Uniform Resource Locator and is pronounced "You Are Ell." URLs identify Internet resources such as Web pages. (See Chapter 5, "Working with Messages")

**username**: A username is the part of the email address before the @ character. In my address, ace@tidbits.com, ace is the username. (See Chapter 3, "Writing Messages")

**Uuencode**: Uuencode is an older method of encoding file attachments such that they can be transferred via email. Use Uuencode when sending Mac documents or PC files to PC users who have old email programs. (See Chapter 3, "Writing Messages")

# CREATING MESSAGES

## 2

One of the most common activities in Eudora is message creation. It might seem like a trivial topic, and in fact it is extremely easy, but newcomers may not realize the many ways messages can be created in Eudora.

You'll definitely want to create new messages to friends, and I guarantee that you will often want to reply to messages you receive. But what about the less common situations? Maybe a colleague sent a joke that you absolutely must forward to your college roommate. Perhaps you received a message that would be best handled by someone else in your department. What if you need to send a piece of boilerplate text to everyone who writes to your company requesting general information?

In each of these cases, you could use basic tools to create a new message with the appropriate content. Instead, you should take advantage of Eudora's power and flexibility in creating new messages, as you'll see in this chapter.

Chapter 2

# Creating a new message

A new blank message is the easiest and most obvious way to create a new piece of email.

### To create a new message

1. From the Message menu, choose New Message ([Cmd]-N/[Ctrl]-N) (**Figure 1**).

    A new outgoing message window appears, with the cursor in the To line of the header and the From line filled in with your name and email address (**Figure 2**).

2. Type the nickname or the email address of the recipient in the To line.

3. Press Tab, or click in the Subject line, then type the subject of your message.

4. Press Tab three more times, or click in the body area of the message, then type your message (**Figure 3**).

5. Click the Queue button ([Cmd]-E/[Ctrl]-E) to queue your message for later sending.

### ✔ Tip

- When you're working on a long, complicated, or important message, you might want to save your message periodically while writing. To do that, choose Save ([Cmd]-S/[Ctrl]-S) from the File menu whenever you like.

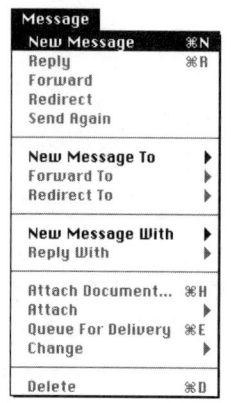

**Figure 1** To create a new outgoing message, choose New Message from the Message menu.

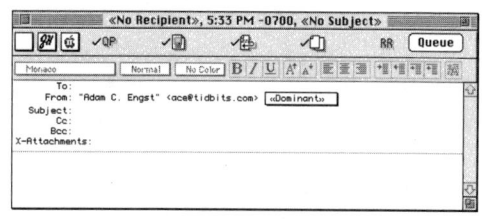

**Figure 2** A new outgoing message window contains a filled-in From line, but has the rest of the window blank.

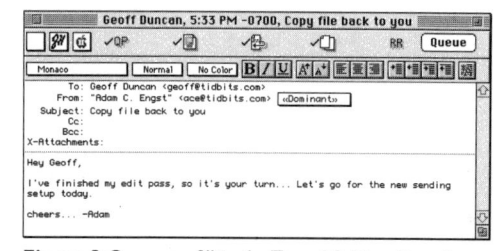

**Figure 3** Once you fill in the To and Subject lines for your message, note how the title bar of the window changes. Click the Queue button to send your message.

---

### Personalities

Eudora Pro has a new feature that enables you to send and receive mail from multiple email accounts. This feature is great for those of us with more than account.

In the Mac screen shots to the right the pop-up menu in the From line controls which personality the message comes from. In the Windows version of Eudora Pro, you choose personalities through a dialog box instead of a pop-up menu.

# Creating Messages

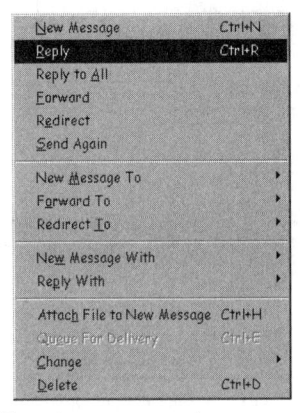

**Figure 4** To reply to a message that you are either reading or have selected in a mailbox window, choose Reply from the Message menu.

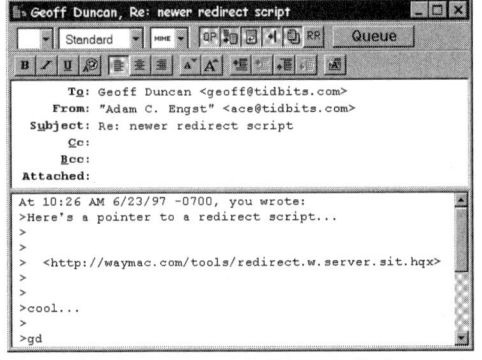

**Figure 5** Eudora automatically fills in the To, From, and Subject lines in a reply, and quotes the original message for you to edit.

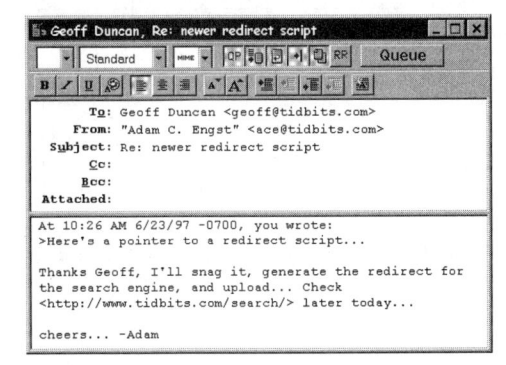

**Figure 6** Edit the body of the message so it's clear what you're replying to. Keep quotes to a minimum.

## Replying to a message

Although you're certain to want to create plenty of new messages to people using New Message, it's far more likely that you'll want to reply to a message that you've received.

### To reply to a message

1. Open or select an incoming message, then choose Reply ( Cmd -R/ Ctrl -R) from the Message menu (**Figure 4**).

   Alternately, in the Windows versions of Eudora, open or select an incoming message, then right-click it and choose Reply from the pop-up menu that appears.

   Eudora creates a new outgoing message, but this time fills in the To line, the From line, and the Subject line.

   The body of the original message is quoted (**Figure 5**) and, in the Mac versions of Eudora, selected.

   You can either delete the original text entirely or edit it if desired.

2. Type your message, and if you wish edit the original message to respond to specific points (**Figure 6**).

3. When you're done, click the Queue button ( Cmd -E/ Ctrl -E) to queue your reply for later delivery.

### ✔ Tip

- When you're working on a long, complicated, or important reply, you may want to save your message periodically while writing. To do so, from the File menu, choose Save ( Cmd -S/ Ctrl -S) whenever you like.

**REPLYING TO A MESSAGE**

19

## Replying to part of a message

What if you want to reply to a message and respond to a specific point in the original without editing the quoted text manually?

### To reply to part of a message

1. With an incoming message window open, select some text (**Figure 7**).

2. Holding Shift down, choose Reply Quoting Selection ([Cmd]-[Shift]-R) from the Message menu (**Figure 8**).

   A new outgoing message window appears, with the To, From, and Subject lines filled in appropriately, and with just the selected text quoted in the body of the message.

3. Make any additional edits you wish, and type your reply (**Figure 9**).

4. When you're done, click the Queue button ([Cmd]-E) to queue your message for later delivery.

### ✔ Tips

- If the menu item says Reply instead of Reply Quoting Selection, you didn't hold the Shift key down before clicking the menu.

- If you wish to include the headers of a message in a reply, you must specifically select them; Eudora never includes headers otherwise. Just select the headers along with any other desired text, then hold down Shift and use Reply Quoting Selection to create the reply message.

**MACINTOSH ONLY!**

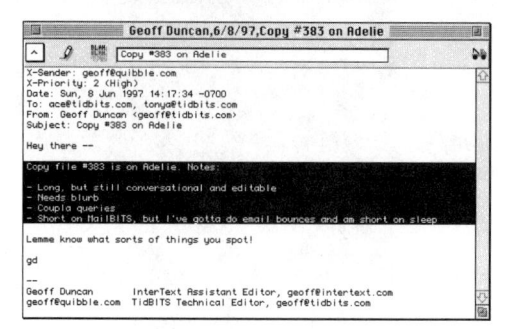

**Figure 7** Select some text in an incoming message window.

**Figure 8** Hold down Shift and select Reply Quoting Selection from the Message menu.

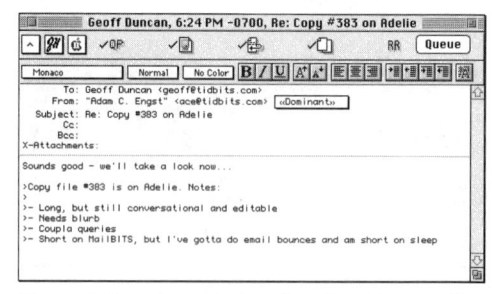

**Figure 9** Note that only the selected text is quoted in the reply. Make any additional edits and type your message before queuing it up for delivery.

# Creating Messages

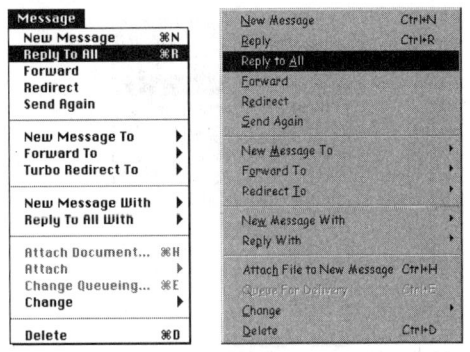

**Figure 10a/10b** From the Message menu, either hold down Option and choose Reply To All (Mac) or just choose Reply to All (Windows).

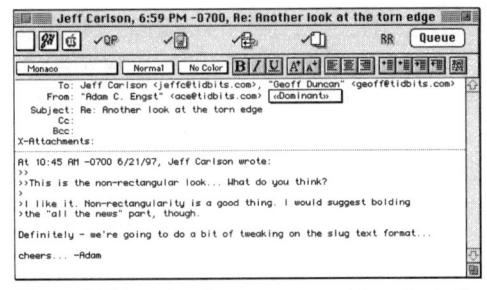

**Figure 11** Note that there are two recipients in the To line, thanks to using Reply To All.

## Reply To All by default

If you're truly foolhardy, you can change a setting in the Replying settings panel of the Settings/Options dialog box to make Reply to All be the default. I strongly recommend that you do not do this—sooner or later you'll send a reply to someone who shouldn't have seen it, and you'll regret it. Believe me on this.

## Replying to all recipients

Often, when you receive a message, it will have been sent to multiple people. For safety's sake, Eudora by default only replies to the sender, but you can address your reply to all of the other recipients.

### To reply to all recipients

1. In the Mac versions of Eudora, open or select an incoming message with multiple recipients. Then hold down Option and choose Reply To All (Cmd-Option-R) (**Figure 10a**).

   In the Windows versions of Eudora, make sure you have an incoming message window open or a message selected in a mailbox and choose Reply to All from the Message menu (**Figure 10b**) or right-click the message and choose Reply to All from the pop-up menu that appears.

   Eudora creates a new outgoing message window with all the recipients in the To line (**Figure 11**). The From line, Subject line, and body of the message are filled out as they would be for any reply.

2. Type your reply, and if you wish to remove a recipient from the To line, do so by selecting it and pressing Delete.

3. When you're done, click the Queue button (Cmd-E/Ctrl-E) to queue your message for later delivery.

### ✔ Tips

- If the menu item in the Mac versions of Eudora says Reply rather than Reply To All, you didn't hold the Option key down before clicking the menu.

- In the Mac versions of Eudora, select some text, then hold down Shift and choose Reply Quoting Selection To All to quote the selected text and address the reply to all recipients.

Chapter 2

# Forwarding a message

If someone sends you a message that you feel another person should see, you can use Eudora's Forward command to send them a copy.

## To forward a message

1.  Open or select an incoming message, then choose Forward from the Message menu (**Figure 12**).

    Alternately, in the Windows versions of Eudora, open a message, right-click it, and choose Forward from the pop-up menu that appears.

    Eudora creates a new outgoing message window, with the From and Subject lines filled in and the original message quoted in the body. The cursor should be in the To line (**Figure 13**).

2.  In the To line, enter the nickname or the email address of the person to whom you wish to forward the message.

3.  If you wish to add a comment to the message or edit part of it, go ahead and do so (**Figure 14**).

4.  When you're done, click the Queue button ( Cmd -E/ Ctrl -E) to queue the message for later delivery.

## ✔ Tips

- If you don't want to quote the original message that you're forwarding, in the Mac versions of Eudora, hold down Option when you choose Forward. Eudora creates the forwarded message the same, but does not include the quote character before each line.

- A forwarded message always includes the headers of the original message. The only way to eliminate headers from forwarded messages is to remove them manually.

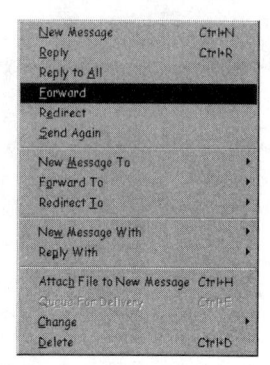

**Figure 12** To forward a message that you are either reading or have selected, choose Forward from the Message menu.

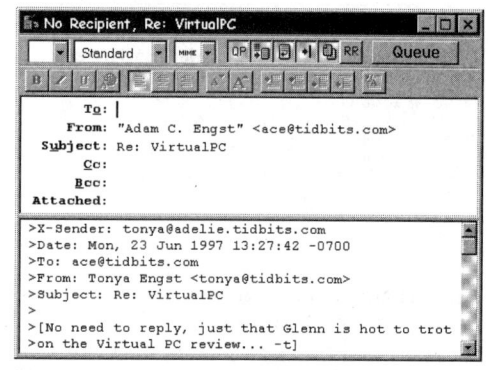

**Figure 13** Eudora creates a new outgoing message with the cursor in the To line and the body of the message quoted.

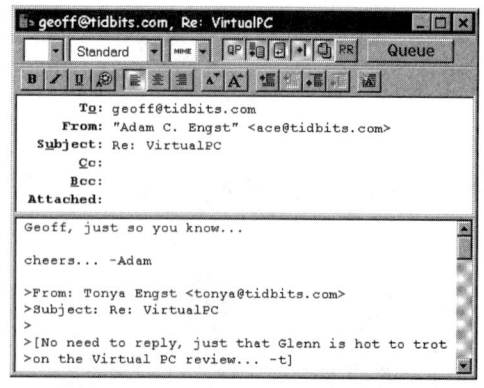

**Figure 14** Enter the email address of the recipient in the To line, and add any comments you may have to the message body.

# Creating Messages

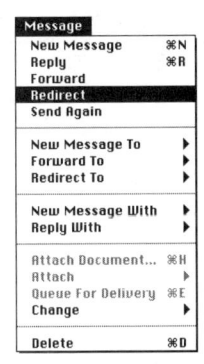

**Figure 15** To redirect a message that you are either reading or have selected, choose Redirect from the Message menu.

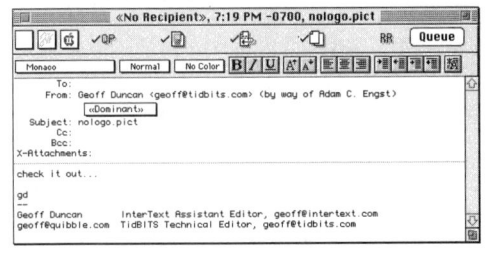

**Figure 16** Eudora creates a new outgoing message with the original message in the body and the cursor in the To line.

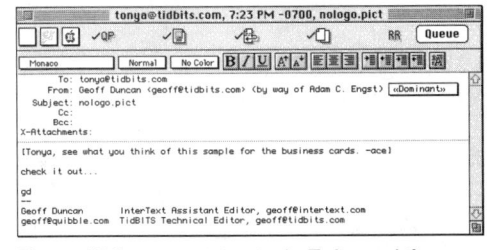

**Figure 17** Enter a recipient in the To line and if you want put a brief explanation in the message body.

### Redirecting etiquette

It's considered extremely bad manners to edit an original message that you're redirecting. Put a short parenthetical at the top of the message explaining why you're redirecting if necessary, but don't change the original text if you can avoid it.

## Redirecting a message

Imagine the situation. You receive a message that should really go to a colleague, since it's not your problem. You could forward the message to your colleague, but if your colleague replies the reply will come back to you by default. A better solution is Eudora's Redirect feature, which sends the original message to your colleague, but keeps the original sender the same so replies go back to that person and not to you. It's one of my favorite features in Eudora.

### To redirect a message

1. Open or select an incoming message, then choose Redirect from the Message menu (**Figure 15**).

    Alternately, in the Windows versions of Eudora, open a message, right-click it, and choose Redirect from the pop-up menu that appears.

    Eudora creates a new outgoing message with the From and Subject lines filled in and the original message in the body. The From line is slightly modified with the parenthetical phrase "(by way of)" and your name and email address, so the eventual recipient knows the message was redirected (**Figure 16**).

    The cursor should be in the To line.

2. Type the nickname or email address of the recipient.

3. If you wish to add a note to the top of the original message, explaining why you're passing the buck, do so (**Figure 17**).

4. When you're done, click the Queue button (Cmd-E/Ctrl-E) to queue the message for later delivery.

## Sending a message again

Eudora's Send Again command is extremely useful but somewhat subtle. Say you send a message to a friend, and later hear that the friend lost all his email and wants another copy of your message. Or, perhaps a message you sent bounces because you typed the email address incorrectly.

### To send a message again

1. Open or select either a saved outgoing message from your Out box or an incoming bounce message that you've received (**Figure 18**).

2. From the Message menu, choose Send Again (**Figure 19**).

   Eudora creates a new outgoing message, filled in exactly the same way your original message was, with the same To, From, and Subject lines, and the same message body.

3. Make any necessary changes, such as fixing an incorrect email address, or adding an important detail to the body of the message that you'd previously forgotten (**Figure 20**).

4. When you're done, click the Queue button (Cmd-E/Ctrl-E) to queue the message for later delivery.

### ✔ Tips

- You can use Send Again on messages you've received, but Eudora will put your address in the To line (since the message was originally sent to you). Change the address to send the message normally.

- When you use Send Again with a message you've sent that's bounced back, your signature appears in the new message. Don't delete it since Eudora won't add a new signature.

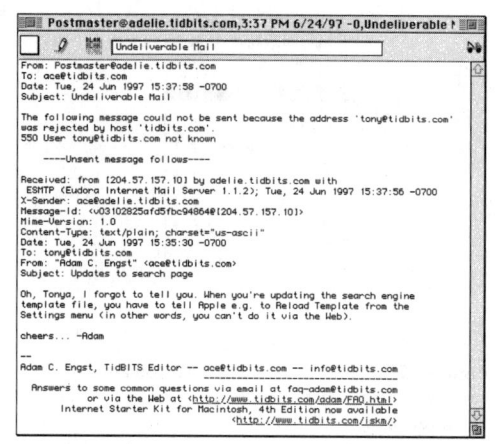

**Figure 18** Open a bounce or a message you've sent previously. Note that in this bounce, I mistyped Tonya's email address, forgetting the a in tonya@tidbits.com.

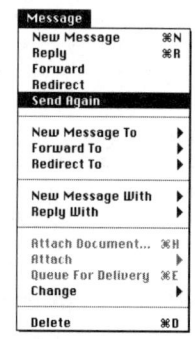

**Figure 19** To send this message again, choose Send Again from the Message menu.

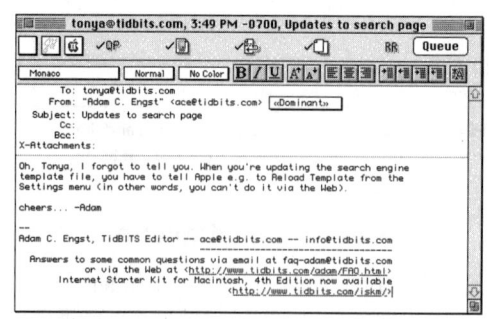

**Figure 20** In the new outgoing message, fix the error in the address if you're resending a bounce, or make any other necessary changes.

# Using the recipient list

In each of the previous examples of creating messages, you've either typed a nickname or email address to address the message or replied to an existing message. A faster method of creating new messages uses Eudora's recipient list, to which you can add people whenever you create a nickname. (See Chapter 9, "Working with the Address Book")

## To address a message using the recipient list

1. Choose a recipient from the recipient list, which you access from the hierarchical New Message menu in the Message menu (**Figure 21**). Or, open or select an incoming message and choose a recipient from the hierarchical Forward to or Redirect To menus in the Message menu

    Eudora creates a new outgoing message window, with the From and, if you chose Forward To or Redirect To, Subject lines filled in. The nickname you chose is in the To line, and the body of the message includes the original message if you chose Forward To or Redirect To (**Figure 22**).

2. Enter your message or add a comment if you wish (**Figure 23**).

3. When you're done, click the Queue button ( Cmd -E/ Ctrl -E) to queue the message for later delivery.

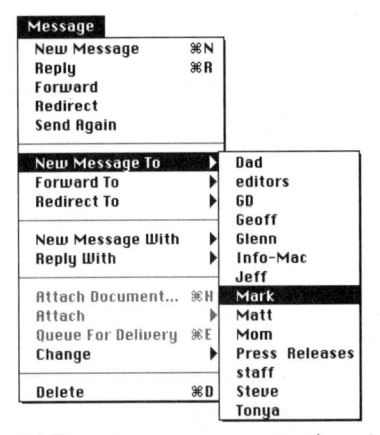

**Figure 21** To create a new message using the recipient list, choose a nickname from the New Message To menu. The Forward To and Redirect To menus contain the same list of recipients.

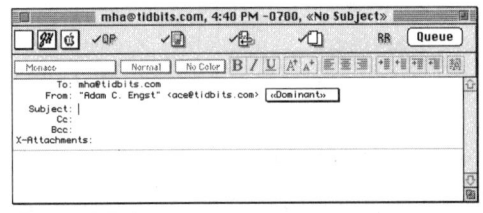

**Figure 22** Eudora creates a new outgoing message window and puts the cursor in the Subject line. If you used Forward To or Redirect To, the rest of the message would be filled in for you.

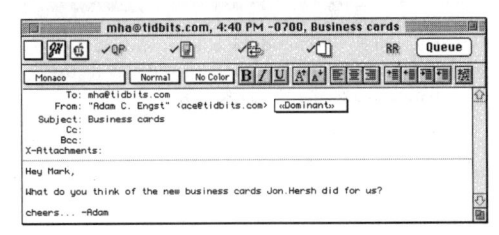

**Figure 23** Fill in the Subject line, and enter your message. If you used Forward To or Redirect To, this step wouldn't be necessary.

# Turbo redirecting a message

Some people find themselves in the position of an email mailroom clerk—they receive lots of email that must be distributed to the appropriate people. For that, Eudora's Turbo Redirect feature is perfect.

## To turbo redirect a message

1. With an incoming message window open or a message selected in a mailbox (**Figure 24**), hold down Option (Mac) or Shift (Windows) and choose a nickname from the Redirect To hierarchical menu. On the Mac, the menu item changes to Turbo Redirect To (**Figure 25**).

   Eudora creates a new outgoing message window addressed to the nickname you chose, with the From and Subject lines filled in, and the original message in the body.

   Eudora then queues the message for later delivery (**Figure 26**), and moves the original message to the Trash mailbox.

## ✔ Tips

- Turbo redirecting a message offers no chance to add a comment to the top of the original message. To do so after the fact, open the Out mailbox, open the queued message, make your changes, and queue the outgoing message again.

- You can set Turbo Redirect to be the default for both the Mac and Windows versions of Eudora in the Miscellaneous settings panel of the Settings/Options dialog box, but the menu item won't change in the Windows versions.

- Be careful with Turbo Redirect—you can easily redirect a message to the wrong person without realizing.

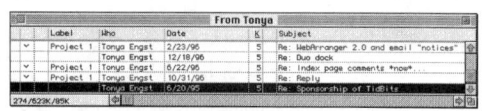

**Figure 24** To turbo redirect a message, open an incoming message window or select a message in a mailbox, as I've done here.

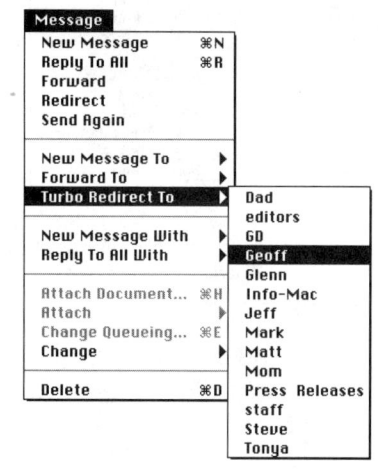

**Figure 25** Hold down Option (Mac) or Shift (Windows) and choose a nickname from the Turbo Redirect To menu (Mac) or the Redirect To menu (Windows).

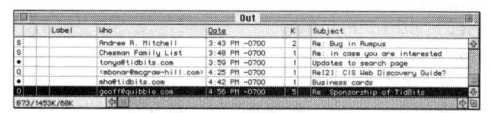

**Figure 26** Eudora responds by queuing the redirected message in the Out box, shown here, and moving the original message to the Trash mailbox.

## Creating a stationery message

If you need to send the same message over and over again, or if you need to reply to numerous messages with the same information, Eudora Pro's stationery is extremely useful.

### To create a stationery message

1. Choose New Message ([Cmd]-N/[Ctrl]-N) from the Message menu.

    Eudora creates a new outgoing message with the From line filled in.

2. Fill in the To, Cc, and Bcc lines with recipients you always want to receive email messages created with the stationery.

3. Fill in the Subject line if you want all messages created with the stationery to have that Subject line.

4. In the body of the message, enter the text you want to appear in each message created with the stationery (**Figure 27**).

5. From the File menu, choose Save As (**Figure 28**).

6. Name the message (if you entered a Subject line, that's the default name).

7. Check the Stationery checkbox (**Figure 29**), and on the Mac, click the Go To Stationery Folder button.

8. Click the Save button to save your stationery message.

### ✔ Tip

- To change an existing stationery message, choose it from the hierarchical New Message With menu in the Message menu. Make any changes and save it according to steps 5 through 8 above, replacing the previous file when prompted.

**EUDORA PRO ONLY!**

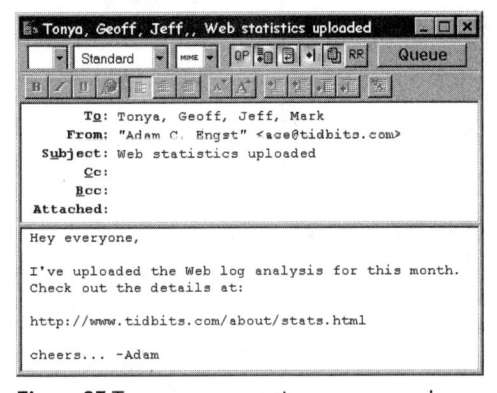

**Figure 27** To create a new stationery message, choose New Message from the File menu, and fill in all the desired parts of the message.

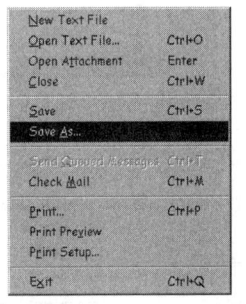

**Figure 28** After you create your message exactly as you want it to appear, choose Save As from the File menu.

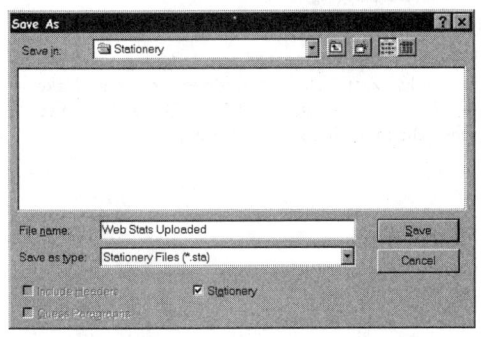

**Figure 29** Enter a file name for your stationery message, click the Stationery checkbox, and then click the Save button to save your stationery message. (In the Mac version of Eudora Pro, click the Go to Stationery Folder button before clicking Save.)

# Creating a new message using stationery

I create new messages with stationery whenever I send the same piece of rote email to a number of different people over time (such as messages asking for permission to include a shareware utility on a book's CD-ROM, for instance).

## To create a new message using stationery

1. From the New Message With hierarchical menu in the Message menu, choose the piece of stationery you wish to use (**Figure 30**).

   Eudora creates a new outgoing message that looks exactly like the stationery message you created (**Figure 31**).

2. Enter a recipient if necessary, fill in any other missing information, and edit the message if necessary.

3. When you're done, click the Queue button ([Cmd]-E/[Ctrl]-E) to queue the message for later delivery.

## ✔ Tips

- In the Windows version of Eudora Pro, you can also hold down Shift when you choose New Message ([Ctrl]-[Shift]-M) to choose a piece of stationery for the new message.

- You can also create a new message using stationery by double-clicking the stationery file to open it.

- Eudora puts the cursor at the most appropriate place in the new outgoing message, depending on the contents of the stationery.

- I often edit my boilerplate messages each time so they don't sound canned.

**EUDORA PRO ONLY!**

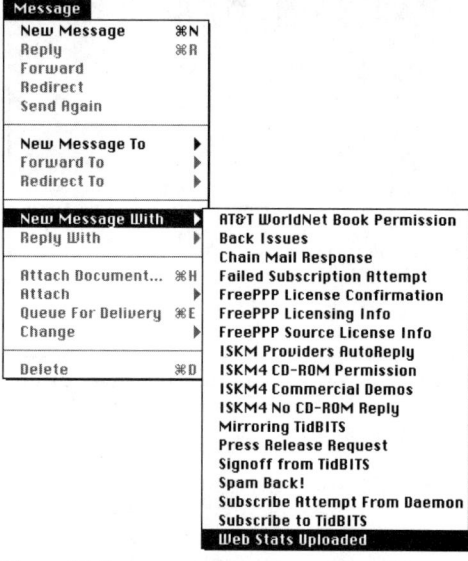

**Figure 30** To create a new message using stationery, choose a stationery message from the New Message With hierarchical menu in the Message menu.

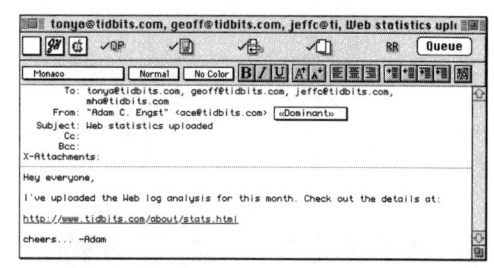

**Figure 31** Eudora creates a new outgoing message that looks exactly like your stationery message. Make any changes you want, and click the Queue button to queue the message for later delivery.

# Creating Messages

## EUDORA PRO ONLY!

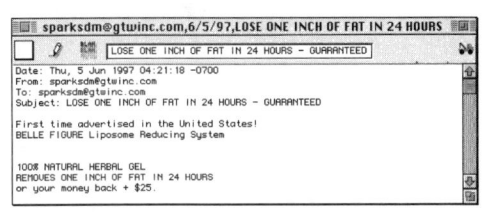

**Figure 32** To reply to a message using stationery, first open or select an incoming message, such as this piece of spam (unsolicited commercial email).

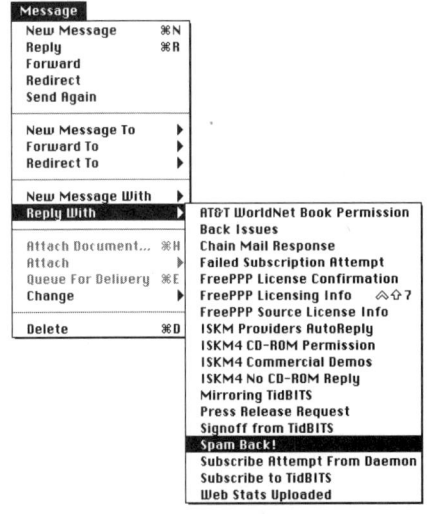

**Figure 33** From the hierarchical Reply With menu in the Message menu, choose the piece of stationery you want to use in your reply.

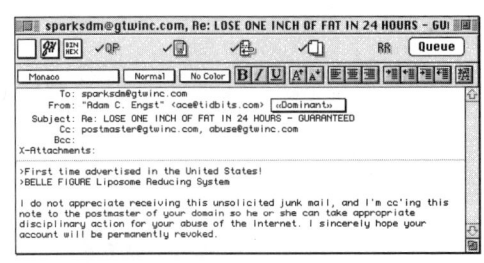

**Figure 34** Eudora creates a new outgoing message that looks like your stationery with the addition of the recipient's address and body text from the original message. Make any changes you want, and click the Queue button to queue your message for later delivery.

## Replying to a message using stationery

Stationery is a godsend for people who get the same questions over and over again in email. Just create a piece of stationery with the appropriate answer and use Eudora Pro's Reply With command to reply to incoming questions with the stationery message.

### To reply to a message using stationery

1.  Open or select the message you want to reply to (**Figure 32**), and then choose a stationery message from the Reply With hierarchical menu in the Message menu (**Figure 33**).

    Eudora creates a new outgoing message that's addressed to the original sender and includes not only the original message, but also all the details from the stationery message.

2.  Fill in any missing information, and edit the message if necessary (**Figure 34**).

3.  When you're done, click the Queue button (Cmd-E/Ctrl-E) to queue the message for later delivery.

### ✔ Tips

- In the Mac version of Eudora Pro, you can use the modifier keys that work with Reply when you're using Reply With. If you hold down Shift with a portion of an original message selected, Reply With changes to Reply Quoting Selection With. If you hold down Option, Reply With changes to Reply To All With. And, both Shift and Option change Reply With to Reply Quoting Selection To All With.

- In the Windows version, you can also hold down Shift when you choose Reply to select a piece of stationery for the reply.

# 3

# WRITING MESSAGES

In the previous chapter, I glossed over the many different ways you can add content to a message after you've created it. I did so in part because although an email message looks simple, those looks can be deceiving, especially in a program as powerful and flexible as Eudora.

When you look at Eudora closely, you realize there are all sorts of ways you can add content to an email message, and those ways aren't always obvious.

For instance, you must address every message, then you must give it a subject. Almost every message has a message body, and Eudora has a capable text entry environment that has some features you might not have noticed, including formatting options in Eudora Pro.

The possibilities for adding content don't end there. Eudora enables you to create multiple signatures that it automatically appends to every message you send, and you can also attach files to messages. Finally, you can set a variety of message options that affect how your message is sent or how the recipient sees it.

In short, there are tons of neat things you can do when writing email messages—read on for the details, arranged as you'll experience them in each message.

# Addressing messages

Every time you send a message, you must address it. There are a number of different ways of adding email addresses to one of the three address lines in an outgoing message, the To line, the Cc line, and the Bcc line (**Figure 1**).

## Methods of addressing messages

- Type an email address in one of the three address lines. Separate multiple addresses with commas.

- Type a nickname in an address line. Separate multiple nicknames with commas.

- Reply to a message. (*See Chapter 2, "Creating Messages"*)

- Use the recipient list with New Message To, Forward To, or Redirect To. (*See Chapter 2, "Creating Messages"*)

- Type the first part of a nickname (enough to make it unique among your nicknames) and then choose Finish Address Book Entry (Cmd-,/Ctrl-,) from the Edit menu to complete the nickname. Hold down Option (Mac) or Shift (Windows) to Finish And Expand Address Book Entry (Cmd-Option-,/Ctrl-Shift-,), which finishes the nickname and replaces it with the corresponding email address.

- Place the cursor in any one of the three address lines and choose a nickname from the Insert Recipient hierarchical menu in the Edit menu. Hold down Option (Mac) or Shift (Windows) to Insert And Expand Recipient, which inserts the nickname and replaces it with its corresponding email address.

- In the Address Book (Cmd-L/Ctrl-L), select one or more nicknames, and click one of the To, Cc, or Bcc buttons to add them to the appropriate line in either the current outgoing message or a new outgoing message.

- Drag a nickname from the Address Book to one of the three address lines.

- Drag an address from another message.

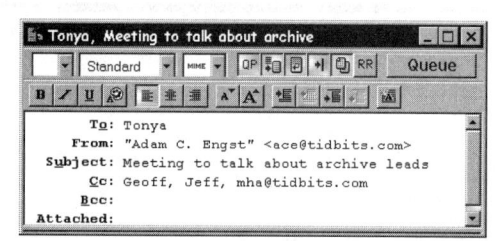

**Figure 1** You can enter email addresses or nicknames in the To, Cc, or Bcc lines. Separate multiple recipients with commas.

### Multiple Recipients Tips

When you enter multiple recipients using any of the methods mentioned (and you can mix and match all of the methods), make sure to separate recipients with commas. This is particularly true when you drag a nickname or address into one of the three address lines, because Eudora won't insert the commas for you, which can be confusing.

Also, when selecting multiple nicknames in the Address Book, hold down Command (Mac) or Control (Windows) to select multiple nicknames. Hold down Shift on both platforms to select a range of nicknames.

# Writing Messages

## EUDORA PRO ONLY!

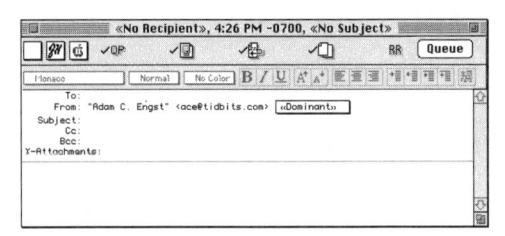

**Figure 2** Create a new message and choose a personality from the personality pop-up menu, which is set to Dominant by default.

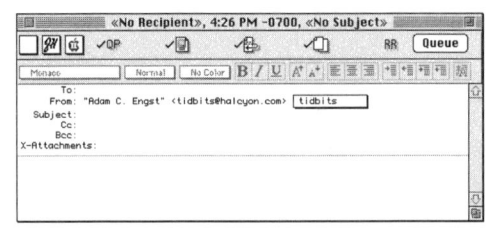

**Figure 3** After you choose the alternate personality, notice how the From address has changed.

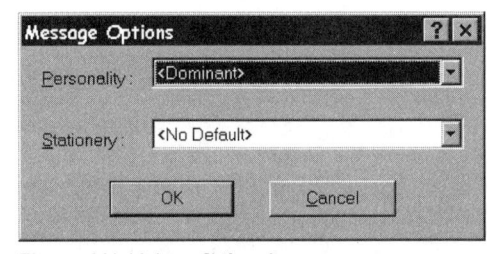

**Figure 4** Hold down Shift and create a new message however you wish to bring up the Message Options dialog. Choose a personality from the Personality pop-up menu, and then click OK to finish creating the outgoing message.

## Choosing a personality

Eudora Pro enables you to send and receive mail from multiple Internet email accounts. This is useful, for instance, if you have a work address and a personal address and wish to handle them on a single computer.

After you've addressed a message, you may want to set it to come from one of your alternate email addresses. (*See Chapter 1,"Eudora Basics" and Chapter 12,"Working with Settings/Options" for information on personalities*)

### To choose a personality (Mac)

1. Create a new outgoing message however you wish. (*See Chapter 2,"Creating Messages"*)

2. Click the personality pop-up menu (**Figure 2**) in the From line and choose an alternate personality.

   Notice how the email address in the From line changes (**Figure 3**). If you set a different name when creating the personality, the name would change too.

### To choose a personality (Windows)

1. Hold down Shift and create a new outgoing message however you wish. (*See Chapter 2,"Creating Messages"*)

   Eudora Pro displays the Message Options dialog (**Figure 4**).

2. From the Personality pop-up menu, choose a personality, then click the OK button to create the outgoing message.

   Notice how the email address in the From line changes (**Figure 3**). If you set a different name when creating the personality, the name would change too.

### ✔ Tip

- Keep in mind that personalities can have different return addresses that control where replies are directed.

# Entering a subject

After addressing your message and perhaps choosing a personality, you should always enter something in the Subject line. If you're replying to, forwarding, or redirecting a message, it will be filled in for you, but even in these cases you may want to change the Subject line to be more appropriate. Here are some things to consider when choosing what to put in the Subject line.

## Things to consider with subjects

- Keep the subject short.

    Not all email programs display long subjects, and even if they do, you want to make your point quickly.

- Make the subject clear and specific.

    Clarity should be a given, but in practice it's all too rare. Subject lines like "General stuff" or "Things to do" aren't useful. You want the recipients to have a good idea of what will be discussed in the message from the Subject line alone, and after they have read the message, the Subject line should act as a reminder as to the contents of the message.

- Don't type in ALL CAPITALS or use exclamation points if possible.

    This piece of advice may seem odd, but I offer it because of the prevalence of spam (unsolicited commercial email) on the Internet today. Most spam messages use uppercase in their Subject lines and throw in an exclamation point or five to indicate how important they are. If you do the same, some recipients may not even read your message, thinking it to be spam.

- If an existing subject in a reply isn't appropriate, change it.

    Never fear to make a subject better fit the contents of a message. Everyone benefits.

# Text selection and navigation

I assume you know the basics of using the mouse, but you may not realize the more subtle methods Eudora provides for selecting and navigating through the text that you type.

## Methods of selecting and navigating through text

- To insert the cursor where the mouse pointer is pointing, single-click the mouse.

- To select the word (or email address in outgoing message window header lines) under the cursor (**Figure 5**), double-click the mouse. To select by word, double-click and drag.

- To select the entire paragraph under the cursor (**Figure 6**), triple-click the mouse. In incoming mail, the lines have hard returns at the end, so a triple-click selects the line instead of the paragraph. To select by paragraph, triple-click and drag.

- To move the cursor a word left or right, hold down Option (Mac) or Control (Windows) and press the left or right arrow key.

- To move the cursor to the beginning or end of the paragraph, hold down Option (Mac) or Control (Windows) and press the up or down arrow key.

- On the Mac, to move to the top or bottom of the message, hold down Command and press the up or down arrow key. To move to the beginning or end of the current line, hold down Command and press the left or right arrow key.

- To select text instead of navigating, combine any of the previous three keyboard navigation methods with the Shift key.

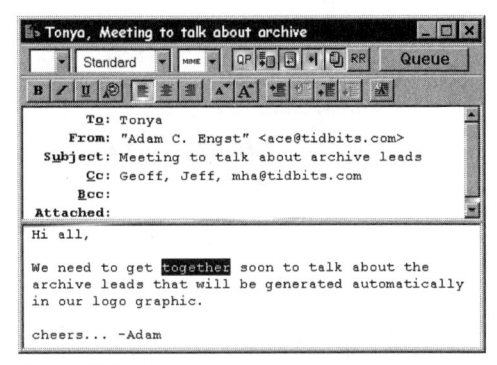

**Figure 5** Double-click a word to select the entire word. Double-click and drag to select by word.

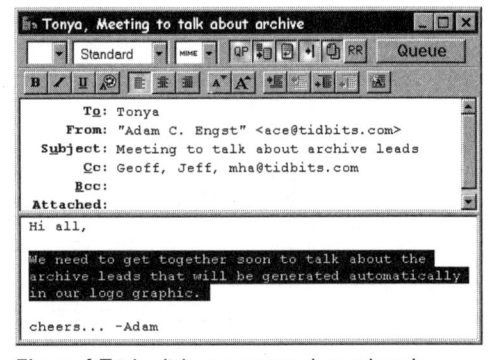

**Figure 6** Triple-click on a paragraph to select the entire paragraph. Triple-click and drag to select by paragraph.

# Entering text

I assume that you've figured out the basics of entering text (fingers on the keyboard, press down), but Eudora supports a number of somewhat unusual methods of getting text into the body of a message that you might not know.

## Methods of entering text

- Copy selected text (using the Copy command ([Cmd]-C/[Ctrl]-C) in any application) and paste it into a Eudora message by choosing Paste ([Cmd]-V/[Ctrl]-V) from the Edit menu.

- To paste text as a quotation (as though you were replying to the text), choose Paste As Quotation ([Cmd]-'/[Ctrl]-') from the Edit menu (**Figure 7**).

- Select text in any other drag-aware application and drag it into your outgoing message window.

- To insert an entire text file in a message, choose Attach Document (Mac) or Attach File (Windows) from the Message menu. Select the document you want to insert, and on the Mac click the Insert button (**Figure 8**). In Windows, click the Open button, but then turn off the Text as Attachment button in the outgoing message header (**Figure 9**). The file won't appear in the body of the message, but that's how the recipient will see it.

## ✔ Tips

- In Eudora Pro only, hold down Shift ([Cmd]-[Shift]-V/[Ctrl]-[Shift]-V) when pasting to remove text styles.

- Dragging is difficult unless both windows are visible. It's often easier to use Copy and Paste.

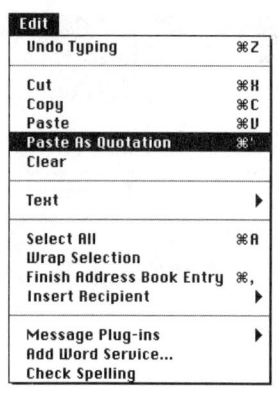

**Figure 7** To paste text as a quotation, copy it, then choose Paste As Quotation from the Edit menu.

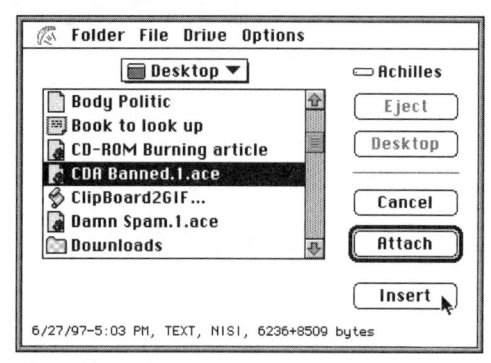

**Figure 8** To insert a text file into a message in the Mac versions of Eudora, choose Attach File, select the file, and then click the Insert button.

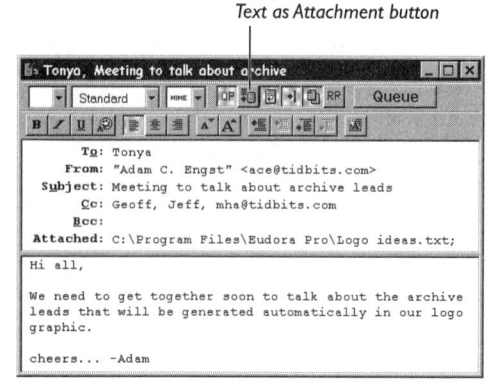

**Figure 9** To insert a text file into a message in the Windows versions of Eudora, attach the file normally, but turn off the Text as Attachment button in the message window's toolbar.

# Editing text

Eudora honors all the standard editing commands on the Mac and in Windows, such as Cut, Copy, Paste, Clear, Undo, and Select All, which are all located in the Edit menu. Eudora also has several less common editing tools that you might find useful.

## Tools for editing text

- To insert hard returns (what you get in text when you press Return or Enter) at the end of each line in normal paragraph of text, select the text and choose Wrap Selection from the Edit menu (**Figure 10**).

- To remove hard returns from the end of every line in an incoming message, select the text, and on the Mac, hold down Option and choose Unwrap Selection from the Edit menu (**Figure 11**). In Windows, hold down Shift and choose Wrap Selection from the Edit menu.

- To paste a paragraph of unwrapped text into another message or application, select the text, hold down Option, and select Copy & Unwrap (**Figure 12**) from the Edit menu ([Cmd]-[Option]-C). This only works on the Mac.

## ✔ Tips

- When trying to unwrap quoted text, the Mac versions of Eudora remove the > characters. The Windows versions don't remove the > characters, but they also won't unwrap quoted paragraphs.

- In the Mac versions of Eudora, hold down Shift and choose Copy Without Styles from the Edit menu to copy text without style information. Also, hold down Shift and Option to change Copy to Copy Without Styles & Unwrap.

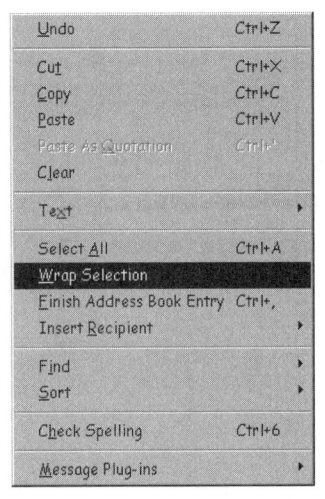

**Figure 10** To insert hard returns in a piece of selected text, choose Wrap Selection from the Edit menu.

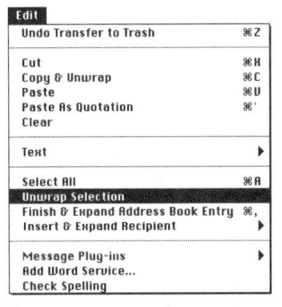

**Figure 11** To remove returns from a piece of selected text, hold down Option on the Mac and choose Unwrap Selection from the Edit menu.

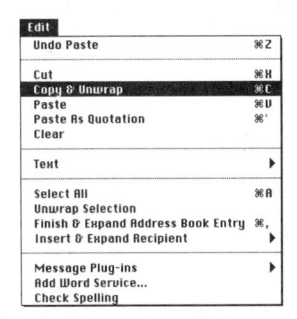

**Figure 12** In the Mac versions of Eudora, you can copy a paragraph of text and remove the returns with a single action—just hold down Option and choose Copy & Unwrap from the Edit menu.

Chapter 3

# About message plug-ins

Eudora comes with several message plug-ins, which are files that extend Eudora's text-editing functionality. The Mac (**Figure 13**) and Windows (**Figure 14**) have slightly different sets of plug-ins, so I note that below. To use a plug-in, select some text and choose the plug-in from the Message Plug-ins hierarchical menu in the Edit menu.

## Message plug-ins

- **Rot13 Text** (Mac only) encodes and decodes text.

- **Tabs to Spaces** (Mac only) replaces all tabs with a visually equivalent number of spaces.

- **Spaces to Tabs** (Mac only) replaces all instances of multiple spaces with a single tab character.

- **Sort** (Windows only) sorts the selected lines in alphabetical order.

- **Unwrap Text** (Windows only) removes hard returns from the selected lines. It is equivalent to holding down Shift and choosing Wrap Selection from the Edit menu.

- **Upper Case** changes the selected letters to uppercase.

- **Lower Case** changes the selected letters to lowercase.

- **Toggle Case** (Windows only) changes the case of each selected letter, changing *A* to *a*, for instance, and *b* to *B*.

- **Word Caps** (Mac) / **Word Case** (Windows) capitalizes each word in the selection.

- **Sentence Caps** (Mac) / **Sentence Case** (Windows) capitalizes the first word in each selected sentence.

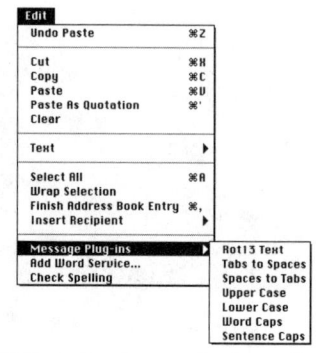

**Figure 13** To apply a message plug-in to selected text in the Mac versions of Eudora, choose it from the hierarchical Message Plug-ins menu in the Edit menu.

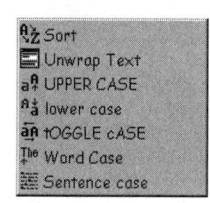

**Figure 14** To apply a message plug-in to selected text in the Windows versions of Eudora, choose it from the hierarchical Message Plug-ins menu in the Edit menu.

### Rot13

Rot13 is a rather interesting, if simple, method of encoding text to prevent prying eyes. Each letter is assigned a number from 1 to 26. Then, each number has 13 added to it, and if the result would be larger than 26, it wraps around.

So, A = 1 and Z = 26. When 13 is added to each, you get 14 and 13 (because any number over 26 wraps around). Then, the results are converted back into letters. That turns the 14 into an N and the 13 into an M. Here's an example of what it looks like:

*The fox ate popcorn.* (Normal text)

*Gur sbk ngr cbcpbea.* (Rot13 text)

## Writing Messages

**EUDORA PRO ONLY!
MACINTOSH ONLY!**

## Spell checking

It would be great if we could all spell correctly, but some of our brains just don't understand the arbitrary rules of English spelling. Eudora Pro for both the Mac and Windows comes with an integrated spelling checker. The Check Spelling dialog boxes are quite different, so flip to the next page for the Windows version.

### To check spelling

1. Create an outgoing message however you like to get some text to check. (*See Chapter 2,"Creating Messages"*)

2. From the Edit menu choose Check Spelling ([Cmd]-6) to bring up the Word Services window (**Figure 15**).

3. Click the Replace or Replace All buttons to replace a misspelled word with the selected word from the suggestions, or click the Skip or Skip All buttons to ignore a properly spelled unknown word.

   When the entire message has been checked, the dialog box disappears.

*The list of suggested replacements appears here, sorted alphabetically or by best guess. Click a word in the list of suggestions to place it in the Replace with field.*

*Use the Skip buttons to skip properly spelled unknown words.*

*The word being checked appears here. Click it to move it to the Replace with field.*

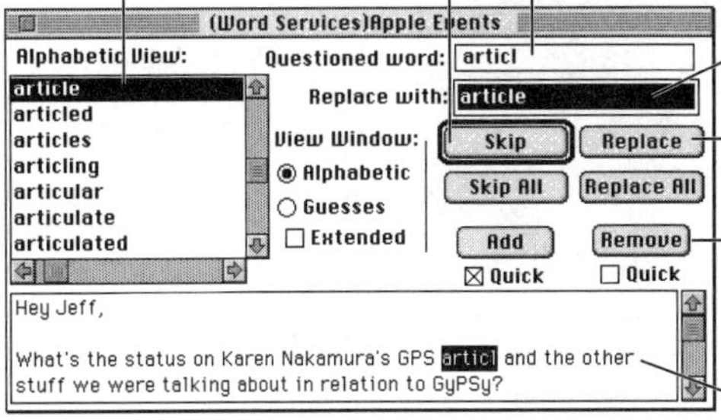

*The Replace with field contains the suggested replacement for the unknown word.*

*Use the Replace buttons to replace the word being checked with the word in the Replace with field.*

*Use the Add button to add the word being checked to the dictionary, or the Remove button to remove the Replace with word from the dictionary. When checked, the Quick checkboxes eliminate confirmation prompts.*

*The word being checked is selected in this preview pane, so you can see the context in which it's being used.*

**Figure 15** Use the controls in the Word Services window to skip properly spelled words, replace incorrectly spelled words, and add words to your user dictionary.

Chapter 3

## Spell checking

**EUDORA PRO ONLY! WINDOWS ONLY!**

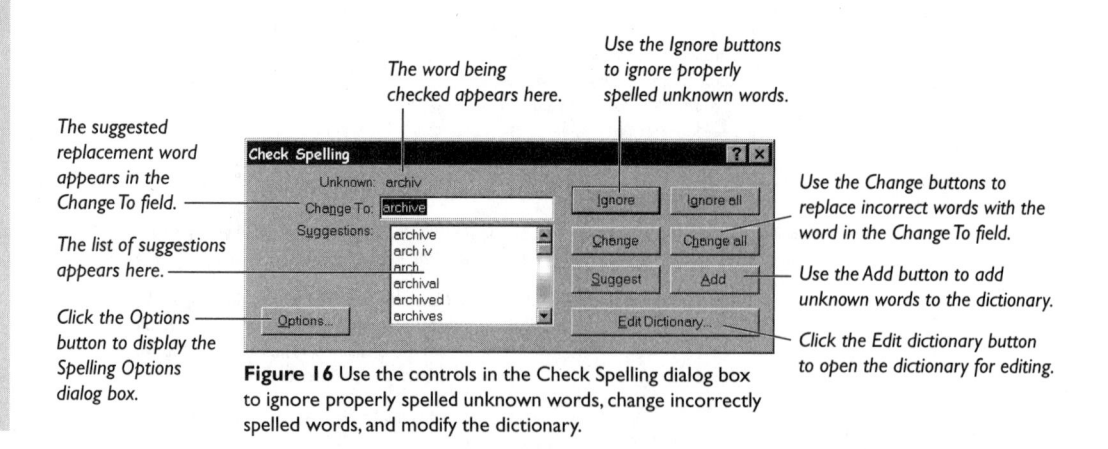

It would be great if we could all spell correctly, but some of our brains just don't understand the arbitrary rules of English spelling. Eudora Pro for both the Mac and Windows comes with an integrated spelling checker. The Check Spelling dialog boxes are quite different, so flip back to the previous page for a look at the Mac version.

### To check spelling

1. Create an outgoing message however you like to get some text to check. (*See Chapter 2, "Creating Messages"*)

2. From the Edit menu choose Check Spelling ([Ctrl]-6) to bring up the Check Spelling dialog box (**Figure 16**).

3. Click the Change or Change all buttons to replace a misspelled word with the selected word from the suggestions, or click the Ignore or Ignore all buttons to ignore a properly spelled unknown word. When the message has been checked, the dialog box disappears.

*The suggested replacement word appears in the Change To field.*

*The list of suggestions appears here.*

*Click the Options button to display the Spelling Options dialog box.*

*The word being checked appears here.*

*Use the Ignore buttons to ignore properly spelled unknown words.*

*Use the Change buttons to replace incorrect words with the word in the Change To field.*

*Use the Add button to add unknown words to the dictionary.*

*Click the Edit dictionary button to open the dictionary for editing.*

**Figure 16** Use the controls in the Check Spelling dialog box to ignore properly spelled unknown words, change incorrectly spelled words, and modify the dictionary.

## Spell checking options

Although the defaults should work fine in almost all cases, you can change a number of settings in both the Mac and Windows versions of Eudora's spelling checker.

### To change preferences in the Mac spelling checker

1. When the spell checking window is showing, choose Preferences from the File menu to display the Preferences dialog box (**Figure 17**).

2. To change a setting, check its checkbox to turn it on or uncheck the checkbox to turn it off.

3. When you're done, click the OK button to save your changes.

### To change preferences in the Windows spelling checker

1. In the Check Spelling dialog box, click the Options button to display the Spelling Options dialog box (**Figure 18**).

2. To change a setting, check its checkbox to turn it on or uncheck the checkbox to turn it off.

3. When you're done, click the OK button to save your changes.

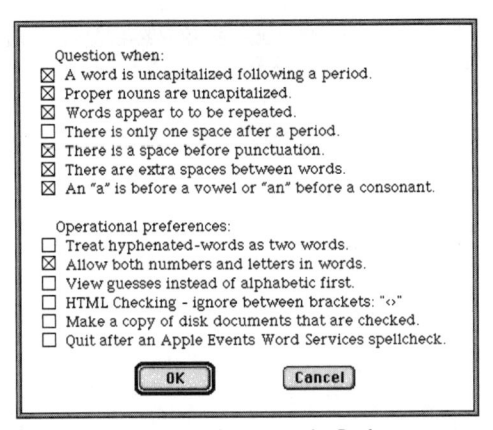

**Figure 17** Use the checkboxes in the Preferences dialog box to control how spelling checks are performed.

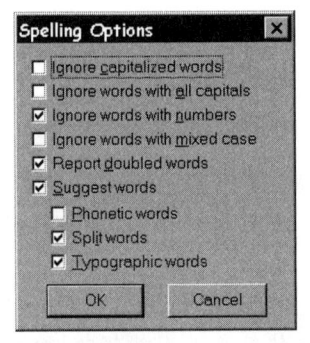

**Figure 18** Use the checkboxes in the Spelling Options dialog box to control how spelling checks are performed.

# Formatting text

Eudora Pro enables you to use fonts, font styles, font sizes, and font colors. You can also format your messages with indents. If you paste or drag styled text in from another message or application, Eudora Pro interprets it properly.

These features can make your email much more attractive, and they're definitely useful in some situations. I cover the various possibilities in the next few pages.

However, I caution you against using styled text in your email much. There are several problems.

## Problems with styled text

- Styled text is not guaranteed to display properly or at all for your recipient unless he or she also uses a recent version of Eudora, and not even always then, depending on what fonts he or she has installed. (**Figure 19**).

- Styled text makes quoting in replies more awkward, because Eudora doesn't use the > character to indicate quoted text (**Figure 20**). Instead, Eudora marks quoted text with black bars, which, though effective, can get ugly when there are too many in a message.

- Applying styles to an email message can be a waste of time, especially on short messages. I personally send and receive way too much email to spend valuable time fussing with how it looks.

### ✔ Tip

- If you don't plan to format text in messages much, you can turn off the formatting toolbar in the Styled Text settings panel of the Mac version of Eudora Pro.

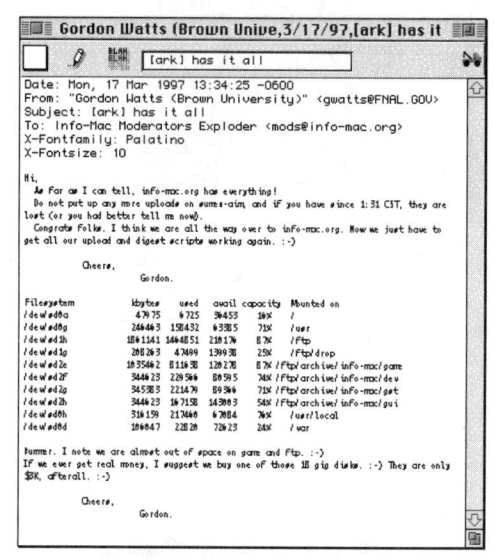

**Figure 19** This message was almost unreadable on my Mac. Although it wasn't sent with Eudora Pro, it shows how styled text can be difficult to read when interpreted differently than was intended.

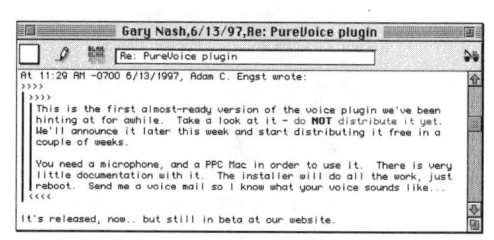

**Figure 20** This message shows how Eudora quotes when styled text has been used. With a single quote like this, it's not too bad, but when you get a message full of back and forth bits of quoted text, it gets ugly fast.

## EUDORA PRO ONLY!

**Figure 21** To change the font in the Mac version of Eudora Pro, select some text, and choose a font from the hierarchical Font menu in the hierarchical Text menu in the Edit menu.

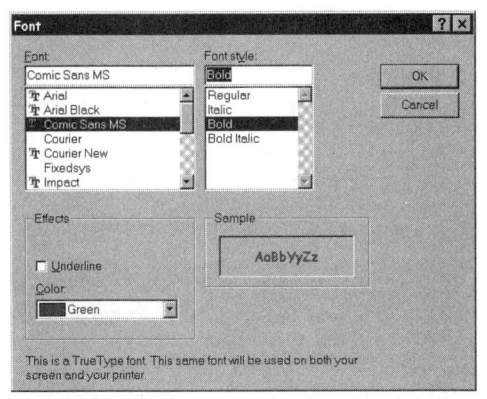

**Figure 22** To style text in the Windows version of Eudora Pro, select some text, choose Font from the hierarchical Text menu in the Edit menu, and then make font, style, and color choices in the Font dialog box.

*The pop-up font menu in the formatting toolbar.*

**Figure 23** In the Mac version of Eudora Pro, you can also select some text and choose a font from the pop-up font menu in the formatting toolbar, if it's showing.

# Changing the font

You can use any of the fonts installed on your computer in email. Beware that if your recipients don't have the same font, the message won't look the same, even if their email programs can display styled text.

### To change the font (Mac)

1. Select some text, and from the hierarchical Font menu in the hierarchical Text menu in the Edit menu, choose a font (**Figure 21**).

### To change the font (Windows)

1. Select some text, and from the hierarchical Text menu in the Edit menu, choose Font to display Eudora's Font dialog box (**Figure 22**).

2. Select a font from the Font scrolling list. If you wish to assign a font style as well, select one from the Font style scrolling list. To assign a color to the selection, choose one from the Color pop-up menu.

3. When you're done, click OK to save your changes (or Cancel to forget them).

### ✔ Tips

- Try to choose common fonts if you're going to change the font so it's more likely that your recipient will see the message as you intended.

- In the Mac version of Eudora Pro, you can also choose a font from the formatting toolbar (**Figure 23**).

## Changing font styles

I think it's more effective to change font styles than to mess with different fonts. Judiciously used font styles like bold can add emphasis to messages without taking much time to create. And, if the recipient can't see the bold, it's no great loss.

### To change font styles

1. Select some text, and from the hierarchical Text menu (**Figure 24**) in the Edit menu, choose Plain, Bold ([Cmd]-B/[Ctrl]-B), Italic ([Cmd]-I/[Ctrl]-I), or Underline ([Cmd]-U/[Ctrl]-U).

   Alternately, select some text and click one of the font style buttons on the formatting toolbar (**Figure 25** and **Figure 26**).

### ✔ Tips

- To remove formatting, select the text and click the Clear Formatting button on the formatting toolbar or, in the Windows version of Eudora Pro, choose Clear Formatting from the hierarchical Text menu in the Edit menu.

- In the Mac version of Eudora Pro, to remove font and size information as well as styles, hold down Option when you click the Clear Formatting button.

**EUDORA PRO ONLY!**

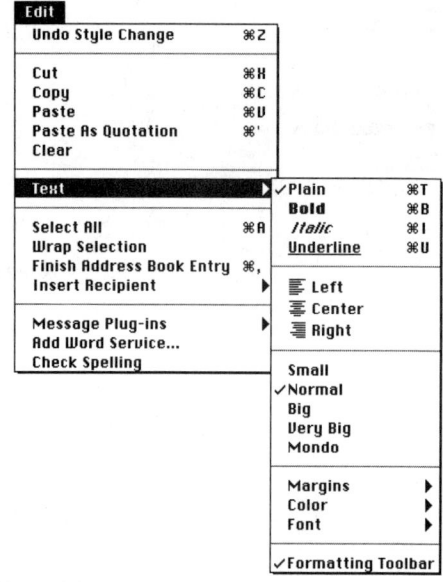

**Figure 24** To change the font style, select some text and from the hierarchical Text menu in the Edit menu, choose the appropriate font style.

*Click the B, I, or U buttons to apply bold, italic, or underline formatting to the selected text.*

*Click the Clear Formatting button to remove font styles. Option-click the Clear Formatting button to remove font and size information as well.*

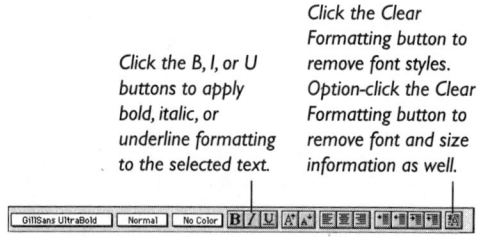

**Figure 25** In the Mac version of Eudora Pro, use the formatting toolbar to apply or clear styles.

*Click the B, I, or U buttons to apply bold, italic, or underline formatting to the selected text.*

*Click the Clear Formatting button to remove font styles.*

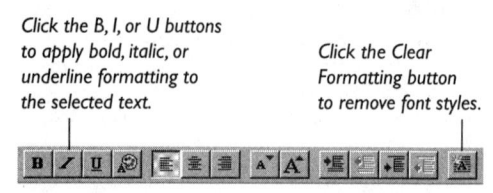

**Figure 26** In the Windows version of Eudora Pro, use the formatting toolbar to apply or clear styles.

# Changing font colors

You can assign one of either five (Mac) or sixteen (Windows) colors to text in your messages. Keep in mind that your recipient may not have a color monitor or may be color-blind.

To be honest, I can't think of a good general example for when you might want to use colored text. I'm sure there are plenty of specific situations where it's useful, though, and you'll recognize them when they happen.

## To change font colors

1. Select some text, and from the Color hierarchical menu in the Text hierarchical menu in the Edit menu, choose a color (**Figure 27**).

   Alternately, select some text and choose a color from the color pop-up menu on the formatting toolbar (**Figure 28** and **Figure 29**).

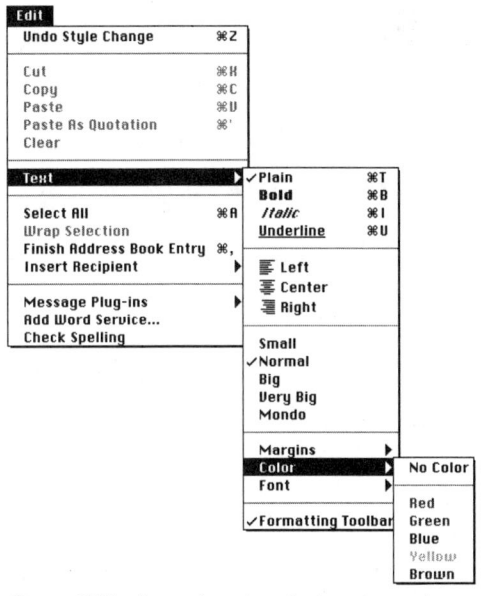

**Figure 27** To change the color of selected text, choose a color from the hierarchical Color menu in the hierarchical Text menu in the Edit menu.

**Figure 28** In the Mac version of Eudora Pro, choose a color from the color pop-up menu to change the color of selected text.

**Figure 29** In the Windows version of Eudora Pro, choose a color from the color pop-up menu to change the color of selected text.

## Changing font sizes

You may be used to font sizes being measured in points. For instance, this is 10 point text. However, in Eudora Pro, font sizes are ambiguous. The Mac version offers five different sizes: Small, Normal, Big, Very Big, and Mondo. The Windows version provides nine unnamed sizes—the only commands available are Smaller and Bigger, which you choose multiple times to move through the various sizes.

### To change font sizes in the Mac version of Eudora Pro

1. Select some text, and from the hierarchical Text menu in the Edit menu, choose a size (**Figure 30**).

    Alternately, select some text and choose a size from the font size pop-up menu (**Figure 31**) on the formatting toolbar.

    As yet another alternative, select some text and click the Bigger or Smaller buttons on the formatting toolbar.

### To change font sizes in the Windows version of Eudora Pro

1. Select some text, and from the hierarchical Text menu in the Edit menu, choose Smaller to reduce the font size or Bigger to increase it (**Figure 32**).

    Alternately, select some text and click the Bigger or Smaller buttons on the formatting toolbar.

### ✔ Tip

- If you receive a message that has the font size set too small to read, click the pencil icon in the message window to enable editing, select the miniature text, and increase its size to one that's readable.

**EUDORA PRO ONLY!**

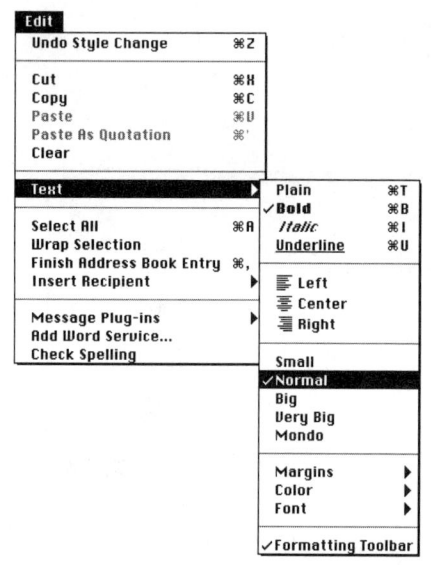

**Figure 30** To change the font size in the Mac version of Eudora Pro, select some text and choose a font size from the hierarchical Text menu in the Edit menu.

*Choose a size from the font size pop-up menu.*

*Use the Bigger or Smaller buttons to increase or decrease the text size.*

**Figure 31** In the Mac version of Eudora Pro, choose a size from the font size pop-up menu to change the size of selected text. Or, select some text and click the Bigger or Smaller buttons.

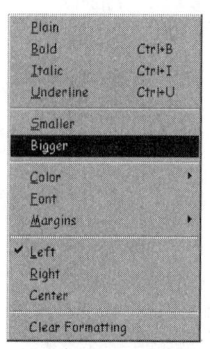

**Figure 32** To change the font size in the Windows version of Eudora Pro, select some text and choose Smaller or Bigger from the hierarchical Text menu in the Edit menu.

# Changing justification

## EUDORA PRO ONLY!

So far, all the formatting I've mentioned has been character formatting. Eudora Pro also provides minimal paragraph formatting via left, right, and center justification.

### To justify text

1. Select some text, and from the hierarchical Text menu in the Edit menu, choose one of the three possible justifications—Left, Center, or Right (**Figure 33**).

   Alternately, select some text and click one of the three justification buttons (**Figure 34**) on the formatting toolbar.

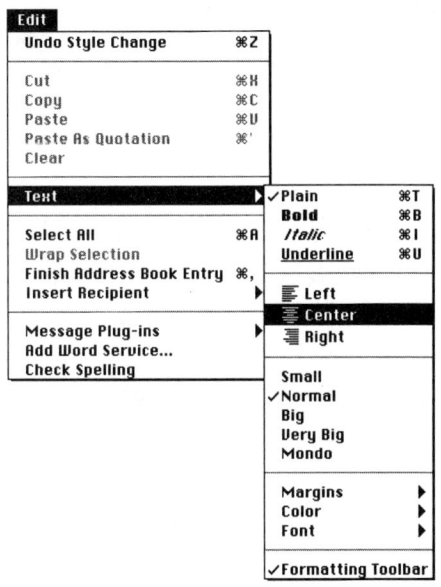

**Figure 33** To change the justification, select some text and from the hierarchical Text menu in the Edit menu, choose the desired justification.

**Figure 34** To use the formatting toolbar to change justification, select some text and click the desired justification button. In the Windows version of Eudora Pro, the button "presses in" to indicate the current justification setting. In the Mac version, the buttons don't change.

## Changing indents

Eudora Pro provides additional paragraph formatting via indents. The Mac version is limited to three levels of indents and three levels of hanging indents; the Windows version has no limitations.

### To modify indents

1. Select some text, and from the hierarchical Margins menu in the hierarchical Text menu in the Edit menu, choose an indent level in the Mac version (**Figure 35**), or, in the Windows version, choose Indent In or Indent Out to increase or decrease the indent level (**Figure 36**).

   Alternately, select some text and click the increase or decrease indent buttons on the formatting toolbar (**Figure 37**).

### To modify hanging indents

1. Select some text, and from the Margins hierarchical menu in the Text hierarchical menu in the Edit menu, choose a hanging indent level in the Mac version or, in the Windows version, choose Hanging Indent In or Hanging Indent Out to increase or decrease the hanging indent level.

   Alternately, select some text and click the increase or decrease hanging indent buttons on the formatting toolbar.

### ✔ Tip

- To reset the indent or hanging indent to normal, choose Normal from the Margins hierarchical menu in the hierarchical Text menu in the Edit menu. Alternately, click the Clear Formatting button on the formatting toolbar.

**EUDORA PRO ONLY!**

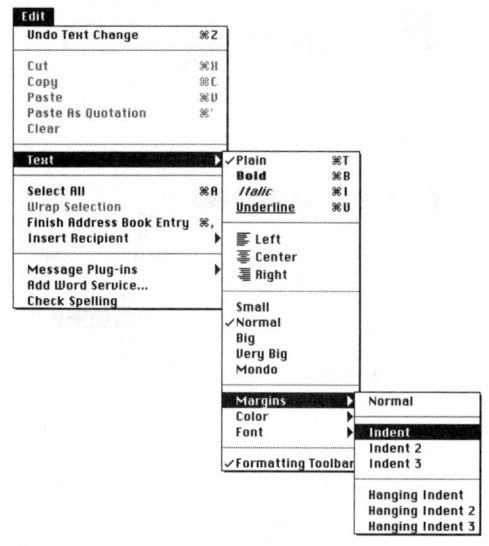

**Figure 35** To increase the indent level of selected text in the Mac version of Eudora Pro, choose an indent level from the hierarchical Margins menu in the hierarchical Text menu in the Edit menu.

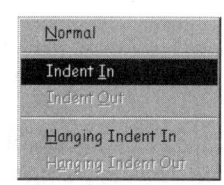

**Figure 36** To increase the indent level of selected text in the Windows version of Eudora Pro, choose an indent level from the hierarchical Margins menu in the hierarchical Text menu in the Edit menu.

*Increase or decrease the hanging indent level by selecting some text and clicking either the increase or the decrease hanging indent buttons.*

**Figure 37** To increase the hanging indent level of selected text, click the increase hanging indent button on the formatting toolbar. The decrease hanging indent button moves text back toward the left margin of the page.

# Writing Messages

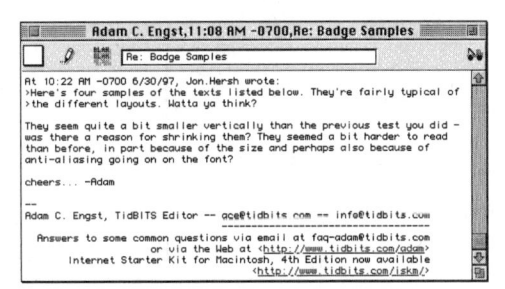

**Figure 38** My standard signature starts with two dashes, provides my name, title, email address, and links to some Web pages for various projects. It's a rather typical signature, although a little long. I change to a shorter signature for some mailing lists.

## About signatures

It's common in email messages to include a signature at the bottom (**Figure 38**). The signature contains bits of personal information that you wish to include with each message.

### Possible signature items

- Your full name, because it's not always clear from other parts of the message.

- Your email address, because it's best to include it in case the headers of the message are munged or are confusing.

- Your title or a description of your job, if you want people to know what you do.

- A URL to your Web page or some other Internet resource. URLs are a bit ugly, so make sure the formatting works.

- If you work on a product, a short pointer or advertisement for your product. We authors do this with our books.

- Your phone number, but only if you want people calling you. I don't recommend it.

- Your office number, if you want people in your organization to be able to find you or send you campus mail.

- Your postal address, if you want people to know where you live or work.

- A tremendously witty saying. Hey, why not? Just keep it short.

### ✔ Tips

- Keep signatures short, preferably no more than four to six lines or so. Longer signatures may cause your messages to be rejected by some mailing lists, and they're a waste of bandwidth no matter what.

- I like starting my signature with two dashes to make sure it's separate from the body of my message.

Chapter 3

# Creating and using signatures

Eudora Light provides two possible signatures, your standard one and an alternate.

## To create a signature

1. From the hierarchical Signatures menu in either the Special menu (Mac) or the Tools menu (Windows) choose either Standard or Alternate (**Figure 39**).

   Eudora opens a standard blank text editing window.

2. Enter the signature (**Figure 40**).

3. When you're done, choose Save ([Cmd]-S/[Ctrl]-S) from the File menu to save your signature.

4. From the File menu, choose Close ([Cmd]-W/[Ctrl]-W) or click the close box to close the signature window.

## To switch between signatures

1. To switch between your signatures, choose one from the Signatures pop-up menu in the message window. On the Mac, it's the JH (John Hancock, get it?) button (**Figure 41**); in Windows, it's a normal pop-up menu (**Figure 42**).

## ✔ Tips

- If you close the signature window without saving first, Eudora prompts you to save before closing the window.

- To see exactly what your signature looks like, send email to your own address.

- Once you create a standard signature, Eudora automatically appends it to all outgoing messages unless you set it otherwise.

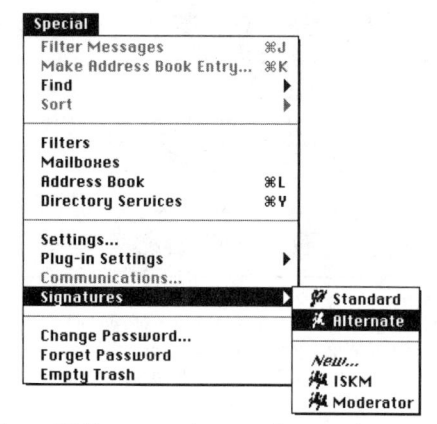

**Figure 39** To create a signature, choose either Standard or Alternate from the hierarchical Signatures menu in the Special menu (Mac) or Tools menu (Windows).

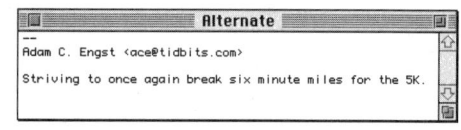

**Figure 40** In the Signature window that appears, type your signature. When you're done, save the signature by choosing Save from the File menu.

The signatures pop-up menu in the Mac version of Eudora looks like a button with a script JH on it.

**Figure 41** To change signatures, choose one of your signatures from the signatures pop-up menu in the message window's toolbar.

The signatures pop-up menu in the Windows version of Eudora is a normal pop-up menu.

**Figure 42** To change signatures, choose one of your signatures from the signatures pop-up menu in the message window's toolbar.

## EUDORA PRO ONLY!

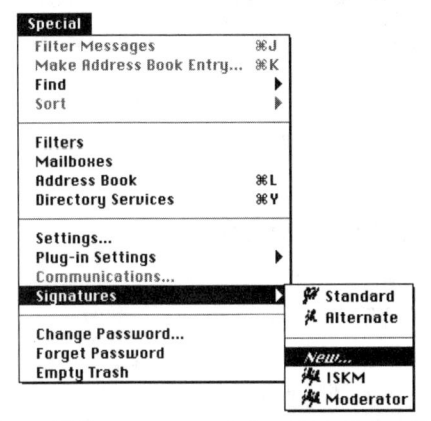

**Figure 43** To create a custom signature in Eudora Pro, choose New from the hierarchical Signatures menu in the Special menu (Mac) or Tools menu (Windows).

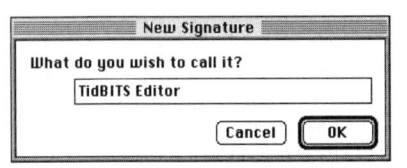

**Figure 44** Name your custom signature, then click the OK button.

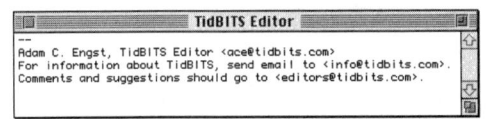

**Figure 45** Enter your signature in the text entry window that appears, and when you're done, save and close the window by choosing Save and then Close from the File menu.

## Custom signatures

Eudora Pro provides the two standard signatures, but it also lets you create additional signatures, which can be helpful if you're the sort of person who wears many hats.

### To create custom signatures

1. From the hierarchical Signatures menu in either the Special menu (Mac) or the Tools menu (Windows) choose New (**Figure 43**).

2. When prompted, enter a name for your custom signature (**Figure 44**) and click the OK button.
   Eudora opens a text editing window.

3. Enter the signature (**Figure 45**).

4. When you're done, choose Save ([Cmd]-S/[Ctrl]-S) from the File menu to save your signature, then choose Close ([Cmd]-W/[Ctrl]-W) from the File menu or click the close box to close the window.

### ✔ Tips

- To delete a custom signature in the Windows version of Eudora Pro, choose Delete from the hierarchical Signatures menu and select the signature to delete in the Delete dialog box.

- Signatures are files stored in the Signature Folder (Mac) or Sigs (Windows) folder, located in your Eudora Folder. You can delete custom signatures by simply dragging them to the Trash on the Mac or the Recycle Bin in Windows.

- You can attach specific signatures to personalities in the Mac version of Eudora Pro. In the Personality Extras settings panel of the Settings/Options dialog box, choose an appropriate signature for each personality. (*See Chapter 12, "Working with Settings/Options"*)

## Editing signatures

You'll undoubtedly want to change your signature every now and then. I find that I tend to change mine when I'm travelling or on vacation so everyone realizes that I may not be as responsive as usual.

### To edit a signature

1. From the hierarchical Signatures menu in either the Special menu (Mac) or the Tools menu (Windows) choose one of your signatures (**Figure 46**).

   Eudora opens a standard text editing window with the text of the signature in it.

2. Edit the signature (**Figure 47**).

3. When you're done, choose Save ([Cmd]-S/[Ctrl]-S) from the File menu to save your signature, then choose Close ([Cmd]-W/[Ctrl]-W) from the File menu or click the close box to close the window.

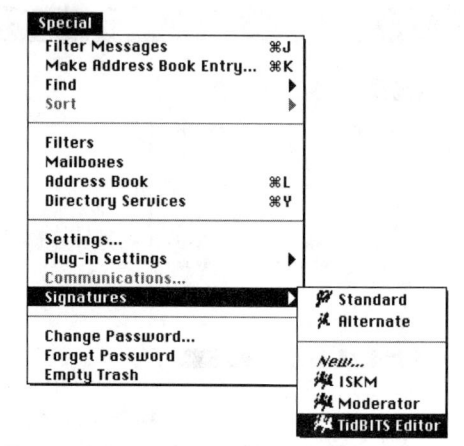

**Figure 46** To edit a signature, choose it from the hierarchical Signatures menu in the Special menu (Mac) or Tools menu (Windows).

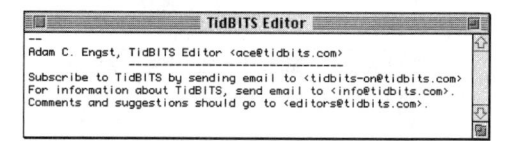

**Figure 47** Make any changes you want, and then save and close the window by choosing Save and then Close from the File menu.

## About attachments

The standard ways of putting text in messages is fine for most messages, but sooner or later you'll need to send a file to a friend or colleague. Perhaps it's just a word processing document that could conceivably be pasted into a message, but what if it's a spreadsheet or page layout document that Eudora couldn't hope to display properly? And, more important, what if you want the recipient to be able to work on the file and return it intact?

In this situation, you should take advantage of Eudora's attachment features. Any document on the Mac or the PC can be attached to an email message, much as you might use a paper-clip to attach a newspaper clipping to a normal paper letter.

When your recipient receives the message, his or her email program (hopefully Eudora as well) saves the attachment to the hard disk, separate from the email message. At that point, it's a normal file such as could have been copied from a floppy disk. Of course, just as with any file that you might send on a floppy disk, the recipient must have a program that can read the file. If you send an Excel spreadsheet, but the recipient doesn't own Excel or have any other method of viewing the file, it's of no use. Check to make sure the recipient can open your file before sending.

Attachments are a tremendously powerful tool, and one that I encourage you to use liberally. Whenever you're collaborating with someone on a project, consider if sending file attachments back and forth might ease the workload.

In this section, I'll discuss how to add attachments to messages; later on we'll look at how to deal with attachments you receive.

Chapter 3

# Attaching files via dialog box

There are several methods of attaching files to outgoing messages. The most obvious method requires selecting the document in a file dialog box.

## To attach files via dialog box

1. Create an outgoing message. (*See Chapter 2, "Creating Messages"*)

2. From the Message menu, choose Attach Document (Mac) or Attach File (Windows) ([Cmd]-H/[Ctrl]-H) (**Figure 48**).

3. In the file dialog box that appears, navigate to the file you want to attach, select it, and click the Attach (Mac) or Open (Windows) button (**Figure 49**).

    Eudora puts the name (and icon, in the Mac versions) of the attached file in the X-Attachments (Mac) or Attached (Windows) line in the header (**Figure 50**). Finish and queue the message as you would any other.

## To remove unwanted attachments

1. Select the attachment by clicking it (you only have to insert the cursor in the name in the Windows versions of Eudora).

2. Press the Delete key to remove the attachment from the message (but not from the hard disk!)

## ✔ Tips

- In the Windows versions of Eudora, you can choose Attach File to New Message from the Message menu if you don't already have an outgoing message open.

- In the Mac versions of Eudora, you can also delete attachments by dragging them to the Trash can in the Finder.

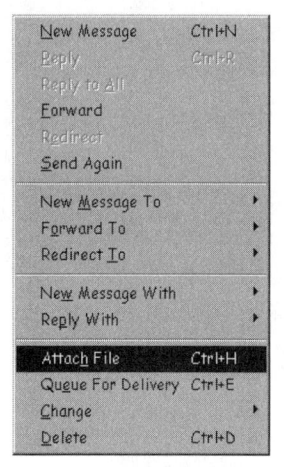

**Figure 48** To attach a file to an outgoing email message, choose Attach File (Windows) or Attach Document (Mac) from the Message menu.

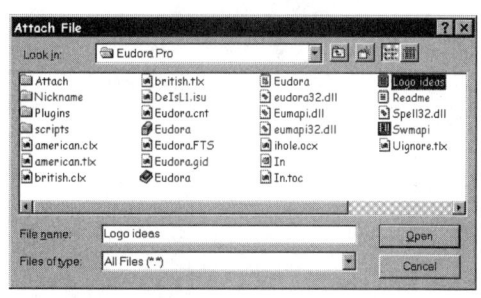

**Figure 49** Select the file to attach and click the Open button (Windows) or the Attach button (Mac).

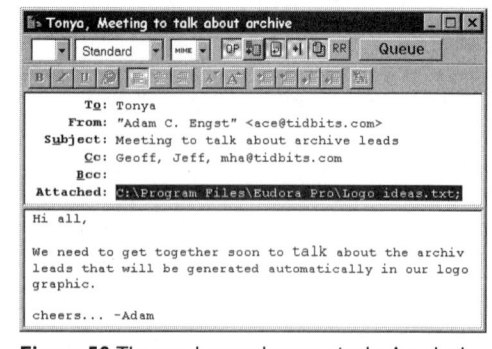

**Figure 50** The attachment shows up in the Attached line (Windows) or the X-Attachments line (Mac) in the header of the message.

54

# Attaching files via drag-and-drop

An easier way of attaching files to messages involves using the mouse to drag the files onto Eudora's icon or onto a message window.

### To create a new message and attach a file

1. From the Macintosh Finder or the Windows desktop, drag one or more files onto the icon for the Eudora program (**Figure 51**).

   Eudora creates a new outgoing message and attaches the file(s) to it (**Figure 52**).

### To attach a file to an existing outgoing message

1. Create a new outgoing message and fill it in. (*See Chapter 2, "Creating Messages"*)

2. From the Macintosh Finder or the Windows desktop, drag one or more files onto the outgoing message window (**Figure 53**).

   Eudora attaches the file(s) to the outgoing message (**Figure 54**).

### ✔ Tips

- It's easier to drag a file onto Eudora's icon if you put an alias (Mac) or a shortcut (Windows) to Eudora on your desktop.

- If you have an outgoing message window open and drag a file onto Eudora, the Mac versions attach the file to that message, whereas the Windows versions attach the file to a new outgoing message.

- In Windows, if your outgoing message window is obscured, drag the file onto the Eudora icon on the Taskbar and wait. Windows brings Eudora to the front so you can drop the file on the message.

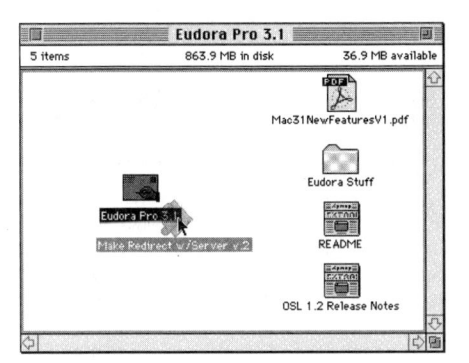

**Figure 51** To create a new message and attach a file to it, drag the file onto the Eudora icon in either the Macintosh Finder or the Windows desktop.

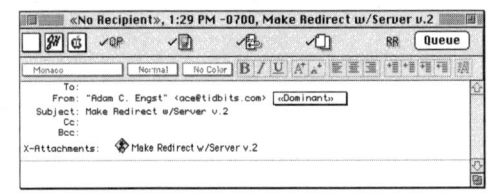

**Figure 52** Eudora creates a new message, attaches the file (and in the Mac versions of Eudora, puts the name of the file in the Subject line as well).

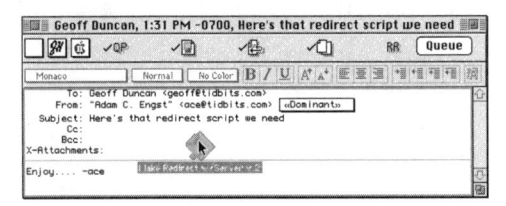

**Figure 53** To attach a file to an existing outgoing message, drop the file's icon on the message window.

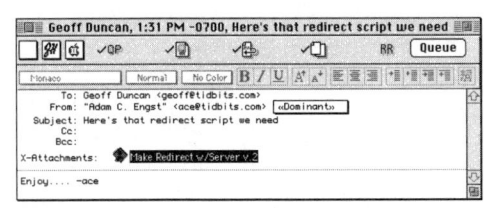

**Figure 54** Eudora attaches files that you drop on a message window to that message.

# Attachment formats

Email attachments can't survive the journey to the recipient without being specially encoded. Think of them as needing envelopes. Unfortunately, there are several encoding formats (**Figure 55a** and **Figure 55b**), and you may have to choose a non-standard one to send attachments to old email programs successfully.

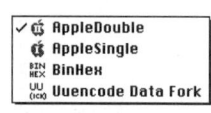

**Figure 55a/55b** Eudora offers a number of encoding formats for attachments. Generally stick with AppleDouble on the Mac and MIME in Windows, but be prepared to try another encoding format if your attachments arrive damaged in your recipient's mailbox.

## Attachment encoding formats

- Use **AppleDouble** (Mac)/**MIME** (Windows) for most messages. They are the best choice for other people using Eudora and for everyone using recent email programs.

- Use **AppleSingle** (Mac only) for sending Mac-specific files (particularly applications) to other Mac users. Try AppleDouble first.

- Use **BinHex** for Mac users with old email programs.

- Use **Uuencode** (all but Mac Eudora Light) when sending documents (never Mac applications) to people with old email programs, particularly on the PC. Mac files have two "forks," and Uuencode only sends the "data fork," which means that any Mac file with information in the "resource fork" will be destroyed in transmission.

## ✔ Tips

- Always test with a small attachment before assuming that attachments will get through to a specific person.

- When sending attachments to America Online users, send only one file per message or the later ones may be damaged.

### Attachment strategies

Here's how I figure out how to send attachments to someone for the first time.

1. First, I try AppleDouble or MIME. That usually works.

2. Next, if I'm sending to a Mac user, I try BinHex, and if I'm sending to a PC user, I try Uuencode. In particular, if my recipient uses the cc:Mail email program on the PC, Uuencode usually works, whereas BinHex works for cc:Mail on the Mac.

3. If all else fails, I talk to my recipients to figure out precisely what they're using and what's going wrong, in the hope that will provide some clues about the next thing to try.

   Every now and then, attachments simply don't work, and at that point, I try an alternate method of transferring the files, such as FTP or the Web.

*Priority menu*
  *Signatures menu*
    *Encoding format menu*

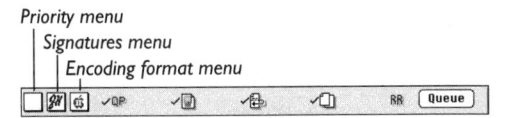

**Figure 56** Use the pop-up message option menus in the Mac version's message window toolbar to change message options.

*Priority menu*
  *Signatures menu*
    *Encoding format menu*

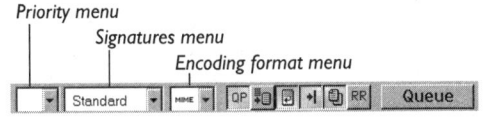

**Figure 57** Use the pop-up message option menus in the Windows version's message window toolbar to change message options.

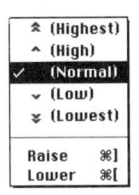

**Figure 58** To change the priority of a message, choose the desired priority from the priority pop-up menu in the message window's toolbar.

**Figure 59** To select a different signature for a specific message, choose the desired one from the signatures pop-up menu in the message window's toolbar.

**Figure 60** To change the attachment encoding format for a specific message and its attachment, choose the desired format from the encoding format pop-up menu in the message window's toolbar.

# Outgoing message toolbar menus

Every outgoing message window has a toolbar with several menus (**Figure 56** and **Figure 57**) that control various options, including message priority, signature, and attachment format.

## To change message priority

1. From the priority pop-up menu (**Figure 58**) in the message window toolbar, choose the appropriate priority. *(See Chapter 5, "Working with Messages")*

## To select a signature

1. From the signatures pop-up menu (**Figure 59**) in the message window toolbar, choose the appropriate signature.

## To select an attachment format

1. From the attachment encoding format pop-up menu (**Figure 60**) in the message window toolbar, choose the appropriate encoding format.

## ✔ Tips

- Keep in mind that not all email programs honor your priority settings.

- Eudora defaults to Normal priority for all email messages. Change priorities sparingly for best effect.

- You can also change the message priority settings from the hierarchical Priority menu in the hierarchical Change menu in the Message menu.

- Eudora defaults to AppleDouble (Mac) or MIME (Windows) for the attachment encoding format, but you can change the default in the Attachments settings panel of the Settings/Options dialog box. *(See Chapter 12, "Working with Settings/Options")*

Chapter 3

# Outgoing message toolbar buttons

Eudora lets you change other settings on a per-message basis by clicking buttons in the outgoing message window's toolbar. The Mac versions (**Figure 61**) consider these buttons On if they have a checkmark next to them. The Windows versions (**Figure 62**) display On by having the buttons "pressed in."

## Message option buttons

- **Quoted-Printable** helps messages with long lines or special characters come through intact. Always leave it on.

- **Macintosh Info** (Mac only) controls whether or not Eudora includes Macintosh resources and types in attachments. Leave it on.

- **Word Wrap** controls whether or not Eudora inserts returns at the end of every line when sending. Generally leave it on.

- **Keep Copies** ensures that outgoing messages remain in your Out box after they're sent. Leave it on for a record of your mail.

- **Return Receipt** (Eudora Pro only), when on, asks the recipient to confirm receipt. It doesn't work with many email programs.

- **Text as Attachment** (Windows only) sends text file attachments in message bodies, rather than as separate files.

- **Tabs in Body** (Windows only) enables you to type tabs in messages. If it's off, the Tab key navigates in the header and body of the message.

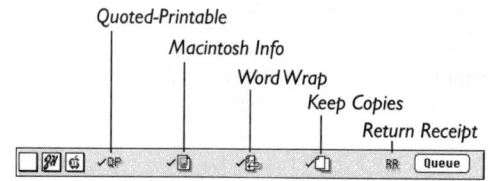

**Figure 61** The message option buttons in the Mac version's message window toolbar. Options are considered to be On when a checkmark appears next to the button.

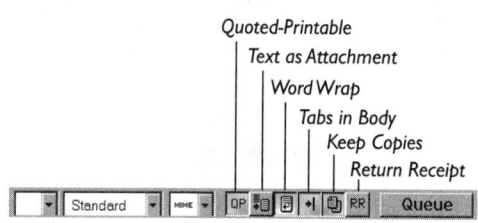

**Figure 62** The message option buttons in the Windows version's message window toolbar. Options are considered to be On when the buttons look "pressed in," as does the QP button above.

### About return receipts

Eudora Pro does return receipts "right." They're not nearly as simple as you might think. For instance, does a return receipt mean that the recipient has received the message, read the message, understood the message, or acted on the message?

Because of this problem, Eudora Pro requires users to click a button on an incoming message to acknowledge receipt. Eudora Pro then generates an automatic message noting that the user has displayed the message—nothing more, nothing less.

# PureVoice plug-in

Qualcomm recently began shipping Eudora with a plug-in called PureVoice that enables you to add voice messages to your email as attachments.

The PureVoice application (**Figure 63**), which is what you use to record or play the voice messages, is completely separate from Eudora, except for the fact that you can attach a recording to a message by choosing PureVoice from the hierarchical Attach menu in the Message menu (**Figure 64**).

PureVoice is simple to use and comes with extensive online help available from the Guide menu (Mac) or the Help menu (Windows) when you have the PureVoice application active.

PureVoice has been available for a only short time, so it remains to be seen how people take to it. Here are a few thoughts about it, based on some early use.

**Figure 63** To record or play sounds with PureVoice, you use the PureVoice application.

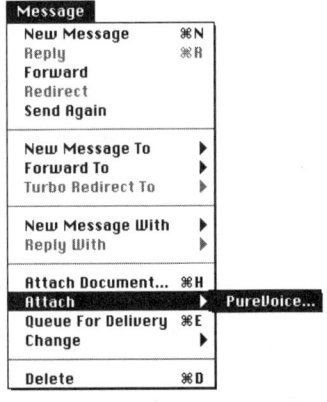

**Figure 64** To attach a voice recording to a new message, create an outgoing message, then choose PureVoice from the hierarchical Attach menu in the Message menu.

## Thoughts about PureVoice

- Technically, PureVoice is extremely impressive. The sound quality is almost as good as normal telephones, and the file sizes are quite small. Usually, high quality audio is accompanied by huge file sizes.

- I found that using PureVoice has the same feel as talking to an answering machine. My telephone manners kicked in instinctively, which seemed awkward, but there's no social convention for voice email yet.

- Voice email isn't as flexible or useful as normal text email in many ways. You can't quote original text for context; you can't edit what you've said; you can't copy and paste text from the message; you can't search through voice email messages; and you can't refer back to only a portion of a message. But it's still a neat trick!

Chapter 3

# PGP plug-in

Qualcomm has also just started shipping Eudora with a plug-in called PGP that enables you to encrypt, decrypt, sign, and verify messages. PGP stands for Pretty Good Privacy and is the name of the company that created the PGP plug-in and its related PGPkeys application.

Entire books could be written about PGP and the field of cryptography, but suffice it to say that you can encrypt messages (**Figure 65**) so no one but the recipient can decrypt them (**Figure 66**). PGP is considered "strong" encryption and cannot currently be broken. You can also use PGP to sign a message so the recipient can verify that you are the sender.

It takes some work to understand how cryptography and PGP work, and I recommend you start with the online documentation that comes with PGP. It should answer your basic questions and show you how to use PGP in conjunction with Eudora.

## Thoughts about PGP

- The PGP package that is integrated into Eudora is the easiest method I've seen for working with cryptographic software. Previous programs were extremely difficult to use, so much so that few people bothered.

- Normal email is not guaranteed to be private, so something like PGP is the only way to be sure that no one but the recipient will read a given message.

- To use PGP's encryption, both you and your recipient must have PGP. Ask before sending encrypted messages to someone.

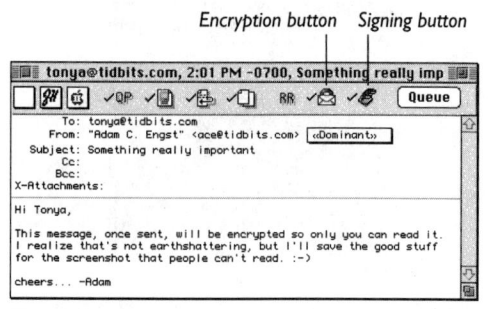

**Figure 65** To encrypt and sign a message, click the encryption and signing buttons in the outgoing message window's toolbar so they're checked (Mac) or pressed in (Windows).

**Figure 66** To decrypt or verify an encrypted or signed message in the Windows versions of Eudora, click the decryption button in the toolbar. In the Mac versions of Eudora, choose PGP Decrypt/Verify from the hierarchical Message Plug-ins menu in the Edit menu.

# Sending and Receiving Messages

# 4

In the last two chapters, we've looked at different ways of creating messages and adding content to them. Throughout those chapters, when you finished creating a message, I said to queue the message for later delivery by clicking the Queue button. That marks the message as being ready to send when Eudora next sends messages.

Eudora is happy to work when you're not connected to the Internet, but that means you need ways to send and receive messages once you connect to the Internet. And to reiterate, you *must* be connected to the Internet to send and receive messages.

Eudora's Check Mail command is generally more than sufficient to send and receive messages, as long as you set the option that has Eudora send queued messages when it checks for new incoming messages. However, Eudora offers numerous ways to send and receive messages that you can tailor to your needs.

For instance, perhaps you want to send a message immediately, or send queued messages without receiving incoming ones. Or, maybe you want Eudora to check for mail every few minutes. You can even have Eudora queue a message and send it automatically several days later. It's all up to you, so let's look at the details now.

# Sending queued messages

After you've created and queued one or more outgoing messages, you probably want to send them. In essence, this is like putting a bunch of letters in your mailbox and then ringing a bell to have the mail carrier suddenly arrive to pick up the letters.

## To send queued messages

1. From the File menu, choose Send Queued Messages (Cmd--/Ctrl-T) (**Figure 1**).

   If necessary, Eudora establishes an Internet connection, and then connects to your SMTP server and sends the queued messages, providing a progress dialog box so you can see what's happening (**Figure 2**).

## ✔ Tips

- The keyboard shortcuts for this process are different between the Mac and Windows versions of Eudora because Eudora Pro on the Mac has to use Cmd-T as the keyboard shortcut for Plain—it's a standard Macintosh keyboard shortcut.

- Bear in mind that sending queued messages does only that; it won't also check for new incoming message. For that, you must use the Check Mail command in the File menu. (*See "Checking for incoming messages" in this chapter*)

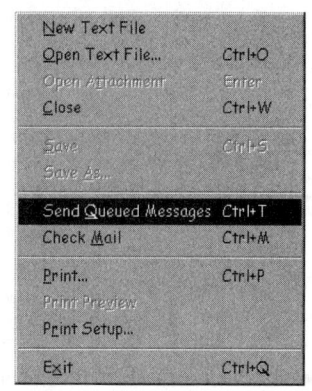

**Figure 1** To send queued messages, choose Send Queued Messages from the File menu.

**Figure 2** Eudora displays a progress dialog box while sending queued messages to your SMTP server.

# Sending and Receiving Messages

## Sending messages immediately

Sometimes you may want a message to go out immediately after you've finished writing it. Although Eudora has a special feature for sending messages immediately (II below), it turns out to be easier to use the standard way of queueing and sending messages manually (I below).

### To send a message immediately (I)

1. Create a new outgoing message. (*See Chapter 2, "Creating Messages"*)

2. Click the Queue button ([Cmd]-E/[Ctrl]-E).

3. Immediately, choose Send Queued Messages ([Cmd]--/[Ctrl]-T) from the File menu to send your message, along with any other queued messages (**Figure 3**).

### To send a message immediately (II)

1. Create a new outgoing message. (*See Chapter 2, "Creating Messages"*)

2. From the hierarchical Change menu in the Message menu, choose Queueing (**Figure 4**) to bring up the Change Queueing dialog box.

    Alternately, hold down Option (Mac) or Shift (Windows) and click the Queue button ([Cmd]-[Option]-E/[Ctrl]-[Shift]-E) to bring up the Change Queueing dialog box.

3. Make sure the Right Now radio button is selected (it is by default) (**Figure 5**).

4. Click the OK button to send the message, along with all other queued messages.

### ✔ Tip

■ There's no way to send just one of several queued messages.

**Figure 3** To send a message immediately, just queue it normally and choose Send Queued Messages from the File menu right after queueing the message. Simple, yet effective.

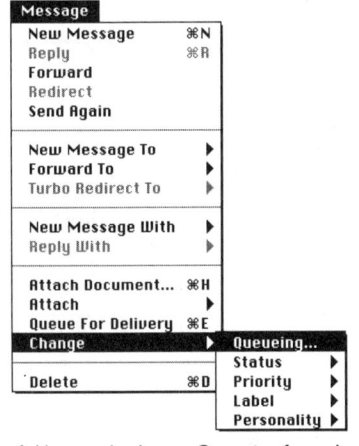

**Figure 4** Alternately, choose Queueing from the hierarchical Change menu in the Message menu to bring up the Change Queueing dialog box.

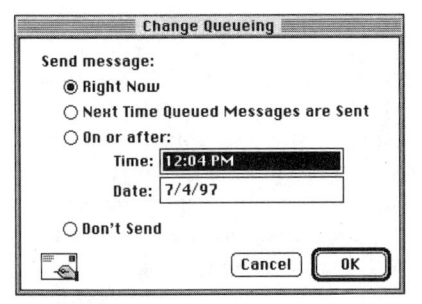

**Figure 5** Make sure the Right Now radio button is selected and click the OK button to send your message (and all other queued messages) immediately.

Chapter 4

# Sending messages at a later date or time

Normally, you want outgoing messages to be sent either immediately or with the next batch of queued messages. Occasionally, however, you may want a specific message to go out after a certain date or time.

## To send a message at a later date or time

1. Create a new outgoing message. (See Chapter 2, "Creating Messages")

2. From the hierarchical Change menu in the Message menu, choose Queueing to bring up the Change Queueing dialog box.

   Alternately, hold down Option (Mac) or Shift (Windows) and click the Queue button ([Cmd]-[Option]-E/[Ctrl]-[Shift]-E) to display the Change Queueing dialog box.

3. Select the On or after radio button and change the time and date fields as needed (**Figure 6**).

4. Click the OK button to queue the message for later sending.

   Eudora saves the message in your Out box and marks it with a T in the message status column (**Figure 7**). Eudora sends the message the next time queued messages go out after the specified date and time.

## ✔ Tips

- Eudora doesn't automatically send the message at the specified time; there must be some other action that causes queued messages to be sent (such as choosing Send Queued Messages from the File menu).

- You can change the queueing for a postponed message if you decide you want it to be delivered sooner.

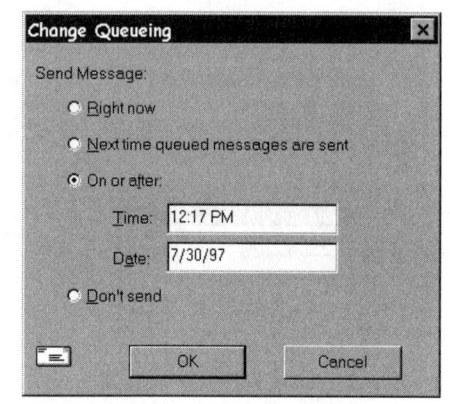

**Figure 6** To send a message at a later date or time, choose Queueing from the hierarchical Change menu in the Message menu, select the On or after radio button, and enter the desired sending time and date.

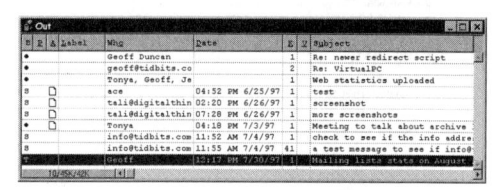

**Figure 7** The last message in the Out box has a T in the status column at the very left.

### Email reminders

I use Eudora's capability to send mail later to remind someone or even myself of something that must happen in several days or weeks. If I sent the email too far ahead of time, the message might be lost or forgotten. Ensuring that the message arrives shortly before the task must be performed works better. Of course, this only works with people who read email religiously.

## Sending and Receiving Messages

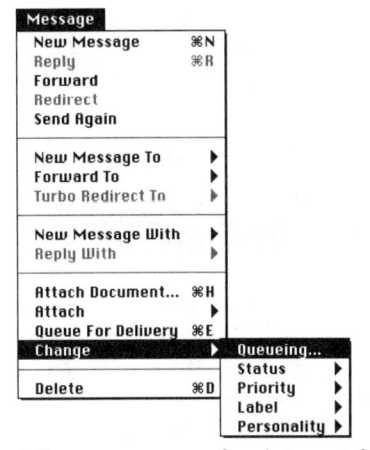

**Figure 8** To prevent a message from being sent, first choose Queueing from the hierarchical Change menu in the Message menu.

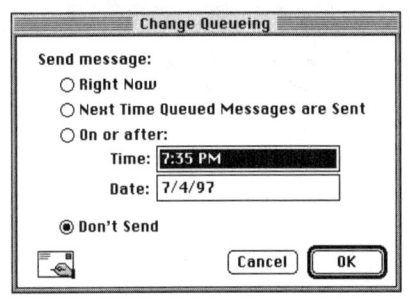

**Figure 9** In the Change Queueing dialog box, select the Don't Send radio button and click the OK button.

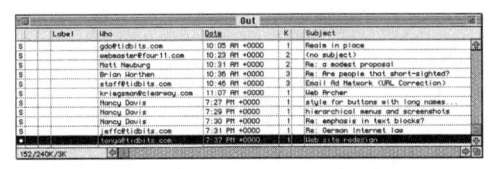

**Figure 10** Notice the last message in the Out box, which has a • in the status column at the very left.

# Preventing a message from being sent

Sometimes, when you're working on an especially complicated or important message, you may want to save it without sending. That's easy—just choose Save ([Cmd]-S/[Ctrl]-S) from the File menu at any time. But what if you queue a message and then decide you don't want to send it the next time queued messages go out?

### To prevent a message from being sent

1. Open or select the message you don't want to send. (*See Chapter 5, "Working with Messages"*)

2. From the hierarchical Change menu in the Message menu, choose Queueing (**Figure 8**) to bring up the Change Queueing dialog box.
   Alternately, hold down Option (Mac) or Shift (Windows) and click the Queue button ([Cmd]-[Option]-E/[Ctrl]-[Shift]-E) to display the Change Queueing dialog box.

3. Select the Don't Send radio button (**Figure 9**).

4. Click the OK button.
   Eudora saves the message in your Out box and marks it with a • in the message status column (**Figure 10**). Eudora won't send the message next time queued messages go out.

### ✔ Tips

- To continue editing your message, double-click it in the Out box, or select it in the Out box and press Return/Enter.

- When you do want to send your message, click the Queue button ([Cmd]-E/[Ctrl]-E) as you would normally.

Chapter 4

# Checking for incoming messages

Enough on sending messages! How do you retrieve incoming messages that others have sent to you? Those incoming messages wait on your POP server until you connect to pick them up.

## To check for incoming messages

1. From the File menu, choose Check Mail ([Cmd]-M/[Ctrl]-M) (**Figure 11**).

   If necessary, Eudora establishes an Internet connection, and then connects to your POP server and receives waiting messages. A progress dialog box shows you what's happening (**Figure 12**).

   Eudora places incoming messages in your In box and then runs any filters you've created on the incoming messages. (*See Chapter 7, "Working with Filters"*)

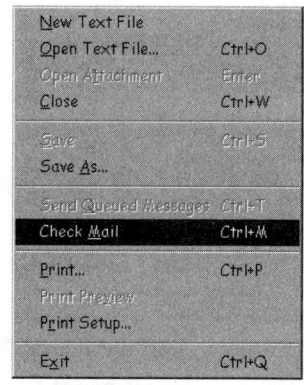

**Figure 11** To check for incoming messages, choose Check Mail from the File menu.

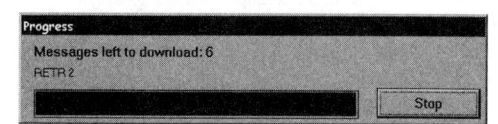

**Figure 12** Eudora displays a progress dialog box while retrieving messages from your POP server.

## ✔ Tip

- I strongly recommend that you check the "Send on check" checkbox in the Checking Mail (**Figure 15** on the next page) or Sending Mail settings panels. This will ensure that Eudora sends queued messages whenever you choose Check Mail. Otherwise, you can forget to send queued messages for some time.

# Checking for incoming messages periodically

If you have a permanent Internet connection, or if you don't mind connecting to the Internet regularly, you can have Eudora check for messages on a periodic basis.

### To check for messages on a periodic basis

1. From the Special menu (Mac) or Tools menu (Windows), choose Settings (Mac) (**Figure 13**) or Options (Windows) to bring up the Settings/Options dialog box (**Figure 14**).

2. Click Checking Mail in the left column to bring up the Checking Mail settings panel.

3. Check the "Check for mail every X minutes" checkbox and enter the number of minutes between checks in the text-entry field (**Figure 15**).

   From then on, Eudora checks for incoming messages on that schedule.

### ✔ Tips

- Macintosh PowerBook users should check the "Don't check when using battery" checkbox to eliminate message checks when the PowerBook isn't plugged in.

- To send queued messages during Eudora's automatic mail checks, check the "Send on check" checkbox in the Checking Mail or Sending Mail settings panels.

- To prevent the Mac versions of Eudora from checking for new mail automatically when you launch Eudora, hold down Shift until Eudora finishes launching.

- Setting Eudora to check for messages periodically can prevent disconnects if your Internet service provider disconnects you after only a short amount of idle time.

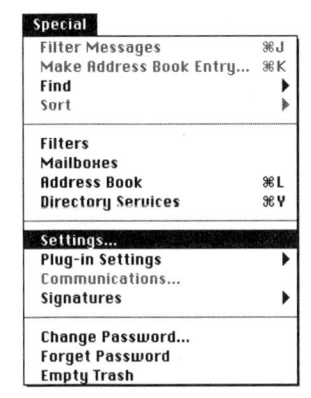

**Figure 13** To check for messages periodically, first open the Settings/Options dialog box by choosing Settings from the Special menu (Mac) or Options from the Tools menu (Windows).

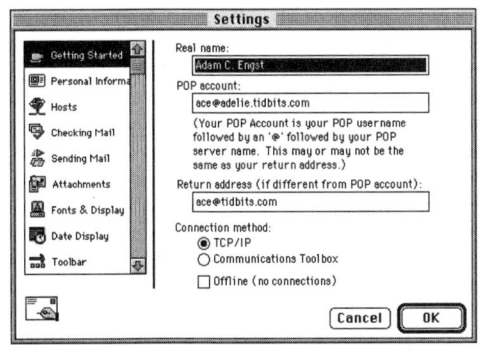

**Figure 14** The Settings/Options dialog box remembers your last choice of panels in the left-hand column but initially defaults to the Getting Started panel. Click Checking Mail to view the Checking Mail panel.

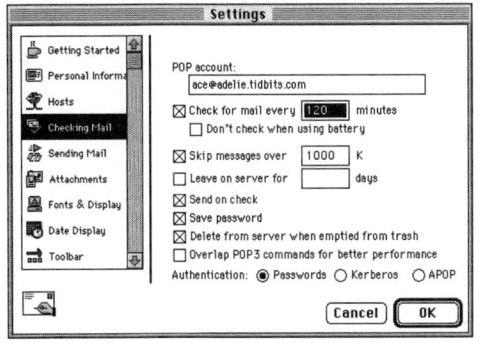

**Figure 15** Check the "Check for mail every X minutes" checkbox, and enter the number of minutes. I set Eudora to check for messages every two hours.

Chapter 4

# About messages left on the server

Before I talk about some of Eudora's other mail checking features, let me explain more about how Eudora interacts with your POP server, where incoming messages wait to be retrieved.

Normally, after Eudora retrieves a message from the server, it deletes the message from the server. However, that's not required, and there are several reasons why a message may remain on the server after Eudora has retrieved it.

- You set Eudora to leave all messages on the server after retrieving them.

- You set Eudora to skip messages over a certain size, and you've received one or more that are too large.

- You asked Eudora Pro to retrieve only message headers.

In any of these situations, Eudora checks old messages left on the server on each mail check to see what it should do with them, and after that retrieves any new messages that are waiting. Eudora can do one of three things with a message left on the server.

- Continue to leave it on the server until something changes.

- Retrieve the entire message, if only the first part had been retrieved previously and you asked Eudora to retrieve the entire thing. Eudora deletes the message from the server after retrieving it.

- Delete the message from the server without retrieving it, either because you explicitly asked Eudora to do so, or because you had put the message in your Trash mailbox and emptied the Trash (with a specific setting turned on).

# Leaving mail on the server

Managing email that you access from two locations (say work and home) can be difficult. To simplify the situation, leave the mail that you read at home on the server so that when you next check from work, the mail is downloaded again (and then deleted from the server). Then you can store or otherwise deal with work email at work.

## To check for new messages but leave them on the server

1. From the Special menu (Mac) or Tools menu (Windows), choose Settings (Mac) or Options (Windows) (**Figure 16**) to bring up the Settings/Options dialog box (**Figure 17**).

2. Click Checking Mail in the left column to bring up the Checking Mail settings panel.

3. In the Windows versions of Eudora, check the "Leave mail on server" and "Delete from server after X days" checkboxes and enter the number of days in the text-entry field (**Figure 18**). In the Mac versions, the "Leave on server for X days" checkbox performs both functions.

    From then on, when (and however) Eudora retrieves incoming messages, it won't delete them from the server until the specified number of days have passed.

### ✔ Tips

- To delete messages left on the server, check the "Delete from server when emptied from Trash" checkbox. After reading the messages, delete them, and choose Empty Trash from the Special menu.

- To leave messages on the server forever in the Mac versions of Eudora, leave the number of days blank.

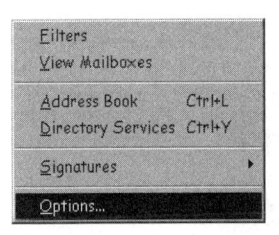

**Figure 16** To leave messages on the server, first open the Settings/Options dialog box by choosing Options from the Tools menu (Windows) or Settings from the Special menu (Mac).

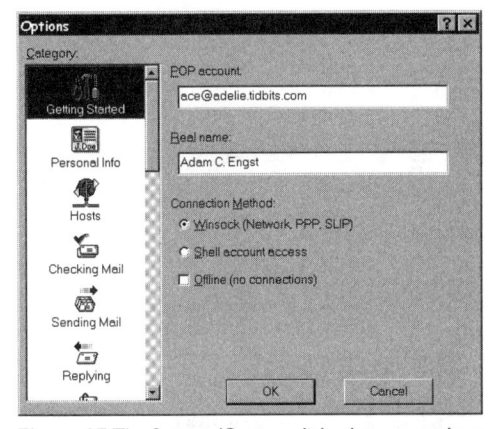

**Figure 17** The Settings/Options dialog box remembers your last choice of panels in the left-hand column, but initially defaults to the Getting Started panel. Click Checking Mail to view the Checking Mail panel.

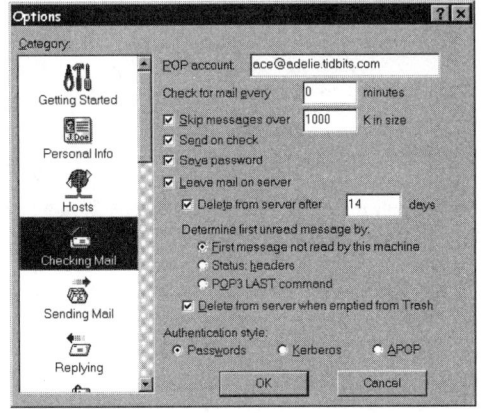

**Figure 18** Check the "Leave mail on server" and "Delete from server after X days" checkboxes, and enter the number of days.

Chapter 4

# Retrieving only small messages

People are sometimes inconsiderate in sending massive attachments in email, and waiting for Eudora to bring in a large attachment may be frustrating, especially over a slow Internet connection or when you're travelling. You can minimize this problem by skipping messages that are larger than you want to download. I skip messages over 40K while travelling and over 1000K at home.

## To retrieve only small messages

1. From the Special menu (Mac) or Tools menu (Windows), choose Settings (Mac) or Options (Windows) to bring up the Settings/Options dialog box.

2. Click Checking Mail in the left column to bring up the Checking Mail settings panel.

3. Check the "Skip messages over X K" checkbox and enter in the text-entry field the maximum acceptable size for messages, measured in kilobytes (**Figure 19**). From then on, Eudora retrieves only the headers and first few lines of too-large messages (**Figure 20**).

## To retrieve a large message

1. In the message window that informs you of the too-large message, click the Fetch (down arrow) button (**Figure 21**).

2. From the File menu, choose Check Mail to ask Eudora to retrieve the entire message and delete it from the server afterwards.

## To delete a large message

1. In the message window that informs you of the too-large message, click the trash can button (**Figure 22**).

2. From the File menu, choose Check Mail to ask Eudora to delete the message.

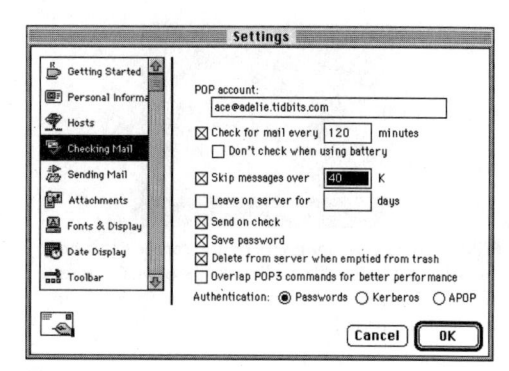

**Figure 19** To retrieve only small messages, check the "Skip messages over X K" checkbox and enter the maximum acceptable size (in kilobytes) in the text-entry field.

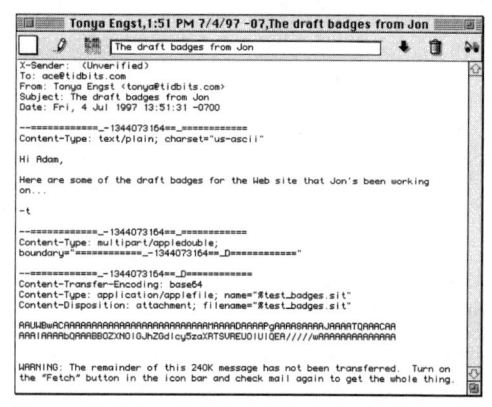

**Figure 20** Eudora displays the header and first few lines of the body of the message.

*Click the Fetch button and choose Check Mail to retrieve a large message.*

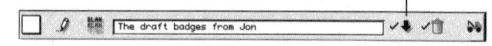

**Figure 21** To retrieve a large message for which you've received only the first bit, click the Fetch button and choose Check Mail from the File menu.

*Click the trash can button and choose Check Mail to delete a large message from the server without reading it.*

**Figure 22** To delete a large message from the server, click the trash can button and choose Check Mail from the File menu.

70

## Special mail transfer options

Eudora Pro users have even more options for sending and receiving messages. For the most part, these options are fairly esoteric, but in the right situation, they are invaluable.

### To use special mail transfer options

1. In the Mac version of Eudora Pro, hold down Option and choose Check Mail Specially ([Cmd]-[Option]-M) from the File menu. In the Windows version of Eudora Pro, hold down Shift and choose Check Mail ([Ctrl]-[Shift]-M) from the File menu (**Figure 23**).

   Eudora displays the Mail Transfer Options dialog box (**Figure 24**). The Windows version of the dialog box looks a bit different but contains the same options.

2. Select the desired options and click the OK button to check mail with those options.

### ✔ Tip

- Using the Option or Shift key to bring up the Mail Transfer Options dialog box also works with Send Queued Messages ([Cmd]-[Option]--/[Ctrl]-[Shift]-T) in the File menu (the Mac version changes to Send Messages Specially). The only difference lies in the checkboxes that are selected by default.

---

### EUDORA PRO ONLY!

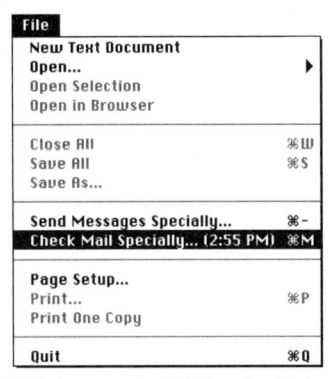

**Figure 23** To bring up the Mail Transfer Options dialog box, hold down Option (Mac) or Shift (Windows) and choose Check Mail Specially (Mac) or Check Mail (Windows) from the File menu.

*Select one or more of your personalities in this list to send or receive messages for the selected personalities.*

*These four options duplicate Eudora Pro's standard behaviors, but you can activate any of them independently here.*

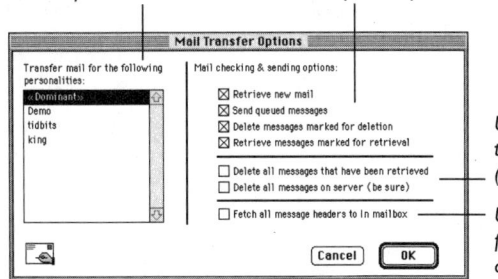

**Figure 24** The Mail Transfer Options dialog box provides numerous tweaky options for sending and receiving messages.

Use these two options to delete mail stored on the server that you've read, or all messages (including unread ones!) currently on the server.

Use this option to retrieve just the headers and first few lines of messages. It's good for quick mail checks when lots of mail is waiting, but note that filters don't operate on these messages.

# Working with Messages

Ironically, the functions in Eudora that we've looked at so far aren't what you'll spend most of your time using. Most people receive much more mail than they send, and they spend much more time reading messages than creating new ones or even replying to old ones.

The ways you work with incoming messages is where Eudora streaks ahead of other email programs. The features may not seem unique, but with interfaces that you use so frequently, the devil is in the details.

The sneaky ways that Eudora makes your life easier abound. For instance, deleting a message can immediately bring up either the next message in the mailbox or the next unread message. A single key (you'll have to read on to find out which one) scrolls the text in the current window, and then, when it reaches the bottom, takes you to the next message. Double-clicking a URL (Uniform Resource Locator, the address of a Web page or other Internet resource) launches your favorite Web browser and takes you there. Or, double-clicking an attachment icon opens the attachment in the appropriate program.

I could go on for a long time, but let's save something for the rest of the chapter. Onward, then!

Chapter 5

# Selecting messages

Selecting messages is simple, but Eudora provides a variety of ways to do so.

## Methods of selecting messages

- To select a single message, click a message summary in a mailbox (**Figure 1**).

- To select a range of messages, click a message summary to select it, then hold down Shift and click another message summary in the same mailbox (**Figure 2**).

- To select a set of messages even if they aren't next to one another, hold down Command (Mac) or Control (Windows) and click several message summaries in a mailbox (**Figure 3**).

- To select all messages in a mailbox whose contents of a column in the message summary are the same, hold down Option (Mac) or Alt (Windows) and click a column in a message summary (**Figure 4**). For instance, click the Sender column of a specific message summary to select all messages sent by that person.

- In the Mac versions of Eudora, when a mailbox is sorted by Sender or Subject, type the first few characters of the sender's name or message subject to select that message.

## ✔ Tips

- The Option/Alt-clicking way of selecting messages is great for selecting all messages with the same subject, from the same sender, with the same priority, or so on.

- When you Option/Alt-click to select similar messages, the Mac versions move the selected messages together into a group in the mailbox. The Windows versions merely select all the similar messages.

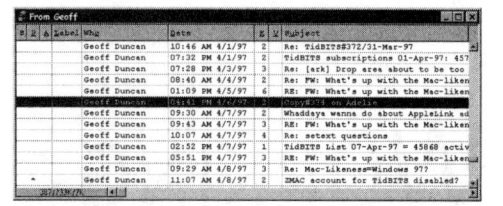

**Figure 1** To select a message, click its message summary.

**Figure 2** To select a range of messages, click a message summary, hold down Shift, and click another message summary.

**Figure 3** To select multiple noncontiguous messages, hold down Control (Windows) or Command (Mac) and click the desired message summaries.

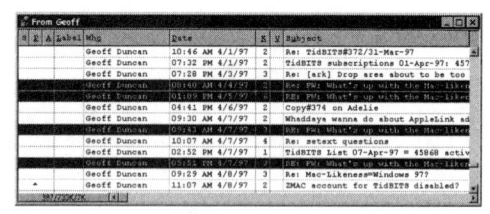

**Figure 4** To select all messages in a mailbox whose contents of a message summary column are the same, hold down Alt (Windows) or Option (Mac) and click a column in a message summary. Here I've Alt-clicked the Subject column of a message to select all other messages with the same subject.

Working with Messages

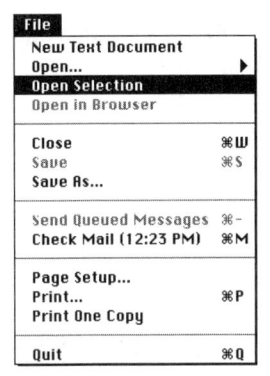

**Figure 5** To open one or more selected messages, choose Open Selection from the File menu in the Mac versions of Eudora.

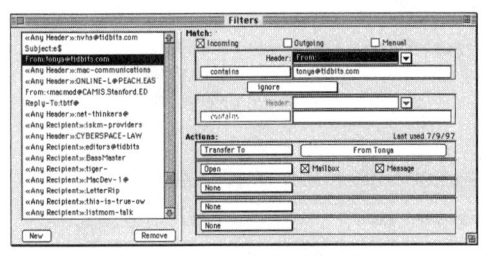

**Figure 6** You can set filters to open messages automatically.

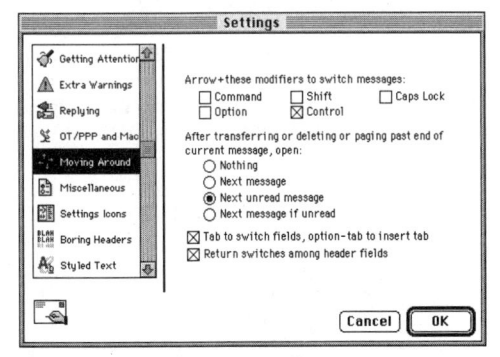

**Figure 7** Eudora can automatically open messages after you transfer, delete, or page past the current message.

## Opening messages

Once you've selected one or more messages, you'll undoubtedly want to open them. Eudora provides numerous ways of opening messages—you'll probably use different ones in different situations.

### Methods of opening messages

- Double-click a message in a mailbox to open its message window.

- Select a message, then press Return/Enter or the Spacebar to open it.

- Select several messages, then press Return/Enter or the Spacebar, or double-click one of the selected messages to open all of them.

- In the Mac versions of Eudora, select one or more messages, then choose Open Selection from the File menu (**Figure 5**) to open all the selected messages.

- Set a filter to open messages that it matches (**Figure 6**). (*See Chapter 7, "Working with Filters"*)

- Set Eudora to open the next message or next unread message after transferring, deleting, or paging past the end of the current message. This setting is in the Moving Around (Mac) (**Figure 7**) or Miscellaneous (Windows) settings panel. (*See Chapter 12, "Working with Settings/Options"*)

### ✔ Tip

- You can switch between message (and mailbox) windows that are already open by choosing them from the Windows menu. The Windows menu also contains commands for managing window display, such as Send to Back, and—in the Windows versions of Eudora—Cascade, Tile Horizontal, Tile Vertical, and Arrange Icons (for minimized windows).

75

Chapter 5

# Changing message priority

You can change the message priority for incoming messages. You might want to do this to organize messages by importance.

### To change message priority (I)

1. Open a message, and then choose a priority from the priority pop-up menu in the message window (**Figure 8**).

### To change message priority (II)

1. In the Mac versions of Eudora, select one or more messages in a mailbox, then move the cursor over the priority column (the second one from the left). When the cursor changes to look like a menu, click and hold to display the priority pop-up menu from which you can choose a priority (**Figure 9**).

   In the Windows versions, right-click one or more selected messages to display a pop-up menu with a hierarchical Change Priority menu from which you can choose a priority (**Figure 10**).

### To change message priority (III)

1. Open a message or select one or more messages, then choose a priority from the hierarchical Priority menu in the hierarchical Change menu in the Message menu (**Figure 11**).

### ✔ Tips

- Message priorities are primarily for your personal use, although they can carry through to replies if you set Eudora to copy the original's priority to the reply in the Replying settings panel.

- You can also use filters to change message priorities. (*See Chapter 7, "Working with Filters"*)

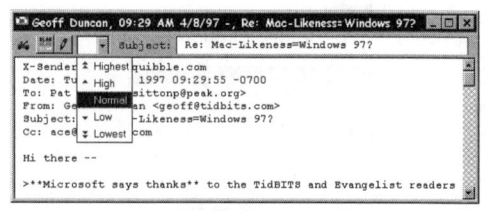

**Figure 8** To change the priority of a message, choose a priority from the priority pop-up menu in the message window.

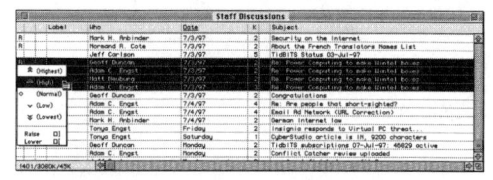

**Figure 9** In the Mac versions of Eudora, move the cursor over the priority column in a mailbox, and when it changes to a menu cursor, click to bring up a menu from which you can choose a priority.

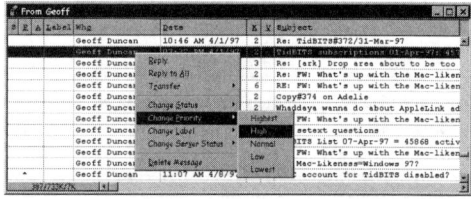

**Figure 10** In the Windows versions of Eudora, right-click one or more selected messages to bring up a pop-up menu with a hierarchical Change Priority menu from which you can choose a priority.

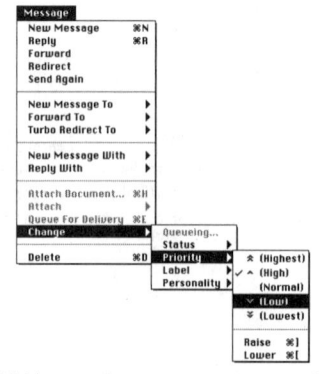

**Figure 11** You can also open a message or select one or more messages and then choose a priority from the hierarchical Priority menu in the hierarchical Change menu in the Message menu.

## Changing message labels

Eudora Pro lets you mark messages with labels, which is helpful for grouping related messages within a mailbox. Labels can have both text and color attributes. (*See Chapter 12, "Working with Settings/Options" for more information on creating labels*)

### To change message labels (I)

1. In the Mac version of Eudora Pro, select one or more messages in a mailbox, then move the cursor over the label column. When the cursor changes to look like a little menu, click and hold to bring up the label pop-up menu from which you can choose a label (**Figure 12**).

   In the Windows version, right-click one or more selected messages to bring up a pop-up menu with a hierarchical Change Label menu from which you can choose a label (**Figure 13**).

### To change message labels (II)

1. Open a message or select one or more messages, then choose a label from the hierarchical Label menu in the hierarchical Change menu in the Message menu (**Figure 14**).

### ✔ Tips

- Message labels are entirely for your personal use—they're never transmitted to others in outgoing messages.

- You can also use filters to change message labels. (*See Chapter 7, "Working with Filters"*)

**EUDORA PRO ONLY!**

**Figure 12** In the Mac version of Eudora Pro, move the cursor over the label column in a mailbox and when it changes to a menu cursor, click to bring up a menu from which you can choose a label.

**Figure 13** In the Windows version of Eudora Pro, right-click one or more selected messages to bring up a pop-up menu with a hierarchical Change Label menu from which you can choose a label.

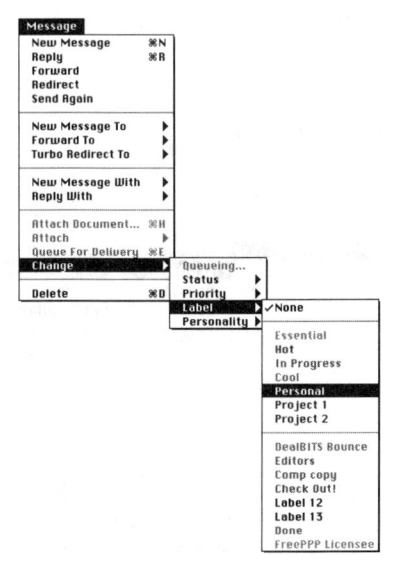

**Figure 14** You can also open a message or select one or more messages and then choose a label from the hierarchical Label menu in the hierarchical Change menu in the Message menu.

# Changing message status

Eudora assigns every message a status, such as Read, Unread, Forwarded, Sent, and Queued. Although Eudora assigns the status of each message automatically, there may be situations where you want to change that status.

## To change message status (I)

1. In the Mac versions of Eudora, select one or more messages, then move the cursor over the status column (the left column). When the cursor changes to look like a menu, click and hold to bring up the status pop-up menu from which you can choose a status (**Figure 15**).

   In the Windows versions of Eudora, right-click one or more selected messages to bring up a pop-up menu with a hierarchical Change Status menu from which you can choose a status (**Figure 16**).

## To change message status (II)

1. Open a message or select one or more messages, then choose a label from the hierarchical Status menu in the hierarchical Change menu in the Message menu (**Figure 17**).

## ✔ Tip

- I sometimes change the status of a message in my In box from Read back to Unread so I'm sure to deal with it again the next day when I read my mail. I also sometimes have a number of messages in my Out box set to Sendable, and it's easier to select them all and change their status to Queued than it is to open each one in turn and click the Queue button.

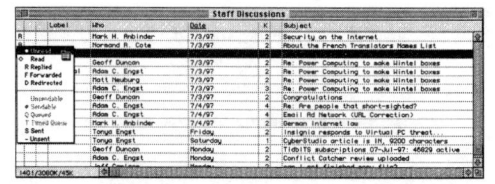

**Figure 15** In the Mac versions of Eudora, move the cursor over the status column in a mailbox and when it changes to a menu cursor, click to bring up a menu from which you can choose a status.

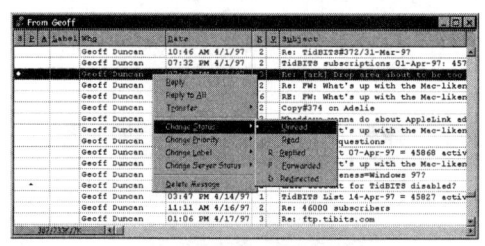

**Figure 16** In the Windows versions of Eudora, right-click one or more selected messages to bring up a pop-up menu with a hierarchical Change Status menu from which you can choose a status.

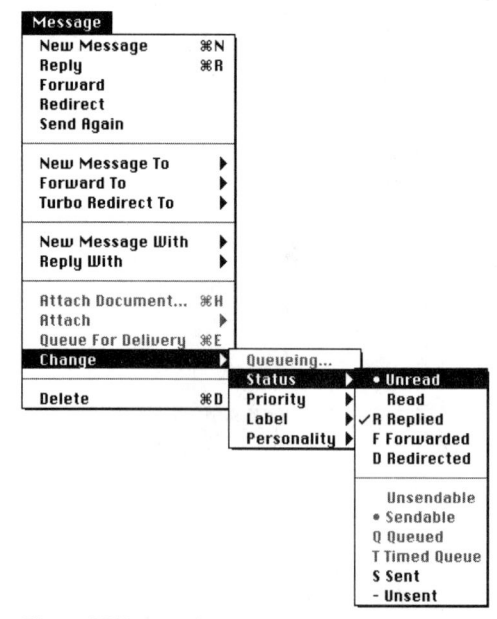

**Figure 17** You can also open a message or select one or more messages and then choose a status from the hierarchical Status menu in the hierarchical Change menu in the Message menu.

## Working with Messages

## Changing message personality

You can select different personalities for outgoing messages in the Mac version of Eudora Pro—since personalities can also receive messages, it makes sense that you could also change the personality of messages that you've received. The Windows version of Eudora Pro doesn't share this feature, but don't worry if that's what you use—you're not missing much.

### To change message personality

1. Open a message or select one or more messages, then choose a personality from the hierarchical Personality menu in the hierarchical Change menu in the Message menu (**Figure 18**).

   You won't see any visible changes; however, when you reply to a changed message, the reply should come from the personality you chose.

**EUDORA PRO ONLY! MACINTOSH ONLY!**

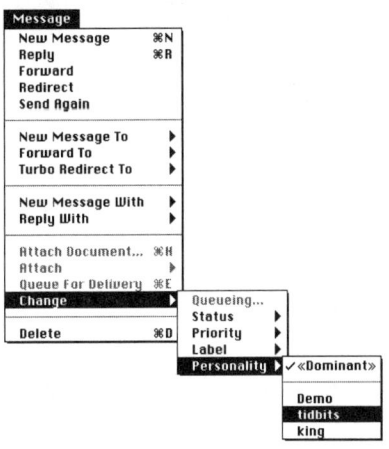

**Figure 18** You can open a message or select one or more messages and then choose a personality from the hierarchical Personality menu in the hierarchical Change menu in the Message menu.

### So why would I want to do this?

You might want to change the personality of some messages if you've received a lot of messages via one personality (say, an old email account you seldom use), but want to reply to them using another personality (your current email account).

If you change the personality of the incoming messages to the new, desired personality, all replies will automatically come from that personality. I realize this is a bit tweaky, but in the right situation, it could save you a lot of work because you wouldn't have to change the personality for each reply individually.

Of course, in my example above, you could just change the old personality to use the return address of the new email account, but for the purposes of argument, let's assume there's a reason you don't want to do that.

# Changing message text

Although you normally only think about changing the text of outgoing messages, Eudora also enables you to change the text of incoming messages. The trick is that you must first unlock the message for editing.

## To change message text

1. Open a message, and in the message window, click the pencil button to enable editing. In the Mac versions of Eudora, the button gets a checkmark next to it (**Figure 19**); in the Windows versions, it indents (**Figure 20**).

2. Make any changes you want in the text of the message.

3. When you're done, choose Save from the File menu ([Cmd]-S/[Ctrl]-S) to save your changes, and then choose Close from the File menu ([Cmd]-W/[Ctrl]-W) or click the window's close box to close the window. If you close the window without saving, Eudora prompts you to see if you wanted to save your changes (**Figure 21**).

## ✔ Tips

- Consider editing the text of a message if you receive a very long message that contains only a small amount of text you want to save. Just delete the unwanted text, then save the changed message.

- People aren't very good at typing URLs (the addresses of Web pages), so they occasionally make glaring errors that prevent you from double-clicking the URL to visit it in a Web browser. If you see the mistake (such as a Web page name ending in .hmtl instead of the correct .html), you can edit the text of the message to fix the problem. That way, double-clicking the URL works and will continue to if you save the message for later use.

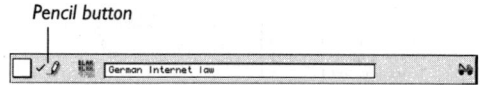

**Figure 19** To switch into edit mode, click the pencil button so there's a checkmark next to it in the Mac versions of Eudora.

**Figure 20** To switch into edit mode, click the pencil button so it's indented in the Windows versions of Eudora.

**Figure 21** If you forget to save your changes after modifying a message, Eudora prompts you when you try to close the message window.

## Revealing boring headers

Eudora tries to protect you from the truly ugly header lines that come with every message—Eudora calls them "boring headers." However, there are times when you may wish to see those header lines, and it's easy to reveal them for further study.

### To reveal boring headers

1. Open a message and note the headers that you can see (**Figure 22**). Then, in the message window, click the Blah button to reveal the boring headers. In the Mac versions of Eudora, the button gets a checkmark next to it (**Figure 23**); in the Windows versions, it indents (**Figure 24**). Eudora then immediately displays the boring headers at the top of the window (**Figure 25**).

### ✔ Tips

- If you look closely at the Received header lines, you can trace the path the message took on its way to you. You can even calculate how long it took, although you have to pay special attention to the time zones, which are generally offsets from Greenwich mean time.

- I sometimes look at the boring headers because it's relatively easy to forge email (spammers do this all the time), but it's more difficult to forge the boring headers, so I can sometimes tell who sent some spam by looking carefully at the X-Sender and Received header lines.

- If someone sends you a message using styled text and it's difficult to read, you can turn off all styling quickly by clicking the Blah button to reveal boring headers. That's because the Blah button also reveals the codes that control styles within the message window.

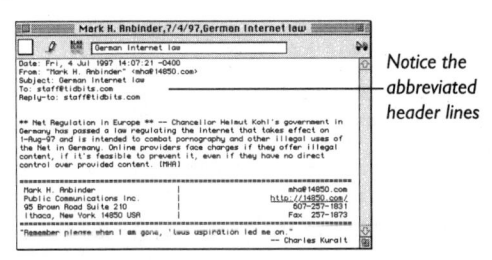

**Figure 22** In a normal message window, the header lines are abbreviated to show only the interesting ones.

*Notice the abbreviated header lines*

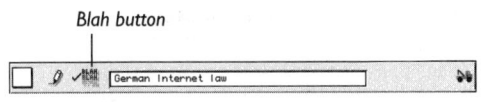

**Figure 23** To display the boring headers in the Mac versions of Eudora, click the Blah button so a checkmark appears next to it.

*Blah button*

**Figure 24** To display the boring headers in the Windows versions of Eudora, click the Blah button so it indents.

*Blah button*

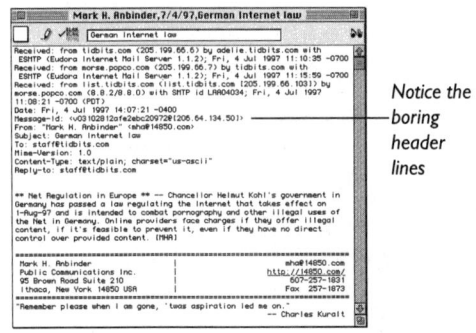

**Figure 25** After you click the Blah button, Eudora reveals all the boring headers.

*Notice the boring header lines*

# Navigating within messages

I'm sure you know how to scroll and move around within a window, and Eudora is no different than most Mac and Windows applications in this regard. However, just to review, here are the ways you can navigate within a message.

## Methods of navigating within messages

- To scroll one line up or down, click the arrows on either end of the scroll bar (**Figure 26**).

- To move up or down one line, press the Up and Down arrow keys when the insertion point is on either the first or last lines. (This is generally too much work.)

- To scroll up or down a page (page size is determined by the window size), click in the scroll bar either above or below the elevator box (**Figure 27**).

- To scroll up or down a page (page size is determined by the window size), press Page Up or Page Down.

- To scroll down a page (page size is determined by the window size), press the Spacebar. When you get to the bottom of the window, pressing the Spacebar again takes you to another message, either the next one or the next unread one, depending on what you set in the Moving Around (Mac) or Miscellaneous (Windows) settings panel.

- To move to the top or the bottom of the message in the Mac versions of Eudora, press Home or End.

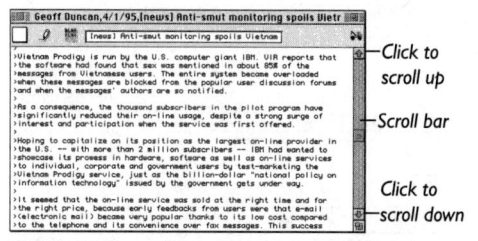

**Figure 26** To scroll one line up or down, click the arrows on either end of the scroll bar.

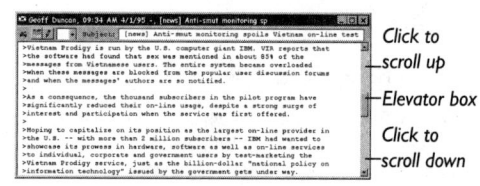

**Figure 27** To scroll up or down a page, click in the scroll box either above or below the elevator box.

# Working with Messages

*Controls for switching messages*

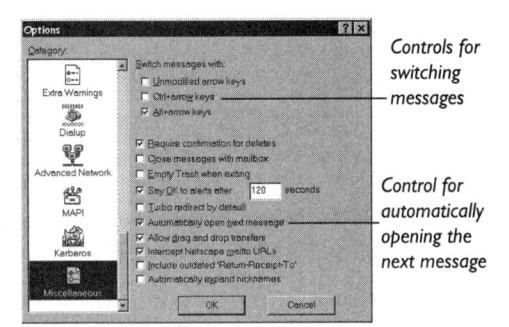

*Control for automatically opening the next message*

**Figure 28** The Miscellaneous settings panel in the Windows versions of Eudora contains the settings for navigating between messages with the arrow keys.

Open Previous Message
Open Next Message

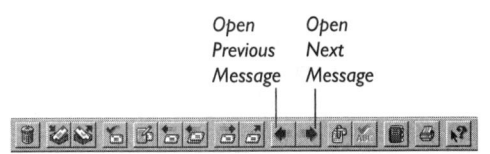

**Figure 29** To switch messages in the Windows versions of Eudora, click the Open Previous Message or Open Next Message button in the toolbar.

## Navigating between messages

Eudora provides a number of ways of moving between messages, some of which are automatic and others of which you must invoke manually.

### Methods of navigating between messages

- Close the current message window by clicking the close box or choosing Close ([Cmd]-W/[Ctrl]-W) from the File menu, then open another message. (*See "Opening messages" in this chapter*)

- When you delete, transfer, or use the Spacebar to page past a message, Eudora closes the message and can open another one, depending on the settings of the Moving Around (Mac) or Miscellaneous (Windows) settings panel (**Figure 28**).

- Press the Left or Up arrow keys to move to the previous message or the Right or Down arrow keys to move to the next message. These keys often require modifiers set in the Moving Around (Mac) or Miscellaneous (Windows) settings panel.

- In the Windows versions of Eudora, click the Open Previous Message or Open Next Message toolbar button (**Figure 29**) to move to the previous or next message.

- To switch between already open messages, choose them from the Windows menu.

### ✔ Tip

- To close all open windows, hold down Option (Mac) or Shift (Windows) and choose Close ([Cmd]-[Option]-W/[Ctrl]-[Shift]-W) from the File menu. Option-clicking a window's close box has the same effect in the Mac versions of Eudora.

### The Windows pane interface

You can create a pane interface (one that doesn't display separate movable windows) in the Windows versions of Eudora. To do this, choose View Mailboxes from the Tools menu, then right-click the Mailboxes window and make sure the Docking View menu is checked (choose it if not). Then, open any message window or mailbox window and click the Maximize button to make that window take up the rest of Eudora's window. From then on, every open message or mailbox window will display at the largest possible size within Eudora's window.

Chapter 5

# Visiting URLs

You'll see many URLs in incoming email messages. Aside from telling friends and colleagues about useful Web pages, people often include URLs in their signatures. You could copy and paste URLs into your Web browser, but that's way too much work.

## To visit a URL

1. URLs in Eudora message windows appear in blue and underlined (**Figure 30**), as do links in many Web browsers. Double-click a Web URL to visit that Web page in your Web browser (**Figure 31**).

## ✔ Tips

- The first time you double-click a URL in the Mac versions of Eudora, it asks you which application to use for that URL type (**Figure 32**). Select your favorite Web browser, or, if you clicked a different URL type (such as ftp, news, or telnet), the appropriate helper application.

- If you want the Mac versions of Eudora to use a different helper application than you initially selected, hold down Option and double-click a URL to bring up the dialog box that asks which helper application to use for that type of URL.

- In the Mac versions of Eudora, if you check the "Read from Internet Config (not recommended)" checkbox in the Miscellaneous settings panel, Eudora will use the preferred helper applications set in Internet Config.

- The Windows versions of Eudora send Web URLs to your default Web browser.

*Notice the underlined, text of the URL. If this book was printed in color, it would be blue too.*

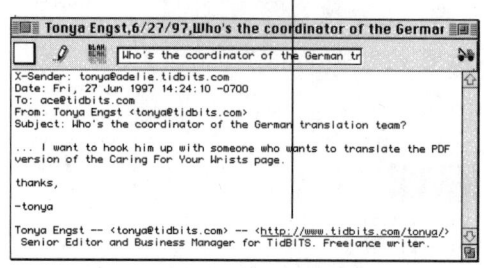

**Figure 30** To visit a URL you see in an email message (it will be blue and underlined), double-click it.

**Figure 31** When you double-click a URL, Eudora either launches or switches to your Web browser and loads the appropriate Web page.

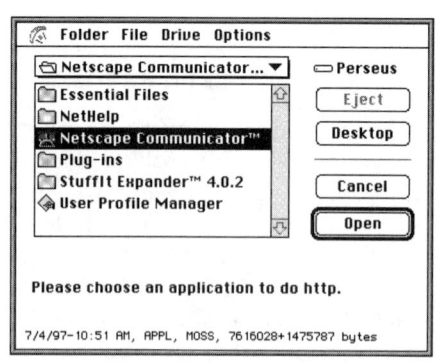

**Figure 32** The first time you double-click a URL (or if you Option-double-click a URL), Eudora asks what application you want to use for that type of URL.

# Deleting messages

Although you may save some incoming mail, you'll want to delete many messages. Keep in mind that Eudora doesn't delete messages immediately; deleted messages are merely moved to the Trash mailbox. They stay there until you empty the Trash by choosing Empty Trash from the Special menu.

## To delete the current message

1. Open a message, read it, and then choose Delete ([Cmd]-D/[Ctrl]-D) from the Message menu (**Figure 33**).

   Alternately, in the Windows versions, right-click the message window and choose Delete from the pop-up menu.

   Eudora moves the message to the Trash and displays the next message, if set to do so in the Moving Around (Mac) or Miscellaneous (Windows) settings panel.

## To delete one or more messages

1. Select one or more messages in a mailbox, then choose Delete ([Cmd]-D/[Ctrl]-D) from the Message menu.

   Alternately, select one or more messages and press either Delete/Backspace or the Forward Delete key.

   Alternately, in the Windows versions, right-click the message window and choose Delete from the pop-up menu.

## ✔ Tips

- To "undelete" a message (or multiple messages, if deleted together) immediately, choose Undo ([Cmd]-Z/[Ctrl]-Z) from the Edit menu. Eudora then moves the message back to the original mailbox.

- In the Mac versions of Eudora, hold down Shift and choose Delete ([Cmd]-[Shift]-D) from the Message menu to delete the current message and not display the next one.

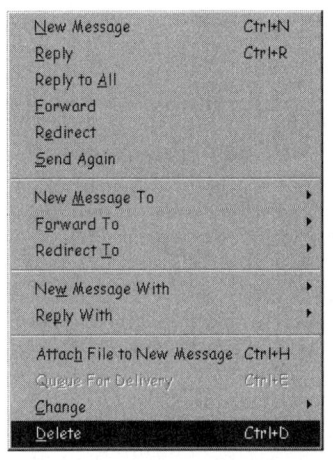

**Figure 33** To delete messages, either open a message or select one or more messages, then choose Delete from the Message menu.

### Nuke it

Every now and then you'll receive a truly sensitive message that you want to delete permanently and immediately, so there's no chance of someone going through your Trash mailbox and finding it. In the Mac versions of Eudora, to delete a message permanently and immediately, hold down Control, Shift, and Option, and choose Nuke from the Message menu.

# Transferring messages to mailboxes

You can and should store important messages in special mailboxes—Eudora provides several different ways to transfer messages into mailboxes. (See Chapter 6, "Working with Mailboxes")

## Methods of transferring messages

- Open a message or select one or more messages, and then choose a mailbox from the Transfer menu (**Figure 34**).

- Open a message, and drag the tow truck icon in the message window to another open mailbox (**Figure 35**) or to a mailbox folder in the Mailboxes window.

- Select one or more messages, then drag them either to another open mailbox or to a mailbox folder in the Mailboxes window (**Figure 36**).

- In the Windows versions, open a message or select one or more messages and then right-click to display a pop-up menu (**Figure 37**) with a hierarchical Transfer menu, from which you can choose a mailbox.

- Create a filter that transfers matching messages to another mailbox. (See Chapter 7, "Working with Filters")

## ✔ Tips

- To undo a transfer, immediately choose Undo (Cmd-Z/Ctrl-Z) from the Edit menu.

- To transfer a copy of a message, hold down Option (Mac) or Shift (Windows) when you transfer the message.

- In the Mac versions of Eudora, hold down Shift when you transfer a message to avoid displaying the next message.

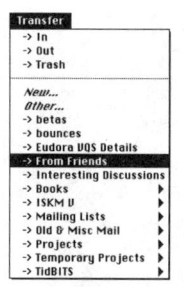

**Figure 34** To transfer messages from one mailbox to another, select one or more messages and then choose a mailbox from the Transfer menu.

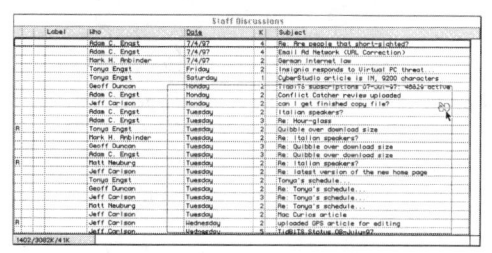

**Figure 35** Alternately, to transfer a message to another mailbox drag the tow truck icon to another open mailbox.

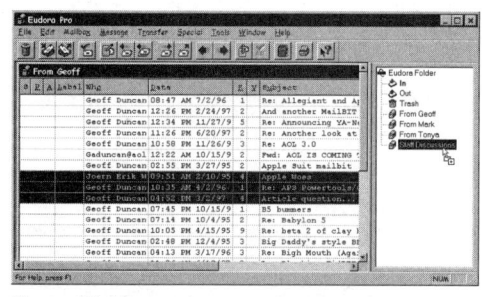

**Figure 36** Alternately, to transfer one or more messages, select them and drag them to another mailbox in the Mailboxes window.

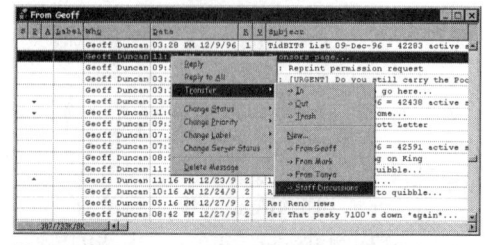

**Figure 37** In the Windows versions of Eudora, you can also right-click a message window or selected messages to display a pop-up menu from which you can choose a mailbox from the hierarchical Transfer menu.

## Opening attachments

When you receive attachments, Eudora places them in the Attachments (Mac) or Attach (Windows) folder in your Eudora Folder, and you can open them like any other file. You can also open them from within Eudora.

### Methods of opening attachments

- Double-click an attachment icon (**Figure 38**).

- Click an attachment icon to select it, then press Return/Enter.

- Click an attachment icon to select it, then choose Open Selection (Mac) or Open Attachment (Windows) from the File menu (**Figure 39**).

- In the Mac versions of Eudora, drag the attachment icon onto the icon of a program that can open the attachment.

### ✔ Tips

- The Mac version of Eudora Pro will display attached graphics within the body of the message if you check the "Display graphics attachments inline" checkbox in the Fonts & Display settings panel.

- In the Mac versions of Eudora, hold down Option and double-click an attachment icon to choose an application to open that attachment.

- In the Mac versions of Eudora, hold down Control and double-click the attachment icon to open the folder that contains the attachment in the Finder.

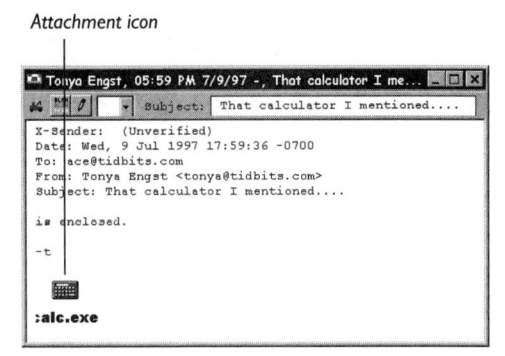

**Figure 38** To open an attachment, double-click the attachment icon, or click once on it to select it and press Return/Enter.

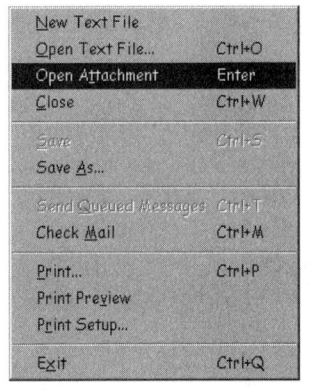

**Figure 39** To open an attachment, select it and choose Open Attachment (Windows) or Open Selection (Mac) from the File menu.

# Moving attachments

All your attachments end up in your Attachments (Mac) or Attach (Windows) folder in the Eudora Folder. You'll probably want to organize those files by moving them to other folders. You can of course do that in the Macintosh Finder or Windows desktop, but you can also do it from within Eudora.

### To move an attachment

**1.** Drag the attachment icon to the folder to which you want to move it.

It may not be obvious immediately, but Eudora moves the file from the Attachments (Mac) or Attach (Windows) folder into the specified destination folder.

### ✔ Tips

- In the Mac versions of Eudora, hold down Option while you drag the attachment icon to another folder to make a copy of the file rather than moving it.

- In the Windows versions of Eudora, watch the cursor while you drag attachment icons. When it's a circle with a slash, you can't drop the attachment; when it's a pointer with a plus sign, you can.

- In the Windows versions of Eudora, if your destination folder or its parent folder is obscured but present on the Taskbar, drag the attachment icon onto the folder's icon on the Taskbar. That folder's window will come to the front so you can drop the attachment in the desired place.

## Deleting attachments

Many attachments won't be interesting after an initial look, and some email programs include style information as attachments (which is really annoying). There are a number of ways you can delete attachments.

### Methods of deleting attachments

- In the Mac versions of Eudora, drag an attachment icon to the Trash in the Finder. This removes the attachment from the message, and moves the file to the Trash, where it will be deleted next time you empty the Trash.

- In the Mac versions of Eudora, delete the message containing the attachment, if the "Trash attachments with messages" checkbox is checked in the Attachments settings panel (**Figure 40**).

- In the Windows versions of Eudora, delete a message containing an attachment, then empty the trash by choosing Empty Trash from the Special menu, if the "Delete attachments when emptying Trash" checkbox is checked in the Attachments settings panel (**Figure 41**).

- Switch to the desktop, open the Attachments (Mac) or Attach (Windows) folder, and drag the file to the Trash (Mac) or Recycle Bin (Windows).

### ✔ Tip

- Although you can drag attachment icons to other folders in the Windows versions of Eudora, you cannot drag them to the Recycle Bin to delete them, as you can drag attachments to the Macintosh Trash.

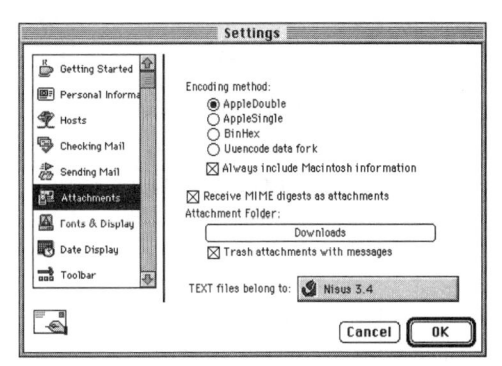

**Figure 40** If you delete a message in the Mac versions of Eudora while the "Trash attachments with messages" checkbox is checked, Eudora moves that message's attachments to the Trash in the Finder.

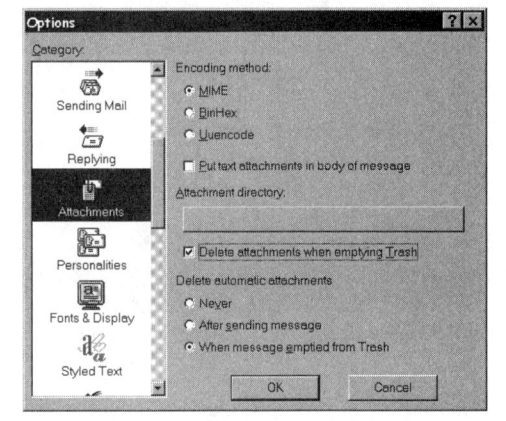

**Figure 41** If you delete a message and then empty the trash in the Windows versions of Eudora while the "Delete attachments when emptying Trash" checkbox is checked, Eudora deletes that message's attachments.

# Saving messages

Eudora offers several ways to extract text from a message, such as copying or dragging it to another application, but you can also save one or more messages to a text file.

## To save messages to a text file

1. Open a message or select one or more messages.

2. From the File menu, choose Save As (**Figure 42**).
   Eudora displays a standard Save dialog box with a suggested file name and two additional checkboxes, Include Headers and Guess Paragraphs (**Figure 43**).

3. To include the headers of each selected message in the text file, check the Include Headers checkbox. To have Eudora attempt to wrap paragraphs of text, check the Guess Paragraphs checkbox.

4. Name the file, navigate to the desired location, and click the Save button.

## ✔ Tips

- If you don't check Include Headers, it may prove difficult to determine where one messages ends and the next one begins in the resulting text file.

- I generally recommend not checking Guess Paragraphs because many messages become difficult to read when wrapped.

- Eudora also enables you to create, open, edit, and save text files using the New Text Document (Mac) or New Text File (Windows), Open (Mac) or Open Text File (Windows), and Save commands in the File menu.

- In the Mac versions of Eudora you can create clippings files by selecting text and dragging it to the Finder.

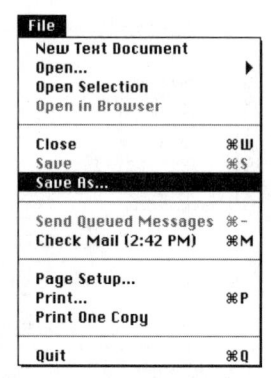

**Figure 42** To save messages to a text file, open a message or select one or more messages, then choose Save As from the File menu.

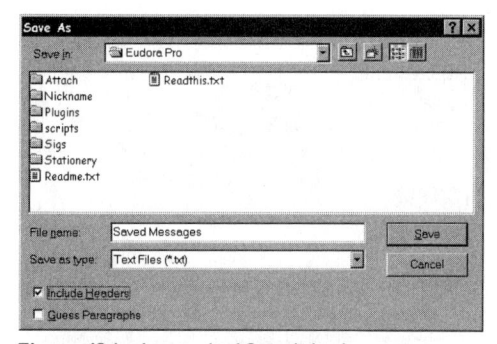

**Figure 43** In the standard Save dialog box, enter a name for the file, check the Include Headers and Guess Paragraphs checkboxes if desired, then click the Save button. The Mac and Windows (shown here) Save dialog boxes look quite different, but are functionally identical.

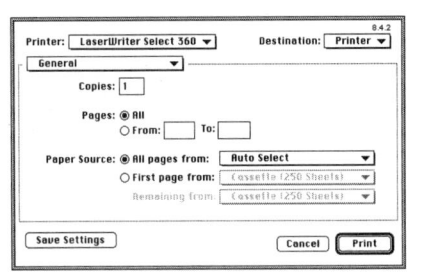

**Figure 44** To print messages, open a message or select one or more messages, then choose Print from the File menu to bring up the Print dialog box. Set any desired print options, then click Print (Mac) or OK (Windows). The Mac (shown here) and Windows Print dialog boxes look quite different, but are functionally the same.

**Figure 45** To see a preview of what will print in the Windows versions of Eudora, choose Print Preview from the File menu.

### Printing other windows

You can print a number of windows in Eudora, including text windows and the contents of the Directory Services window. In the Mac versions, you can also print the contents of the Filters and Address Book windows. Just open the desired window and choose Print from the File menu.

## Printing messages

I generally discourage people from printing email messages since I consider it a waste of paper. However, there are instances where printing is absolutely necessary, such as when you receive driving directions in email.

### To print a message

1. Open a message, or select one or more messages.

2. From the File menu, choose Print ([Cmd]-P/[Ctrl]-P).
   Eudora displays the Print dialog box (**Figure 44**).

3. Make any desired changes to the print options, then click the Print button (Mac) or OK button (Windows).
   Eudora prints the message with a header containing the sender's name, the message date and time, and the message subject. Also included is a footer with a page number and a line that says "Printed for" and your name and email address (**Figure 45**).

### ✔ Tips

- In the Mac versions of Eudora, to print selected messages without seeing the Print dialog box, choose Print One Copy from the File menu.

- In the Windows versions of Eudora, to see what your printout will look like before committing it to paper, choose Print Preview from the File menu.

- In the Mac versions of Eudora, to print just selected text in a message, hold down Shift and choose either Print Selection or Print One Copy from the File menu.

- You set the font used for printing in the Fonts & Display settings panel. (*See Chapter 12, "Working with Settings/Options"*)

# Working with Mailboxes

## 6

### Introduction to Working with Mailboxes

In the last chapter, we looked at how to work with the individual messages that you receive. Dealing with all those messages could prove daunting, especially for people like me who get hundreds of messages a day. Fortunately, Eudora has superior capabilities for storing messages in user-created mailboxes.

You can create as many mailboxes as you want, and you can even nest mailboxes within mailbox folders, which simplifies the task of organizing collections of messages you want to save.

What's most important about Eudora's mailboxes though, is that they're accessible in numerous ways. Everyone works in different ways, and Eudora presents no obstacles to individual methods of organizing messages.

Along with the basic instructions on how to work with Eudora's mailboxes, I also delve into a few strategies that I've used over the years for managing my mailboxes. Perhaps I'm in an unusual situation because of the amount of email I receive, but if a strategy works well for me, it may prove useful, or at least instructive, for you as well.

With that, let's turn our attention to working with mailboxes in Eudora.

# Opening mailboxes

Eudora creates three mailboxes by default: In, Out, and Trash. Before we get into how you create your own mailboxes, let's look at how you open mailboxes.

## Methods of opening mailboxes

- From the Mailboxes menu or one of its hierarchical mailbox folder menus, choose a mailbox (**Figure 1**) to open it.

- Open the Mailboxes window (**Figure 2**) by choosing Mailboxes from the Special menu (Mac) or View Mailboxes from the Tools menu (Windows). Then, either double-click a mailbox or select one and press Return/Enter to open it.

- In the Getting Attention settings panel in the Settings/Options dialog box, set Eudora to open mailboxes when new mail arrives in them (**Figure 3**). (*See Chapter 12, "Working with Settings/Options"*)

- Set a filter to open mailboxes that are matched by that filter. (*See Chapter 7, "Working with Filters"*)

- Open a message window, then hold down Command (Mac) or Control (Windows) and double-click the message's title bar to open its mailbox.

- In the Mac versions of Eudora, select one or more mailboxes in the Mailboxes window and choose Open Selection from the File menu to open them.

## ✔ Tip

- The Mac versions of Eudora mark mailboxes with unread messages by underlining them in the menus and Mailboxes window. The Windows versions do this by bolding mailbox names in the Mailboxes window and placing a letter icon next to them in the Mailbox menu.

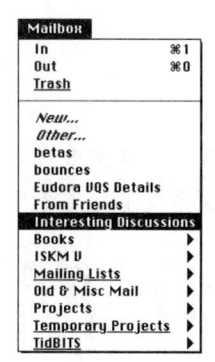

**Figure 1** To open a mailbox, choose it from the Mailboxes menu or one of its hierarchical mailbox folder menus.

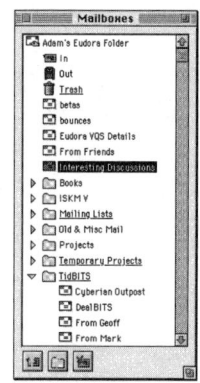

**Figure 2** To open a mailbox from the Mailboxes window, double-click it or select it and press Return/Enter.

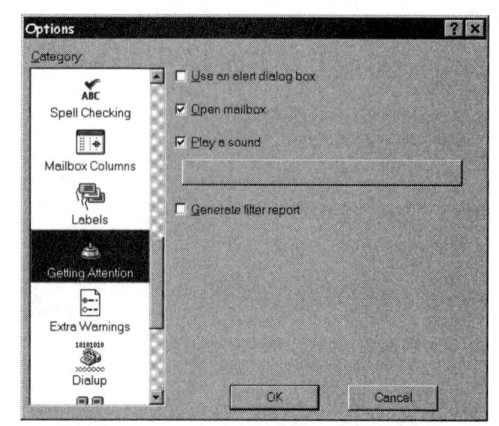

**Figure 3** To set Eudora to open mailboxes automatically when new mail arrives in them, check the Open mailbox checkbox in the Getting Attention settings panel.

## Sorting messages in a mailbox

Once you have opened a mailbox window, you can sort the messages in that mailbox.

### To sort messages (I)

1. Open the mailbox you want to sort, then choose the desired sort from the hierarchical Sort menu (**Figure 4**) in the Special menu (Mac) or Edit menu (Windows).

   Eudora sorts the messages according to the sort you chose.

### To sort messages (II)

1. Open the mailbox you want to sort, then click the header of the column by which you want to sort (**Figure 5**).

   This works in all versions of Eudora except the Mac version of Eudora Light.

### ✔ Tips

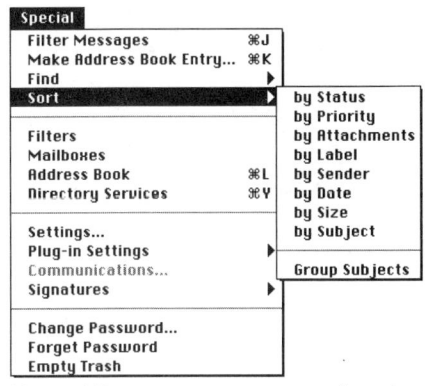

- Hold down Option (Mac) or Shift (Windows) when performing a sort to sort in descending order (Z to A) rather than ascending order (A to Z).

- In the Mac version of Eudora Pro, hold down Shift when performing a sort to add that sort to the current sort rather than replacing the current sort order. This tells Eudora Pro to sort first by Sender then by Date, for instance. The Windows versions of Eudora always add a new sort order to the previous one.

**Figure 4** To sort messages, open a mailbox, then choose the desired sort from the hierarchical Sort menu in the Special menu (Mac) or Edit menu (Windows).

*Click a column header to sort the mailbox by that column.*

**Figure 5** Alternately, in all versions of Eudora except the Mac version of Eudora Light, click a header to sort the mailbox by that column.

### Group Subjects

The Group Subjects command in the Mac versions of Eudora is a fabulous feature if you participate in lots of mailing lists. Open the mailbox where you store messages from a specific mailing list, and choose Group Subjects from the hierarchical Sort menu in the Special menu to turn on subject grouping for that mailbox.

From then on (unless you turn off Group Subjects by choosing it again), Eudora tries to group messages with the same subject, overriding the current sort order. Thus, it's a lot easier to read all the messages about the same topic, even if they didn't all arrive at once.

# Different types of sorts

Most of the options for sorting messages are obvious (**Figure 6**), but some may not be.

## Different types of sorts

- **Status** sorts messages according to message status, in the following order: Unread, Read, Replied, Forwarded, and Redirected. The order of a status sort in the Out box varies somewhat—just scroll to the top or bottom of the mailbox to see messages with less common statuses.

- **Priority** places messages with the highest priority messages at the top of the mailbox and those with the lowest priority at the bottom.

- **Attachment(s)** groups messages with attachments at the bottom of the mailbox.

- **Label** (Eudora Pro only) sorts messages in the same order as the label menu, with unlabeled messages at the top of the mailbox.

- **Sender** sorts messages alphabetically by the name of the sender. If the sender's name doesn't appear in the message, Eudora sorts alphabetically by the sender's email address.

- **Date** sorts messages chronologically by date, with the newest messages at the bottom of the mailbox. Be aware that messages can come in with incorrect dates, thus messing up your date sorts.

- **Size** sorts messages by size, with the smallest messages appearing at the top of the mailbox.

- **Server Status** (Windows Eudora Pro only) sorts messages by their status on the server.

- **Subject** sorts messages alphabetically by the subject of each message.

```
Sort by Status
Sort by Priority
Sort by Attachment
Sort by Label
Sort by Sender
Sort by Date
Sort by Size
Sort by Server Status
Sort by Subject
```

**Figure 6** Eudora provides numerous ways of sorting mailboxes, all available from the hierarchical Sort menu in the Edit menu (Windows) or the Special menu (Mac).

### Remembrance of sorts past

Eudora always remembers the way you last sorted each individual mailbox, and new messages that filter into a mailbox are sorted automatically by that last sort.

This can cause some confusion if you think all new messages should end up at the bottom of a mailbox—a message might sort to the top of a mailbox and thus remain unnoticed for a while.

In the Mac version of Eudora Pro, to remove all sorting and have messages appear in the order in which they arrive, hold down Shift and click the current underlined column header to remove that sort (repeat if other columns are involved in the sort as well).

# Creating mailboxes

I strongly recommend you create mailboxes to store related messages, especially those that come from specific mailing lists—there's no reason they should crud up your In mailbox.

## To create a mailbox (I)

1. From the Mailbox menu or one of its hierarchical mailbox folder menus, choose New (**Figure 7**).

    Eudora displays the New Mailbox dialog box (**Figure 8**).

2. Enter a name for your mailbox and click OK to save it.

    If you chose New from within one of the hierarchical mailbox folder menus, the new mailbox is created inside that folder.

## To create a mailbox (II—Mac)

1. Open the Mailboxes window by choosing Mailboxes from the Special menu.

2. Select a mailbox folder or a mailbox, then click the New Mailbox button (**Figure 9**) to create a new untitled mailbox in the selected folder or at the same level as the selected mailbox.

3. Name your new mailbox—it works just like renaming a file in the Finder.
    *(See "Renaming mailboxes and mailbox folders" in this chapter)*

## To create a mailbox (II—Windows)

1. Open the Mailboxes window by choosing View Mailboxes from the Tools menu.

2. Right-click the folder where you want to store the new mailbox, then choose New from the pop-up menu (**Figure 10**) to display the New Mailbox dialog box.

3. Enter a name for your mailbox and click OK to save it in the selected folder.

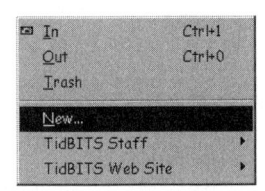

**Figure 7** To create a new mailbox, choose New from the Mailbox menu or one of its hierarchical mailbox folder menus.

**Figure 8** Eudora then displays the New Mailbox dialog box. Enter the name of your mailbox and when you're done, click OK.

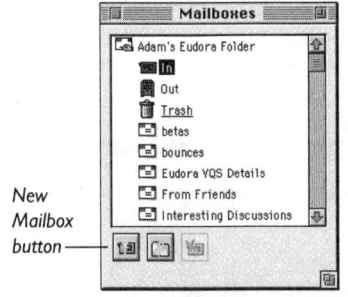

**Figure 9** In the Mac versions of Eudora, click the New Mailbox button in the Mailboxes window to create a new mailbox.

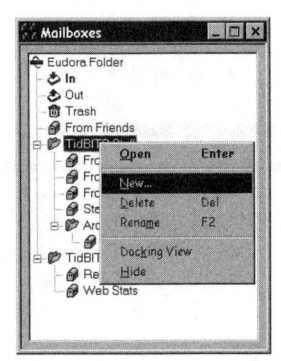

**Figure 10** In the Windows versions of Eudora, right-click the Eudora Folder or another mailbox folder, then choose New from the pop-up menu that appears.

# Transferring messages into mailboxes

We looked at transferring messages back in Chapter 5, "Working with Messages," but the topic is equally relevant here because once you've created a mailbox, you'll want to transfer messages into it.

## Methods of transferring messages

- Open a message or select one or more messages, and then choose a mailbox from the Transfer menu (**Figure 11**).

- Open a message, then drag the tow truck icon in the message window to another open mailbox (**Figure 12**) or to a mailbox folder in the Mailboxes window.

- Select one or more messages in a mailbox, then drag them either to another open mailbox or to a mailbox folder in the Mailboxes window (**Figure 13**).

- In the Windows versions of Eudora, open a message or select one or more messages and then right-click to display a pop-up menu (**Figure 14**) with a hierarchical Transfer menu, from which you can choose a mailbox.

- Create a filter that transfers matching messages to another mailbox. (*See Chapter 7, "Working with Filters"*)

### ✔ Tips

- To undo a transfer, immediately choose Undo ( Cmd -Z/ Ctrl -Z) from the Edit menu.

- To transfer a copy of a message, hold down Option (Mac) or Shift (Windows) when you transfer the message.

- In the Mac versions of Eudora, hold down Shift when you transfer a message to avoid displaying the next message.

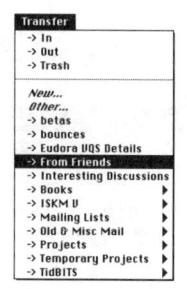

**Figure 11** To transfer messages from one mailbox to another, select one or more messages and then choose a mailbox from the Transfer menu.

**Figure 12** Alternately, to transfer a message to another mailbox, drag the tow truck icon to another open mailbox.

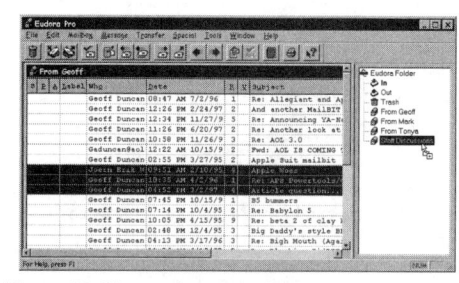

**Figure 13** Alternately, to transfer one or more messages, select them and drag them to another mailbox in the Mailboxes window.

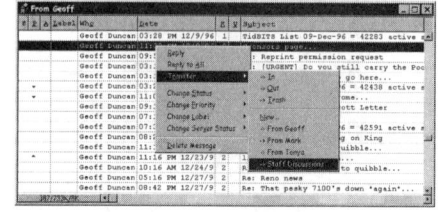

**Figure 14** In the Windows versions of Eudora, you can also right-click a message or selected messages to display a pop-up menu from which you can choose a mailbox from the hierarchical Transfer menu.

# Creating a mailbox during a message transfer

Another way to create messages is probably the most common because it fits best with the way we think. Imagine you're reading a message you want to store in a new mailbox folder. Rather than create a mailbox and then transfer the message into it, you can perform both actions in a single step.

## To create a mailbox and transfer a message into it

1. Open a message or select one or more messages in a mailbox. Then, from the Transfer menu or one of its hierarchical mailbox folder menus, choose New (**Figure 15**).

   Eudora displays the New Mailbox dialog box (**Figure 16**).

2. Enter a name for your mailbox and click OK to save it. If you chose New from one of the hierarchical mailbox folder menus, the new mailbox is created inside that folder. After creating the new mailbox, Eudora transfers the selected message or messages into the new mailbox.

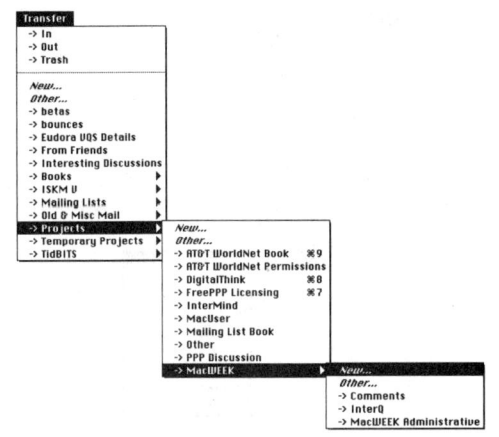

**Figure 15** To create a mailbox and transfer a message into it, open a message or select one or more messages, then choose New from the Transfer menu or one of its hierarchical mailbox folder menus.

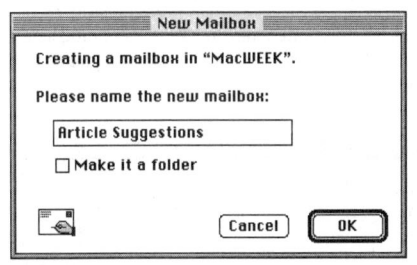

**Figure 16** Eudora then displays the New Mailbox dialog box, asking you to name your mailbox. Enter a name and click OK to save it.

# Creating mailbox folders using menus

Eudora enables you to create nested folders for storing mailboxes, just like the Macintosh Finder or Windows desktop.

## To create a mailbox folder and a mailbox

1. From the Mailbox menu or one of its hierarchical mailbox folder menus, choose New (**Figure 17**).

   Alternately, open a message or select one or more messages in a mailbox, then choose New from the Transfer menu or one of its hierarchical mailbox folder menus.

   Eudora displays the New Mailbox dialog box (**Figure 18**).

2. Enter a name for your mailbox folder, check the "Make it a folder" checkbox, and click OK to save the folder.

   If you chose New from one of the hierarchical mailbox folder menus, the new mailbox folder appears inside that folder.

   Eudora then displays the New Mailbox dialog box again.

3. Enter a name for your mailbox and click OK to save it in your newly created mailbox folder (**Figure 19**). (To avoid creating the mailbox, click Cancel.)

   If you chose New from the Transfer menu or one of its hierarchical menus, Eudora transfers the selected messages to the new mailbox in the new folder.

## ✔ Tip

- In the Windows versions of Eudora, check the "Don't transfer, just create mailbox" checkbox in the New Mailbox dialog box to create a mailbox without transferring any selected messages.

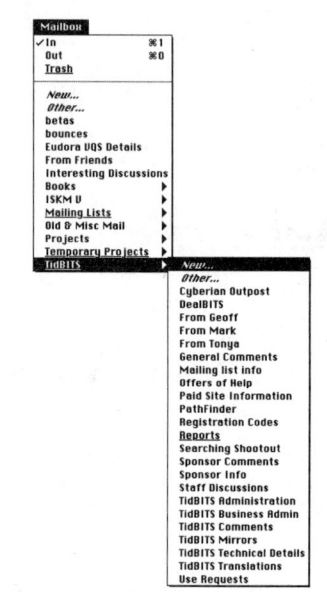

**Figure 17** To create a new mailbox folder and a mailbox, choose New from the Mailbox menu or one of its hierarchical mailbox folder menus.

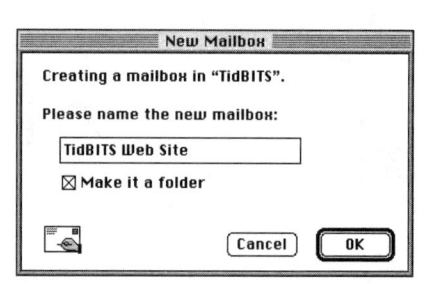

**Figure 18** Eudora then displays the New Mailbox dialog box. Enter a name for your mailbox folder, check the "Make it a folder" checkbox, and click OK to create the mailbox folder.

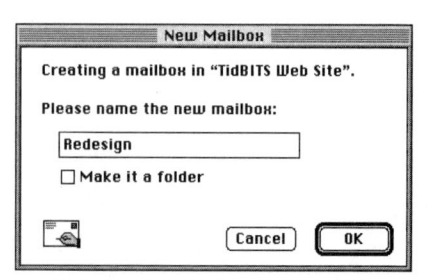

**Figure 19** Eudora then displays the New Mailbox dialog box again, so you can name the new mailbox that Eudora will create inside the new mailbox folder. Click OK when you're done.

Working with Mailboxes

# Creating mailbox folders in the Mailboxes window

You can also create mailbox folders from the Mailboxes window.

## To create a mailbox folder (Mac)

1. Open the Mailboxes window by choosing Mailboxes from the Special menu.

2. Select a mailbox folder or a mailbox, then click the New Folder button (**Figure 20**) to create a new untitled mailbox folder in the selected folder or at the same level as the selected mailbox.

3. Enter a name for the new mailbox folder.

## To create a mailbox folder (Windows)

1. Open the Mailboxes window by choosing View Mailboxes from the Tools menu.

2. Right-click a mailbox folder, then choose New from the pop-up menu (**Figure 21**) to display the New Mailbox dialog box.

3. Enter a name for your mailbox folder, check the "Make it a folder" checkbox, and click OK to save it inside the selected folder (**Figure 22**).

   Eudora then displays the New Mailbox dialog box again.

4. Enter a name for your mailbox and click OK to save it in the new mailbox folder. (To avoid creating the mailbox, click Cancel.)

## ✔ Tip

- In the Windows versions of Eudora, to "dock" (or "float," if it's already docked) the Mailboxes window to the left or right edges of the Eudora window, right-click the Mailboxes window and choose Docking View from the pop-up menu.

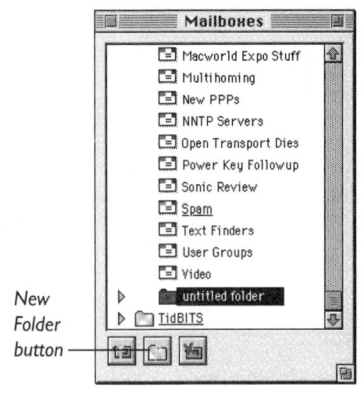

**Figure 20** To create a new mailbox folder from the Mailboxes window in the Mac versions of Eudora, select a mailbox or mailbox folder, then click the New Folder button.

**Figure 21** To create a new mailbox folder from the Mailboxes window in the Windows versions of Eudora, right-click the Eudora Folder or another folder in the list, then choose New from the pop-up menu.

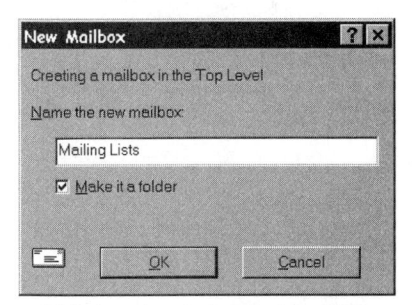

**Figure 22** Eudora then displays the New Mailbox dialog box. Name your mailbox folder and check the "Make it a folder" checkbox, then click OK.

101

# Opening and closing mailbox folders

You can work with the contents of mailbox folders in several ways.

## To open and close mailbox folders (Mac)

1. Open the Mailboxes window by choosing Mailboxes from the Special menu.

2. Double-click a closed mailbox folder to open it and display its contents. Double-click an open mailbox folder to close it and hide its contents.

   Alternately, to open a mailbox folder, click the triangle to its left so that it points down. To close the folder, click the triangle so it points right (**Figure 23**).

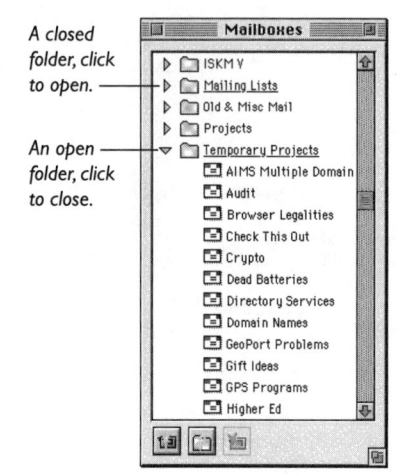

*A closed folder, click to open.*
*An open folder, click to close.*

**Figure 23** In the Mac versions of Eudora, to open or close mailbox folders, click the triangles to the left of the mailbox folder names.

## To open and close mailbox folders (Windows)

1. Open the Mailboxes window by choosing View Mailboxes from the Tools menu.

2. Double-click a closed mailbox folder to open it and display its contents. Double-click an open mailbox folder to close it, and hide its contents.

   Alternately, to open a mailbox folder, click the plus icon to its left. The plus icon changes to a minus icon when the folder is open; click it to close the folder (**Figure 24**).

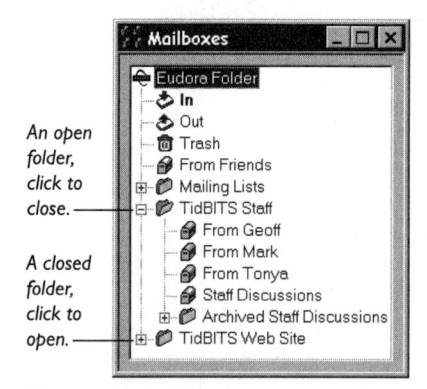

*An open folder, click to close.*
*A closed folder, click to open.*

**Figure 24** In the Windows versions of Eudora, to open or close a mailbox folder, click the plus or minus icon to the left of the mailbox folder names.

# Renaming mailboxes and mailbox folders

Don't worry if you don't like the names you've given your mailboxes—you can always change them later.

### To rename a mailbox or mailbox folder (Mac)

1. Open the Mailboxes window by choosing Mailboxes from the Special menu.

2. Click a mailbox name or mailbox folder name to select it, then wait briefly for Eudora to switch into editing mode, just like the Finder (**Figure 25**).

3. Enter a new name or edit the existing one. When you're done, click somewhere else or press Return to save your changes.

### To rename a mailbox or mailbox folder (Windows)

1. Open the Mailboxes window by choosing View Mailboxes from the Tools menu.

2. Click a mailbox or mailbox folder to select it, then click the name again (**Figure 26**) to switch into editing mode (just like the Windows desktop).

   Alternately, right-click a mailbox or mailbox folder and choose Rename (F2) from the pop-up menu (**Figure 27**).

3. Enter a new name or edit the existing one. When you're done click somewhere else or press Enter to save your changes.

### ✔ Tip

- In the Mac versions of Eudora, you must click the *name* of a mailbox or mailbox folder and pause briefly to enter editing mode. Clicking the icon won't work.

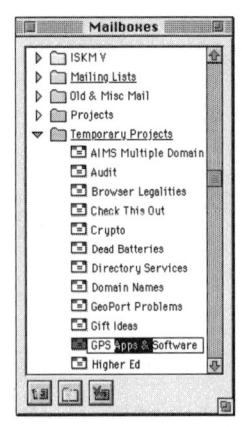

**Figure 25** To rename a mailbox or mailbox folder in the Mac versions of Eudora, click its name, pause briefly, and then edit the name or enter a new one.

**Figure 26** To rename a mailbox or mailbox folder in the Windows versions of Eudora, click a mailbox or mailbox folder to select it, click the name again to enter editing mode, then edit the name or enter a new one.

**Figure 27** Alternately, in the Windows versions of Eudora, right-click a mailbox or folder, then choose Rename from the pop-up menu to enter editing mode.

Chapter 6

# Reorganizing mailboxes and folders

As time passes, you'll undoubtedly want to reorganize your mailboxes and mailbox folders—no organizational scheme lasts forever.

## To reorganize mailboxes and mailbox folders (Mac)

1. Open the Mailboxes window by choosing Mailboxes from the Special menu.

2. Select one or more mailboxes or mailbox folders, then drag them over another folder so the destination folder highlights (**Figure 28**). If the mailbox is closed, it automatically opens to display its contents. Drop the mailboxes or mailbox folders to move them to the highlighted folder.

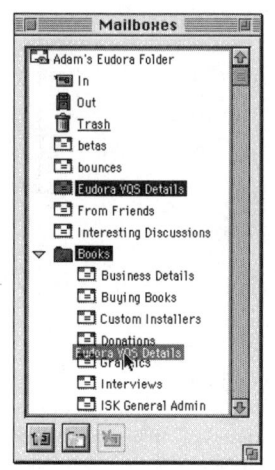

**Figure 28** To move a mailbox from one folder to another in the Mac versions of Eudora, select it and drag it over the new folder, which opens automatically if it was closed.

## To reorganize mailboxes and mailbox folders (Windows)

1. Open the Mailboxes window by choosing View Mailboxes from the Tools menu.

2. Select a mailbox or mailbox folder, then drag it over another folder so the destination folder highlights (**Figure 29**). Drop the mailbox or mailbox folder to move it to the highlighted folder.

## ✔ Tips

- In the Windows versions of Eudora, you can select only one mailbox or mailbox folder at a time.

- In the Windows versions of Eudora, if you drag a mailbox or mailbox folder where it doesn't make sense to drop it, the cursor turns to a circle with a slash through it. The cursor looks like a normal arrow when you can drop the mailbox or mailbox folder.

**Figure 29** To move a mailbox from one folder to another in the Windows versions of Eudora, select it and drag it over the new folder.

Working with Mailboxes

# Deleting mailboxes and mailbox folders

Eventually, you'll decide that you no longer need a mailbox or even an entire mailbox folder. Deleting mailboxes and mailbox folders is simple but destructive, so be careful!

### To delete a mailbox or mailbox folder (Mac)

1. Open the Mailboxes window by choosing Mailboxes from the Special menu.

2. Select one or more mailboxes or mailbox folders, then click the Delete Mailbox button (**Figure 30**) or press Delete.

   Eudora asks if you want to delete the selected mailboxes or mailbox folders, warning you if the mailboxes contain messages (**Figure 31**).

3. Click Cancel to cancel, Remove It to delete just the mailbox or folder mentioned in the dialog box and be prompted for the rest again, or Remove All to delete all the selected mailboxes or folders.

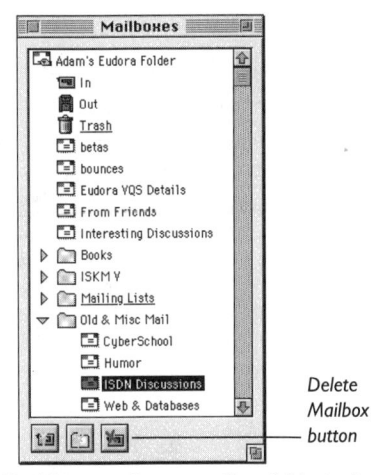

**Figure 30** To delete a mailbox or mailbox folder in the Mac versions of Eudora, select it and click the Delete Mailbox button.

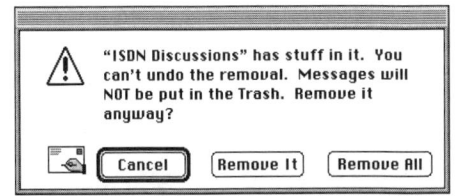

**Figure 31** When you delete a mailbox or mailbox folder, Eudora warns you explicitly if you stand to lose messages in the process.

### To delete a mailbox or mailbox folder (Windows)

1. Open the Mailboxes window by choosing View Mailboxes from the Tools menu.

2. Right-click a mailbox or mailbox folder, then choose Delete (**Figure 32**) from the pop-up menu.

   Eudora asks if you want to delete the selected mailboxes or mailbox folders, warning you if the mailboxes contain messages.

3. Click Cancel to cancel, Remove It to delete just the mailbox or folder mentioned in the dialog box and be prompted for the rest again, or Remove All to delete all the selected mailboxes or folders.

**Figure 32** To delete a mailbox or mailbox folder in the Windows versions of Eudora, right-click it and choose Delete from the pop-up menu.

105

# Compacting mailboxes

When you transfer a message from a mailbox or delete a message, Eudora doesn't immediately reclaim the space that message used. Instead, it tracks the amount of wasted space in each mailbox and compacts mailboxes automatically when there's more wasted space than used space. You can also manually compact mailboxes to save the space.

## To compact mailboxes

1. Open a mailbox, and look in the lower-left corner at the size display (**Figure 33**).
   The three numbers are the number of messages in the mailbox, the size of the mailbox in kilobytes, and the amount of wasted space.

2. To recover the wasted space in a mailbox, either hold down Command and click the size display (Mac) or just click the size display (Windows).

## ✔ Tips

- In the Windows versions of Eudora, to compact all your mailboxes, choose Compact Mailboxes from the Special menu (**Figure 34**).

- In the Mac versions of Eudora, to compact all your mailboxes, hold down Command-Option and click the size display of any mailbox.

*Size display: messages/size/wasted space*

**Figure 33** To compact a mailbox, hold down Command and click the size display in the lower-left corner of the mailbox window. In the Windows versions of Eudora, just click the size display.

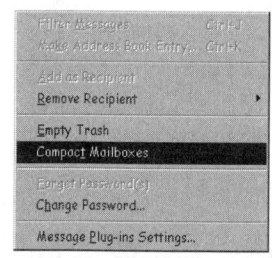

**Figure 34** To compact all your mailboxes in the Windows versions of Eudora, choose Compact Mailboxes from the Special menu.

### Why waste the space?

You probably wonder why Eudora wastes space and then recovers it later. The reason is simple—speed. It's faster to mark a message as deleted than it is to remove it from the mailbox file. If Eudora compacted mailboxes every time you closed them, it would take a lot of extra time.

Eudora tracks which messages are deleted (and other pieces of information about messages, such as status, label, and priority) in a table of contents file. Table of contents files, or TOC files in Eudora parlance, have the same name as their mailbox but also have a *.toc* extension.

In the most recent Mac versions of Eudora, separate TOC files aren't necessary since Eudora can optionally store the message information in the mailbox file itself (in the resource fork, if you care).

# Eudora and aliases

The Mac versions of Eudora honor aliases that you make of mailboxes and mailbox folders (select a mailbox file or a folder that contains mailboxes in the Finder, then choose Make Alias from the File menu). Thus, you can use aliased mailboxes and mailbox folders for a variety of interesting purposes.

## Using aliased mailboxes and mailbox folders

- You can make an alias to a mailbox or a folder that contains mailboxes and place the alias in your Eudora Folder to make Eudora treat the alias as though it were a real mailbox or mailbox folder. This is a great way to store old or large mailboxes outside your Eudora Folder where they can be more readily managed.

- To open a mailbox not in your Eudora Folder and make an alias to it in your Eudora Folder, choose Other (**Figure 35**) from the Mailbox menu or one of its hierarchical mailbox folder menus, and then select a mailbox (**Figure 36**). You might use this if someone sends you a Eudora mailbox that you want to store somewhere other than in your Eudora Folder.

- In Eudora Pro, to open a mailbox not in your Eudora Folder and make an alias to it in your Eudora Folder, double-click the mailbox file in the Finder.

- In Eudora Pro, to open an external mailbox, make an alias to it in your Eudora Folder, and transfer the selected messages into that mailbox, select one or more messages, choose Other from the Transfer menu or one of its hierarchical mailbox folder menus and select a mailbox.

---

**MACINTOSH ONLY!**

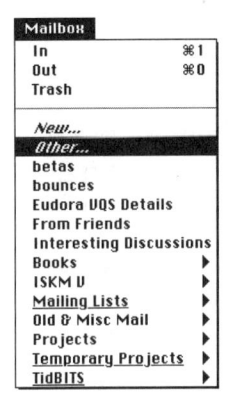

**Figure 35** To open a mailbox outside of your Eudora Folder, choose Other from the Mailbox menu.

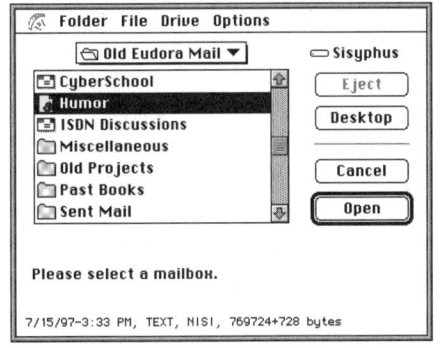

**Figure 36** Then, find a mailbox outside your Eudora Folder, select it, and click the Open button to open the mailbox and create the alias.

## Uses of aliased mailboxes and mailbox folders

I use aliases to mailboxes and mailbox folders in two main ways. First, I alias my massive folder of archived mail into my Eudora Folder so I don't have to take it with me on my PowerBook when I travel. Second, people occasionally send me Eudora mailboxes that I prefer to keep outside of my Eudora Folder for organizational purposes.

Chapter 6

# Being a pack rat

I'm sure there are numerous strategies for archiving messages. I tend to save a lot of my email because disk space is cheap and I like going back to see what happened in the past. Here are a few strategies I use, many of which rely on filters to transfer messages into mailboxes automatically. (*See Chapter 7, "Working with Filters"*)

## Archiving strategies

- Set Eudora to keep copies of outgoing messages in the Sending Mail settings panel of the Settings/Options dialog box, then transfer all your already sent outgoing messages to another mailbox every month.

- Organize mailing lists by setting Eudora to filter mailing list messages into their own mailboxes (**Figure 37**). Keep only the most interesting messages from mailing lists; otherwise the volume will overwhelm you.

- Set Eudora to filter messages from friends and family into a single mailbox. Save most of those messages since they're from the people who are closest to you and will have the greatest value in the future. Archive the contents of this mailbox every year.

- Set Eudora to filter messages from your most prolific correspondents into their own mailboxes. I do this with my wife Tonya and a few people who work on TidBITS (**Figure 38**).

- If you're concerned about not being able to find an especially important message, store it in multiple mailboxes by holding down Option (Mac) or Shift (Windows) to copy the message rather than moving it. I do this when my organizational scheme can't quite cope with a message.

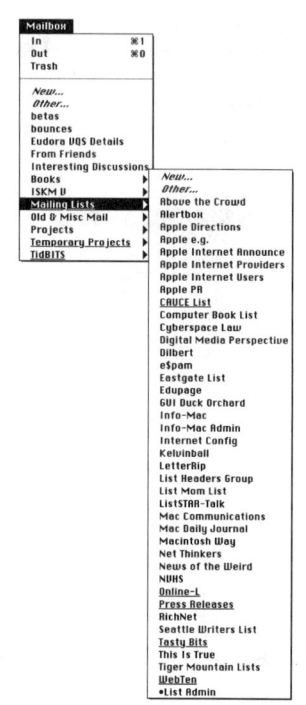

**Figure 37** Here you can see the contents of my Mailing Lists mailbox folder.

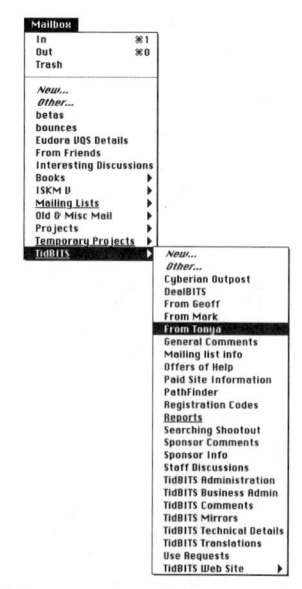

**Figure 38** Here you can see the contents of my TidBITS mailbox folder, including the From Geoff, From Mark, and From Tonya mailboxes.

# Taking out the trash

The Trash mailbox is just another mailbox to Eudora, with one exception—Eudora can delete the messages in it permanently. I prefer to save messages in the Trash for a while because I never know when I'll want to go back for an email address or something. Here, then, are my strategies for deleting messages to recover disk space when the Trash mailbox has grown too large. (*See "Sorting messages in a mailbox" in this chapter*)

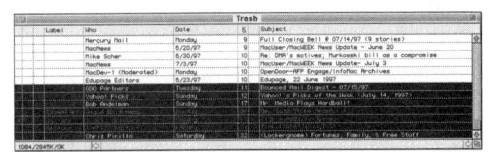

**Figure 39** Sort messages by size, select those over a certain size (over 10K here), then delete them.

**Figure 40** Sort messages by sender, Option/Alt-click the sender of an automated message to select all messages from that sender, then delete them.

**Figure 41** To delete all messages from the Trash mailbox, choose Empty Trash from the Special menu.

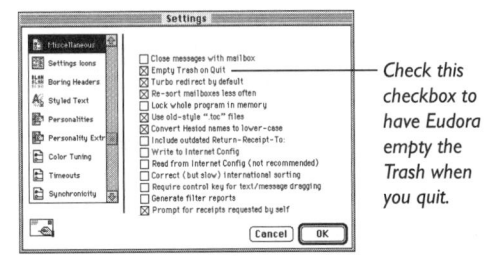

**Figure 42** To set Eudora to empty the trash each time you quit, check the Empty Trash on Quit (Mac) or Empty trash when exiting (Windows) checkbox in the Miscellaneous settings panel of the Settings/Options dialog box.

*Check this checkbox to have Eudora empty the Trash when you quit.*

## Trash strategies

- Sort messages by date, select roughly the top half (the oldest messages) and delete them.

- Sort messages by size, select all the messages over a certain size (look at the bottom of the Trash mailbox) and delete them. This recovers space quickly (**Figure 39**).

- Sort messages by status, select all unread messages (since they were probably boring messages from mailing lists) and delete them.

- Sort messages by sender, Option/Alt-click the senders of automated messages (such as bounces, or daily stock reports) to select them, then delete those messages (**Figure 40**).

- If you really need the disk space, choose Empty Trash (**Figure 41**) from the Special menu to delete all the messages in the Trash.

- If you're chronically short on disk space, set Eudora to empty the trash whenever you quit the program (**Figure 42**).

# Working with Filters

Filters automatically perform a number of actions on email messages based on a message's content. If you receive only several email messages each day, you don't need filters. However, if you subscribe to even a single mailing list or, if you receive lots of email, filters are the life preserver that prevents you from drowning in a sea of email.

Every filter has two parts, a match string and the action Eudora performs on messages that contain the match string. The match string is merely text that Eudora looks for in an email message; the action is what Eudora does when a message contains the match string.

Eudora can look for match strings in specific lines in the message header, in the entire header, or even in the message body, although searching message bodies is a bit slower.

Eudora can perform a wide range of actions when a message contains the match string. Eudora can, for instance, transfer it to a mailbox (the most common use for filters), forward the message, reply to it, redirect it, open it, open its mailbox, print it, change its label, or modify its priority. It's up to you, so let's start filtering now!

### Filter flexibility

This chapter is a little tricky because Eudora's filters are so flexible that it's impossible to walk you through the steps necessary to create every type of filter. Instead, I show you how to create a basic filter and then look at all the different ways you can modify filters.

# Creating filters

Filters are extremely flexible, so the steps below are for creating a generic filter; I provide ideas for specific filters later.

## To create a basic filter

1. From the Special menu (Mac) or the Tools menu (Windows), choose Filters.
   Eudora opens the Filters window (**Figure 1**).
2. Click the New button to create a new Untitled filter (Eudora names the filter automatically based on what it does).
3. From the Header pop-up menu, choose a header line to match.
4. From the Contains pop-up menu, choose how you want the match string to relate to the content of the message. (Contains is the most common.)
5. Enter a match string in the field next to the Contains pop-up menu.
6. From the first Action pop-up menu, choose an action.
7. If necessary, configure the action in the controls that appear to the right of the Action pop-up menu. For instance, choose a mailbox to transfer the message to.
8. In the Mac versions, choose Save from the File menu to save your new filter. In the Windows versions, close the Filters window and click Yes when prompted to save.

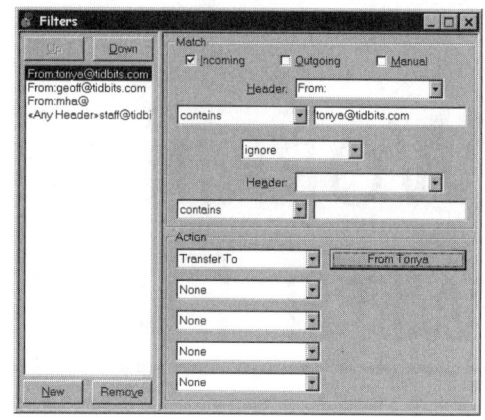

**Figure 1** To create a basic filter in the Filters window, click the New button, choose a header line from the Header pop-up menu, choose how you want the header line to be matched from the Contains pop-up menu, enter a match string, and then choose an action from one of the Action pop-up menus.

## ✔ Tip

- Although you'll want to choose a header line from the Header pop-up menu most of the time, you can enter a specific header line into the Header field. That might be useful if you want to match messages with a strange header line that's not included in the Header pop-up menu.

*Check one or more of these three checkboxes to determine which messages Eudora should consider when running filters.*

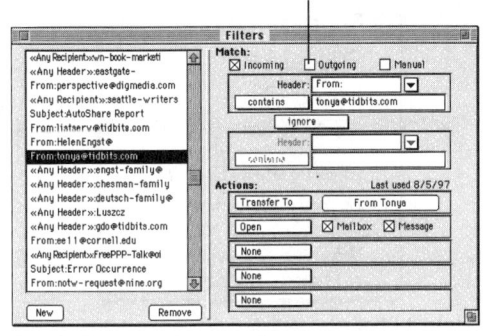

**Figure 2** To set a filter so it filters incoming messages, check the Incoming checkbox. To set a filter so it filters outgoing messages, check the Outgoing checkbox. And, to set a filter so it filters a selected set of messages at any time, check the Manual checkbox.

# Selecting messages to filter

At the top of the Filters window there are three checkboxes, Incoming, Outgoing, and Manual (**Figure 2**). They control which messages the filter looks at.

## Incoming

- To match new incoming messages, make sure the Incoming checkbox is checked for each filter (it's done for you by default).

  Almost all of my filters are incoming filters.

## Outgoing

- To match outgoing messages once they're sent, check the Outgoing checkbox.

  I seldom use outgoing filters, but you could use them to archive only certain outgoing messages for later reference.

## Manual

- To match only the messages you've selected in a mailbox, check the Manual checkbox.

  Manual filters, though not as commonly used as incoming filters, enable you to perform actions on arbitrary sets of messages whenever you like.

## ✔ Tip

- When you're considering creating a manual filter, consider if there isn't an easier way of accomplishing the same task. For instance, if you're using Eudora Pro, you can Option/Alt-click a message summary cell to select all messages like that one, and once you've selected them, transfer them to another mailbox. A manual filter could do the same thing, but is probably more work.

## Header lines

Eudora's filters can examine any line in message headers or even in message bodies (**Figure 3**).

### Header lines for filters

- To look for the match string in a specific message header line, choose To, Cc, From, Subject, or Reply-To from the Header pop-up menu.

- To look for the match string in the To or Cc line of message headers, choose «Any Recipient» from the Header pop-up menu.

- To look for the match string in any header line, choose «Any Header» from the Header pop-up menu.

- To look for the match string in the bodies of messages, choose «Body» from the Header pop-up menu.

- In Eudora Pro, to look for the match string in the name of the personality associated with the messages, choose «Personality» from the Header pop-up menu.

### ✔ Tips

- «Any Recipient» is useful because people don't use the To or the Cc lines consistently, and «Any Recipient» matches both.

- Subject filters seldom work well, since people aren't good at writing subjects consistently.

- Reply-To filters are most useful with mailing lists that set explicit Reply-To lines.

- Scanning message bodies is slower than scanning message headers, and scanning the entire header is a little slower than scanning a specific line. Speed isn't an issue until you amass a lot of filters.

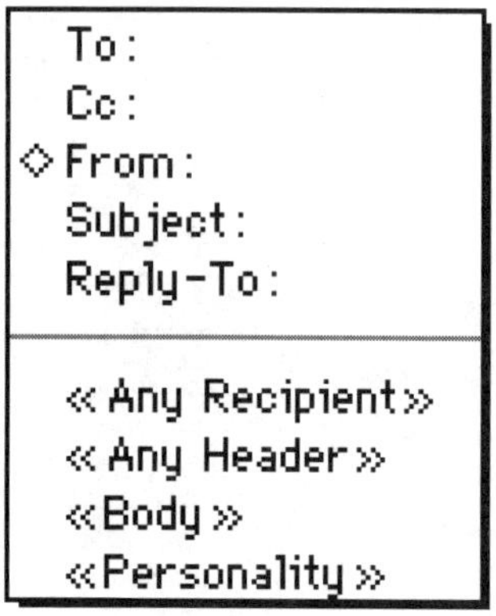

**Figure 3** Choose an item from the Header pop-up menu to have Eudora scan that part of the header for the match string. The currently selected item is indicated with a diamond in the Mac versions of Eudora and by being highlighted in the Windows versions.

### Header line advice

The only way to determine which header line to use is to look at a message of the sort you want to filter. For instance, to filter messages from a mailing list into a different mailbox, look for a header line that contains the name of the mailing list.

Eudora enhances what you can look for in headers by providing two sets of controls for matching header lines, separated by a menu containing "ignore," "and," "or," and "unless." This enables you, for instance, to match messages from someone who regularly sends mail from two addresses (From *geoff@tidbits.com* or *gaduncan@halcyon.com*).

Choosing "and" requires that both matches be true. Choosing "or" requires that one or the other be true. Finally, choosing "unless" only matches if the first one is true and the second one isn't.

I mainly use "unless" to avoid filtering messages redirected by friends whose messages I otherwise store in special mailboxes.

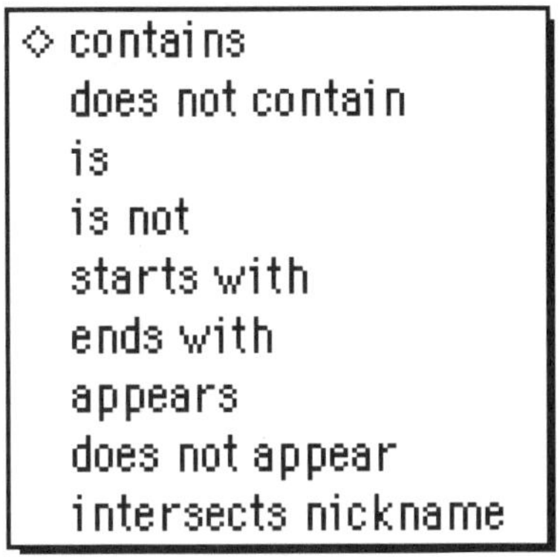

## Contains menu

After you've told a filter which header line to scan, you must determine how it should compare the match string to the chosen item in the Header pop-up menu (**Figure 4**).

### Contains menu items

- To match header lines that contain a portion of the match string, choose "contains." For instance, *ace@tidbits.com* contains the match string *ace*.

- To match header lines that don't contain a portion of the match string, choose "does not contain." For instance, *ace@tidbits.com* does not contain the match string *gurgle*.

- To match header lines that contain the complete match string, choose "is." For instance, the match string *ace@tidbits.com* is *ace@tidbits.com*.

- To match header lines that don't contain the complete match string, choose "is not." For instance, the match string *ace* is not *ace@tidbits.com*.

- To match header lines that start with the match string, choose "starts with." For instance, *ace@tidbits.com* starts with the match string *ace*.

- To match header lines that end with the match string, choose "ends with." For instance, *ace@tidbits.com* ends with the match string *tidbits.com*.

- To match header lines that appear in the header, choose "appears."

- To match header lines that don't appear in the header, choose "does not appear."

- To match header lines that contain an address that's part of the nickname entered as the match string, choose "intersects nickname."

**Figure 4** Choose an item in the Contains pop-up menu to control how Eudora compares the chosen header line with the match string. The currently selected item is indicated with a diamond in the Mac versions of Eudora and by being highlighted in the Windows versions.

---

### Matching advice

Most simple filters use "contains" since it works in almost all situations and generally supplants "starts with" and "ends with." "does not contain" is mostly useful when trying to determine if an address isn't in the message header. "is" and "is not" are much pickier and more likely to fail when something changes. "appears" and "does not appear" are primarily useful for automated mailings that have special headers.

The most interesting item in the Contains menu is "intersects nickname" since it enables Eudora to determine if a message is from or to someone in a specific group of people whose addresses you've added to a nickname.

# Filter actions

Filters must do something, and Eudora Pro provides numerous possibilities (**Figure 5**). Eudora Light can only change priorities and subjects, copy or transfer messages, and skip the rest of the filters.

## Action menu items

- To have the filter do nothing to a message or have that message skipped by all other filters choose None or Skip Rest.

- To change the personality (Mac Eudora Pro only), status, priority, or label of the matched message, choose Make Personality, Make Status, Make Priority, or Make Label, and then choose a personality, status, priority, or label from the pop-up menus to the right.

- To change the subject of the matched message, choose Make Subject, and enter a subject in the text field to the right.

- To notify an application like paging software (Windows Eudora Pro only), play a sound, open the message or the message's mailbox, print the message, notify you, or change the server status of the message, choose Notify Application, Play Sound, Open, Print, Notify User, or Server Status, and set the controls to the right.

- To forward or redirect the matched message, choose Forward To or Redirect To, and enter an email address or nickname in the text field to the right.

- To reply to the matched message, choose Reply With and then choose a stationery from the pop-up menu to the right.

- To copy or move the matched message to a mailbox, choose Copy To or Transfer To and then choose a mailbox from the Transfer menu (Mac) or the pop-up menu (Windows).

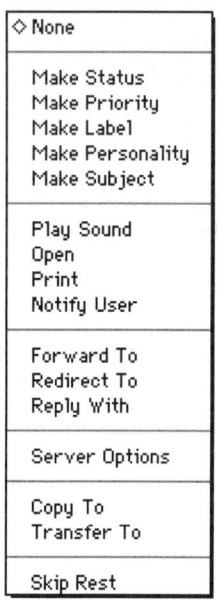

**Figure 5** Choose an item in the Action pop-up menu to perform that action on matched messages. The currently selected item is indicated with a diamond in the Mac versions of Eudora and by being highlighted in the Windows versions.

### Action advice

The most commonly used action is Transfer To, which you use to separate mailing lists into mailboxes. I also use Open to open messages and mailboxes.

The actions for changing status, priority, label, and subject are especially useful for organizing and categorizing messages within a mailbox.

The Forward To and Redirect To items won't work with mail that was automatically generated, such as bounces.

Eudora can perform up to five different actions in a single filter, so you could easily have a filter change the label of a message, raise its priority, transfer it to a mailbox, open that mailbox, and play a sound, all from a single filter.

## Activating filters

I noted previously in this chapter three ways of selecting which messages filters look at, controlled by the Incoming, Outgoing, and Manual checkboxes. It follows, then, that there are three ways of activating filters, depending on the type.

### To activate incoming filters

1. To activate incoming filters, which are the most common type, simply choose Check Mail from the File menu or use any other method of having Eudora retrieve new messages. (*See Chapter 4, "Sending and Receiving Messages"*)

   Eudora retrieves the new incoming messages, and once it's done, applies your incoming filters to them.

### To activate outgoing filters

1. To activate outgoing filters, simply choose Send Queued Messages from the File menu or use any other method of having Eudora send outgoing messages. (*See Chapter 4, "Sending and Receiving Messages"*)

   Eudora sends the queued outgoing messages, and once it's done, applies your outgoing filters to them.

### To activate manual filters

1. To activate manual filters, select some messages in a mailbox, then choose Filter Messages (Cmd-J/Ctrl-J) from the Special menu (**Figure 6**).

   Eudora immediately applies your manual filters to the selected messages.

**Figure 6** To activate manual filters, select some messages in a mailbox, then choose Filter Messages from the Special menu.

Chapter 7

# Filter ideas

How might you use filters? Lots of ways, but here are a few suggestions that I use.

## Filter ideas

- Create filters that transfer messages from mailing lists to their own mailboxes. This sort of filter keeps down the clutter in your In mailbox and allows you to read mailing lists whenever you want.

- Create a set of filters that transfer messages from your close friends and family into a specific mailbox. I like to do this, and I keep those messages as a kind of email diary.

- Create filters that open messages or play sounds when you receive messages from important people. That way you're more likely to see the messages and reply promptly.

- Create a filter that marks messages by whether your address appears in the To line, the Cc line, or in none of the recipient lines. You can usually assume that mail that's cc'd to you is less important than messages sent directly to you, and mail that doesn't contain your address at all seldom requires a response or might even be spam.

- If you frequently receive misdirected mail, create a filter that forwards or redirects messages to the appropriate person automatically.

- Create a set of filters that transfer bounce messages into a special mailbox where you can figure out how to deal with them. Set the filter to look for addresses containing *postmaster*, *Mailer-Daemon*, or *Mail Delivery Subsystem*.

> **Filtering spam**
>
> Many people use filters to transfer spam messages to another mailbox, and although I too do a little of that, it's not a great way of dealing with spam. Some suggestions:
>
> - Don't transfer spam directly to the Trash mailbox until you're sure your filters won't catch mail you might want. I once filtered on two exclamation points in the subject, but that occasionally caught a good message.
>
> - Spammers almost always forge addresses, so it's difficult to filter successfully on any given address. I capture some spam by looking in «Any Header» for *cyberpromo*, *iemmc.org*, *ispam.net*, and *savetrees.com*. But, such a system is always doomed to failure, because spammers are always trying to circumvent filters.
>
> - There are a variety of utilities and preconfigured filters for eliminating spam from your In mailbox, but frankly, I haven't found them all that useful.

## Working with Filters

**MACINTOSH ONLY!**

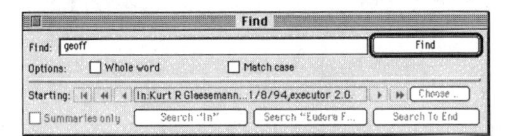

**Figure 7** To find a filter in the Mac versions of Eudora, open the Filters window, open the Find window, enter a search term in the Find field, and click the Find button.

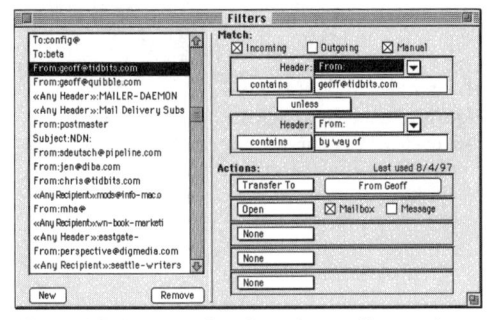

**Figure 8** Eudora searches through your filters and selects the first one that matches the search term.

## Finding filters

After you've been creating filters for a while, it becomes difficult to find any given one in the list. In the Mac versions of Eudora, you can use the Find window to find a filter.

### To find a filter

1. From the Special menu, choose Filters.
   Eudora opens the Filters window.

2. From the hierarchical Find menu in the Special menu, choose Find (Cmd-F).
   Eudora opens the Find window (**Figure 7**).

3. Enter the search term in the Find field.
   The search term should include the text for which the filter looks, such as an email address.

4. Click the Find button.
   Eudora starts searching through your filters. If Eudora finds a match, it stops and selects the matching filter (**Figure 8**). If not, Eudora tells you that it was unable to find the search term.

5. To continue searching if you find a filter that's not the one you want, click the Find button again.

### ✔ Tips

- Don't worry about the starting point when trying to find a filter. Eudora searches your entire set of filters, starting at the selected filter and wrapping around if necessary.

- The Match case checkbox works as you would expect, so if it's checked, a search for *ACE* will not find a filter that looks for *ace@tidbits.com*.

- Avoid the Whole word checkbox because it's not clear what a "word" is in the context of a filter.

119

# Modifying filters

Sooner or later someone's email address will change or you'll want to modify a filter for different actions.

### To modify a filter

1. From the Special menu (Mac) or the Tools menu (Windows), choose Filters.

   Eudora opens the Filters window (**Figure 9**).

2. From the list on the left side of the Filters window, click the filter you want to modify to select it.

3. Modify the filter settings as desired.

4. In the Mac versions of Eudora, choose Save from the File menu to save your new filter. In the Windows versions, close the Filters window and click Yes when prompted to save.

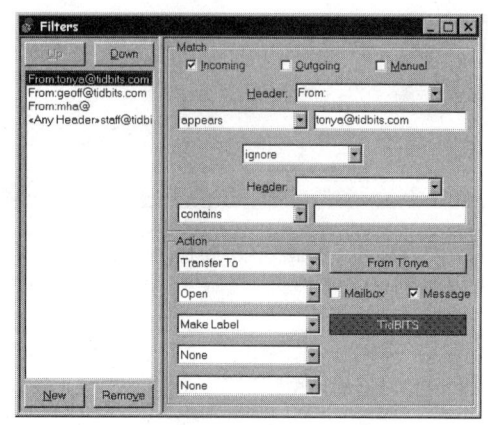

**Figure 9** To modify a filter, open the Filters window, click the filter you want to modify, and then change the actions or any other part of the filter.

---

### Mac filter effectiveness

In the Mac versions of Eudora, you can determine how well your filters work (and if they're working at all). Eudora creates a Last Used date field above the Action menus and updates it every time that filter activates. I periodically scan my filters to make sure they're being used. If the Last Used date is many months old, I look more closely at the filter to see if something about it has broken, or if I've simply stopped receiving messages that it would match (perhaps I unsubscribed from a mailing list). If it's no longer necessary, I delete the filter to speed up the filtering process.

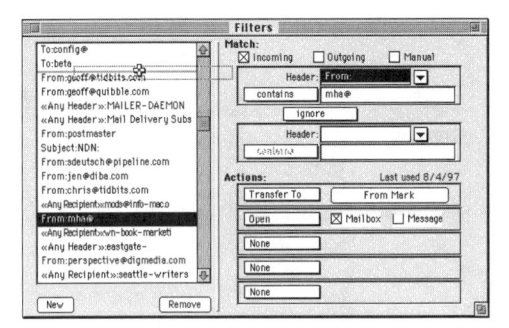

**Figure 10** To reorder a filter in the Mac versions of Eudora, drag it up or down in the list of filters. A small line indicates where it will go when you drop it.

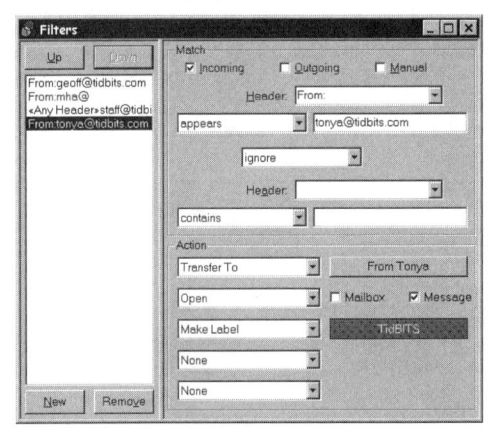

**Figure 11** To reorder a filter in the Windows versions of Eudora, select the filter then click the Up or Down buttons to move it up or down in the list. Here I've moved my filter for Tonya down in the list.

# Reordering filters

When filters are invoked, either automatically or manually, Eudora matches each message against each filter, working from the top of the filter list to the bottom. If you include the Skip Rest action in a filter, Eudora skips all other filters below that one for that message. Thus, the order of filters can prove important. In addition, I like to group related filters (such as all those that look for messages from friends and family) for easier access.

## To reorder a filter (Mac)

1. From the Special menu, choose Filters. Eudora opens the Filters window.

2. Click the filter you want to reorder and drag it up or down in the list (**Figure 10**).

3. Drop the filter in the desired location, as indicated by a small blue line that appears in the list.

4. Choose Save from the File menu to save your changed filter order.

## To reorder a filter (Windows)

1. From the Tools menu, choose Filters. Eudora opens the Filters window.

2. Click the filter you want to reorder, and then click either the Up or Down button at the top of the list to move the filter up or down in the list (**Figure 11**).

3. Choose Save from the File menu to save your changed filter order.

## ✔ Tip

- In the Mac versions of Eudora, you can move multiple filters at the same time. Shift-click to select a range of filters, or Command-click to select a noncontiguous set of filters, then drag them all at once.

# Deleting filters

If you unsubscribe from a mailing list or stop receiving mail that requires filtering, you should delete the unused filters.

### To delete a filter

1. From the Special menu (Mac) or the Tools menu (Windows), choose Filters.
   Eudora opens the Filters window.

2. Click the filter you want to delete (**Figure 12**).

3. Click the Remove button.
   Eudora deletes the filter instantly, without asking first.

4. In the Mac versions of Eudora, choose Save from the File menu to save your new filter. In the Windows versions, close the Filters window and click Yes when prompted to save.

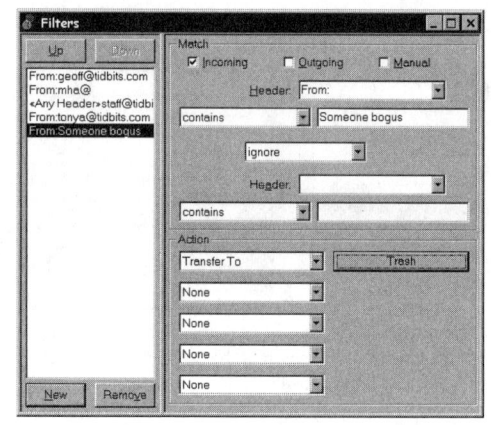

**Figure 12** To delete a filter, select it and then click the Remove button.

### ✔ Tips

- In the Mac versions of Eudora, you can delete multiple filters at the same time. Shift-click to select a range of filters, or Command-click to select a noncontiguous set of filters, then click the Remove button to delete them.

- Be careful when deleting filters because Eudora doesn't warn you before deleting them.

# FINDING AND SEARCHING

In Chapter 6, "Working with Mailboxes," I encouraged you to store old messages in mailboxes for later reference. Much of my communication takes place in email, which makes my stored email the record of both my personal and my business lives.

In previous chapters I introduced you to a number of features that simplify the task of finding messages, including features like sorting and Option/Alt-clicking messages to select similar messages in the same mailbox.

But, what if you need to find a message that you stored away some time ago, and you're not sure who sent it or when it came in? In such a situation, you must rely on Eudora's finding and searching capabilities.

Unfortunately, although Eudora's finding and searching capabilities are fast and powerful, they can be confusing, especially in the Mac versions of Eudora. After you read this chapter, though, you shouldn't have problems.

To aid in understanding, I recommend that you read all the pages relevant to your version of Eudora in this chapter, since later pages build on earlier ones in significant ways.

These features differ a good bit between the Mac and Windows versions of Eudora, so I'll cover the two separately where necessary. Let's see what we can find!

## Finding text in a message

The first task is to find text within a single message. Occasionally you receive a long message, and it's easier to use Eudora's Find feature than it is to scan the message.

I call the text you want to find the "search term" throughout this chapter.

### To find text in a message

1. Open a message window, then choose Find ([Cmd]-F) from the hierarchical Find menu (**Figure 1**) in the Special menu.

   Eudora opens the Find window. For now, ignore everything below the horizontal line under Options.

2. Type the search term in the Find field (**Figure 2**).

3. Click the Find button to find the first instance of the search term.

   Eudora selects the found text (**Figure 3**).

4. To find subsequent instances of the search term within the message, continue to click the Find button or choose Find Again ([Cmd]-G) from the hierarchical Find menu in the Special menu.

### ✔ Tips

- To restrict the found text to whole words, check the Whole word checkbox. Without Whole word checked on a search for *sing*, Eudora finds *sing*, *singer*, and *singing*. With Whole word checked, Eudora finds only *sing*.

- To restrict the found text to words with the same case as the search term, check the Match case checkbox. Without Match case checked on a search for *sing*, Eudora finds *sing*, *Sing*, and *SING*. With Match case checked, Eudora finds only *sing*.

**MACINTOSH ONLY!**

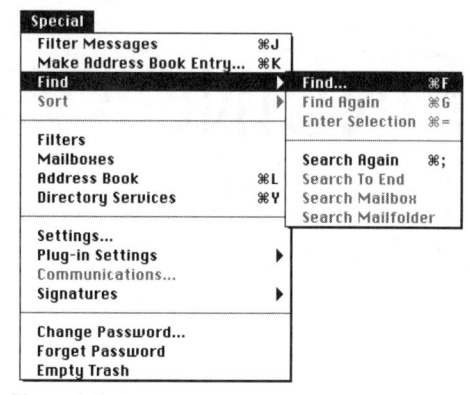

**Figure 1** To find text in a message, open the message window, then choose Find from the hierarchical Find menu in the Special menu.

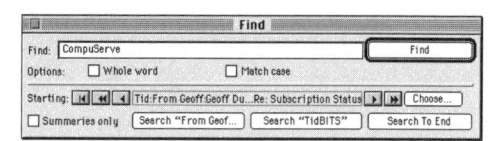

**Figure 2** Eudora then opens the Find window. Enter your search term in the Find field, and click the Find button to find the first instance of the search term in the current message window.

**Figure 3** Eudora selects the found text within the current message. Click the Find button in the Find window to find the next instance of the search term.

## Finding text in a message

The first task is to find text within a single message. Most messages are fairly short, but occasionally you receive a long message, and it's easier to use Eudora's Find feature than it is to scan the message.

I call the text you want to find the "search term" throughout this chapter.

### To find text in a message

1. Open a message window, then choose Find ([Ctrl]-F) from the hierarchical Find menu (**Figure 4**) in the Edit menu.
   Eudora opens the Find window.

2. Type the search term in the Find field (**Figure 5**).

3. Click the Find button to find the first instance of the search term.
   Eudora selects the found text (**Figure 6**).

4. To find subsequent instances of the search term within the message, continue to click the Find button or choose Find Again ([F3]) from the hierarchical Find menu in the Special menu.

### ✔ Tips

- To restrict the found text to words that have the same case as the search term, check the Match case checkbox. Without Match case checked on a search for *sing*, Eudora finds *sing*, *Sing*, *SING*, and so on. With Match case checked, Eudora finds only *sing*.

- Checking the Summaries only checkbox has no effect when you are finding text within a single message.

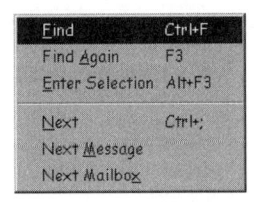

**Figure 4** To find text in a message, open the message window, then choose Find from the hierarchical Find menu in the Edit menu.

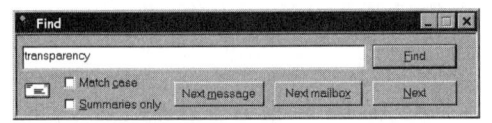

**Figure 5** Eudora then opens the Find window. Enter your search term in the Find field, and click the Find button to find the first instance of the search term in the current message window.

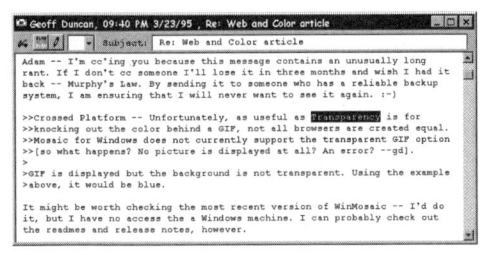

**Figure 6** Eudora selects the found text within the current message. Click the Find button in the Find window to find the next instance of the search term.

# Searching for text in a mailbox

You'll also want to search all messages in a mailbox. Note that "finding" happens in a single message; "searching" spans messages.

## To search for text in a mailbox

1. Open a mailbox, scroll to the top, select the first message, and then choose Find (`Cmd`-F) from the hierarchical Find menu in the Special menu.

   Eudora opens the Find window.

2. Type the search term in the Find field.

3. Click the Search "Mailbox" button (**Figure 7**) to locate the first instance of the search term. The name of the button changes to reflect the current mailbox.

   Eudora displays the Finding dialog box and, when it finds a message containing the search term, opens the message and selects the found text.

4. To locate subsequent instances of the search term within that mailbox (moving from top to bottom), continue to click the Search "Mailbox" button or choose Search Again (`Cmd`-;) from the hierarchical Find menu in the Special menu.

## ✔ Tips

- To make a message the starting point, select it, then open the Find window. Selecting a message when the Find window is already open has no effect on the starting point *unless* you also change the search term.

- Click the buttons that look like VCR buttons (**Figure 7**) to change the starting point or click the Choose button and choose a mailbox from the Mailbox menu to make the first message in that mailbox your starting point.

## MACINTOSH ONLY!

*Moves the starting point to the first message in the previous mailbox.*

*The current starting point appears here, with commas used as the delimiters between folders, mailboxes, and messages.*

*Click to choose a mailbox to use as the starting point.*

*Resets the starting point to the first message in the In mailbox.*

*Moves the starting point to the previous message.*

*Click to search within the current mailbox.*

*Moves the starting point to the next message.*

*Moves the starting point to the first message in the next mailbox.*

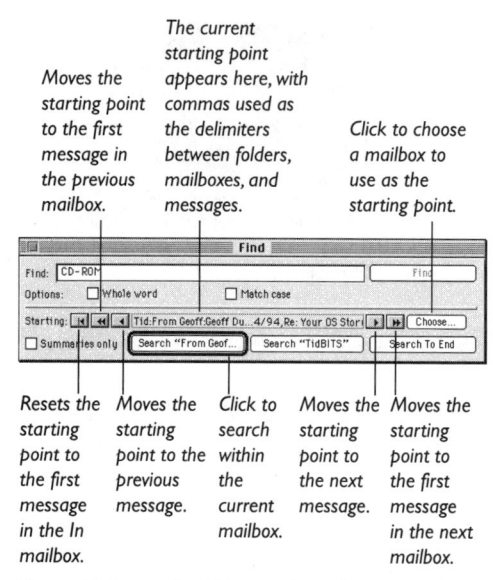

**Figure 7** To search within a single mailbox, open the mailbox, select the top message to make it the starting point, open the Find window, enter your search term in the Find field, then click the Search "Mailbox" button.

### Watch the starting point!

The starting point for a search is crucial! If the starting point is below the message containing the search term, the search will fail. But, if a search fails, changing the search term resets the starting point to the currently selected message (which is why it's best to select the first message in a mailbox before starting).

Another way to make the first message in a mailbox the starting point is to open a mailbox, open the Find window, click the Previous Mailbox VCR button, and then click the Next Mailbox VCR button.

## MACINTOSH ONLY!

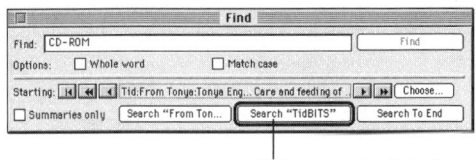

**Figure 8** To search within a mailbox folder, open the first mailbox in the mailbox folder, select the top message to make it the starting point, open the Find window, enter your search term in the Find field, then click the Search "Mailbox folder" button.

*Click to search within the current mailbox folder.*

## Searching for text in a mailbox folder

A desired message may live in one of several mailboxes within a mailbox folder. If so, you can restrict your search to messages in mailboxes in a specific mailbox folder. (*See Chapter 6, "Working with Mailboxes"*)

### To search for text in a mailbox folder

1. Open the first mailbox in a mailbox folder, scroll to the top, select the first message, and then choose Find (Cmd-F) from the hierarchical Find menu in the Special menu.

    Eudora opens the Find window.

2. Type the search term in the Find field.

3. Click the Search "Mailbox folder" button (**Figure 8**) to locate the first instance of the search term.

    Eudora displays the Finding dialog box and, when it finds a message containing the search term, opens the message and selects the found text.

4. To locate subsequent instances of the search term within a mailbox folder (moving from top to bottom, as defined by the order of the Mailbox menu), continue to click the Search "Mailbox folder" button or choose Search Again (Cmd-;) from the hierarchical Find menu in the Special menu.

### ✔ Tip

- Refer to **Figure 7** on the previous page for descriptions of the buttons that look like VCR buttons.

Chapter 8

## Searching in multiple mailboxes

You may not know what mailbox contains a desired message, and in the Mac versions of Eudora you can expand your search to include multiple mailboxes.

### To search in multiple mailboxes

1.  Set a starting point by opening a mailbox, scrolling to the top, selecting the first message, then choosing Find ([Cmd]-F) from the hierarchical Find menu in the Special menu.

    Alternately, use the VCR buttons or the Choose button in the Find window to set the starting point.

    Eudora opens the Find window.

2.  Type the search term in the Find field.

3.  Click the Search To End button (**Figure 9**) to search messages in all mailboxes below the starting point.

    Eudora displays the Finding dialog box and, when it finds the search term, opens the message and selects the found text.

4.  To locate subsequent instances of the search term within any mailbox below the current mailbox, continue to click the Search To End button or choose Search Again ([Cmd]-;) from the hierarchical Find menu in the Special menu.

### ✔ Tips

- If no mailboxes are open, Eudora sets the starting point at the first message in the first mailbox, which is the In mailbox.

- When a search hits the end of all mailboxes, it stops.

- To stop a search, click the Stop button in the Finding dialog box (**Figure 10**).

**MACINTOSH ONLY!**

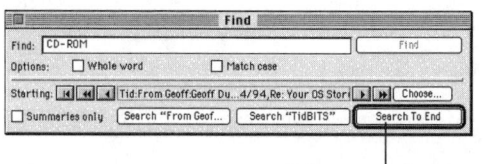

*Click to search from the starting point to the end of all mailboxes.*

**Figure 9** To search multiple mailboxes, open the first mailbox you want to search, select the top message to make it the starting point, open the Find window, enter your search term in the Find field, then click the Search To End button.

**Figure 10** To stop a search, click the Stop button in the Finding dialog box.

## WINDOWS ONLY!

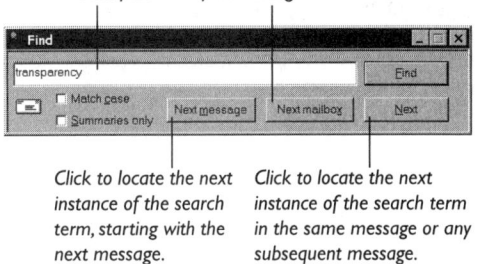

**Figure 11** To search multiple mailboxes, open the first mailbox you want to search, select the top message, open the Find window, enter your search term in the Find field, then click the Find button.

- Find field
- Click to locate the next instance of the search term, starting with the first message in the next mailbox.
- Click to locate the next instance of the search term, starting with the next message.
- Click to locate the next instance of the search term in the same message or any subsequent message.

**Figure 12** To stop a search, click the Stop button in the Progress dialog box.

# Searching in multiple mailboxes

The Windows versions of Eudora can't restrict a search to a mailbox or a mailbox folder, but as a result, it's a bit easier to use.

## To search in multiple mailboxes

1. Open a mailbox, scroll to the top, select the first message, and then choose Find (Ctrl-F) from the hierarchical Find menu in the Edit menu.

   Eudora opens the Find window.

2. Type the search term in the Find field.

3. Click the Find button (**Figure 11**) to locate the first instance of the search term.

   Eudora displays the Progress dialog box and, when it finds a message containing the search term, opens the message and selects the found text.

4. To locate subsequent instances of the search term within the current message, the current mailbox, or all mailboxes (moving from top to bottom in both the current mailbox and the list of mailboxes as displayed in the Mailbox menu), click the Next button (Ctrl-;).

   Alternately, to skip to the next message and continue searching, click the Next message button.

   Alternately, to skip to the next mailbox and continue searching, click the Next mailbox button.

## ✔ Tips

- When a search reaches the bottom of the current mailbox, it wraps around throughout all your mailboxes.

- To stop a search, click the Stop button in the Progress dialog box (**Figure 12**).

# Searching for text in message summaries

Searching the full text of every message can take a while if you have many stored messages. To speed up the search, consider limiting your search to the Sender and Subject columns of the message summaries that you see in mailboxes. The Mac and Windows versions of Eudora share this feature.

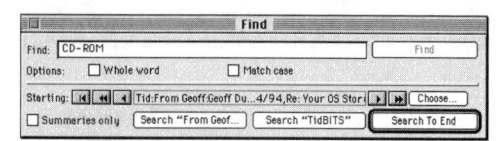

**Figure 13** To search just message summaries, which is much faster than a full text search, check the Summaries only checkbox in the Find window before performing any other sort of search.

## To search for text in message summaries

1. Set up any of the previously mentioned methods of searching.

2. Before clicking the Find button or any of the search buttons, check the Summaries only checkbox in the Find window (**Figure 13**).

3. Continue with the search as you would normally, and note how much faster Eudora searches.

## ✔ Tips

- Remember that searching only in message summaries restricts you to searching for text you can see in the Sender or Subject columns of the message summaries.

- The Sender column generally contains only names, not email addresses.

- Although searching for text in message summaries proceeds much more quickly than full text searching, it's much easier to enter a search term that won't match any messages.

- Eudora's full text finding and searching capabilities are sufficiently fast that searching for text in message summaries is primarily useful if you're searching through numerous large mailboxes.

# Searching tips and tricks

The best way to become comfortable with Eudora's finding and searching capabilities is to try them. However, here are a few tips and tricks that might be especially handy.

## ✔ Tips

- If a search has gone too far, especially in the Windows versions of Eudora, click the Stop button to stop it.

- After stopping a search or after a search fails, remember that you *must* reset the starting point in the Mac versions of Eudora before trying again.

- To move selected text in a message to the Find field in the Find window, choose Enter Selection ([Cmd]-=/[Alt]-[F3]) from the hierarchical Find menu (**Figure 14**) in the Special menu (Mac) or Edit menu (Windows).

- To search all mailboxes in the Mac versions, set the starting point to the first message in the In mailbox, which you can do by clicking the First Message VCR button in the Find window (**Figure 15**), then use the Search To End button.

- The Whole word (Mac only) and Match case checkboxes apply to both finding and searching.

- The hierarchical Find menu (**Figure 16** and **Figure 17**) contains menu items that duplicate the Search Mailbox, Search Mailfolder, and Search To End buttons (Mac) and the Next Message and Next Mailbox buttons (Windows). I can't imagine why you'd use them instead of the buttons, but they're there if you want them.

- In case I haven't sufficiently beaten this deceased equine, in the Mac versions of Eudora, pay attention to the starting point!

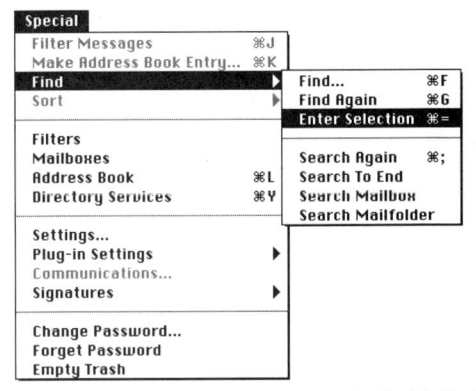

**Figure 14** To transfer selected text to the Find field of the Find window, choose Enter Selection from the hierarchical Find menu in the Special menu (Mac) or the Edit menu (Windows).

Resets the starting point to the first message in the In mailbox.

Click to search from the starting point to the end of all mailboxes.

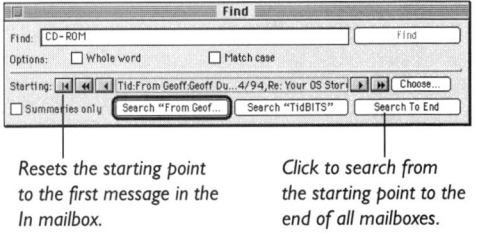

**Figure 15** To search all mailboxes in the Mac versions of Eudora, set the starting point to the first message in the In mailbox by clicking the First Message VCR button, then use the Search To End button.

**Figure 16** The hierarchical Find menu in the Special menu duplicates several of the Find window's buttons.

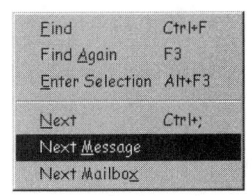

**Figure 17** The hierarchical Find menu in the Edit menu duplicates several of the Find window's buttons.

# Working with the Address Book

Let's face it—lots of email addresses are confusing and hard to type. And, if you type an email address incorrectly, your message will probably bounce or be delivered to the wrong person.

Eudora addresses this problem (pun intended, sorry) by providing a powerful address book in which you can store email addresses and link them to nicknames that are short, easy to remember, and easy to type. So, since I send email to my wife Tonya all the time, instead of typing her email address in each message, I just type the letter t, which is my nickname for her. Eudora then substitutes the address for the nickname.

In addition to making it easier to address messages, Eudora's address book enables you to associate a single nickname not just with an individual, but also with a group of people. Want to create a nickname that expands to the email addresses of your entire family, all your college friends, or the people in your department? No problem.

Nicknames are so useful that I strongly recommend you make heavy use of Eudora's address book capabilities. If you send someone or a group of people mail frequently, using a nickname is the easiest way to go.

# Chapter 9

# Creating nicknames for individuals

Eudora offers several ways to create nicknames for individuals.

## To create individual nicknames (I)

1. Open or select a message, and then choose Make Address Book Entry ([Cmd]-K/[Ctrl]-K) from the Special menu (**Figure 1**). This creates a nickname for the sender of the selected message.

   Or, in the Mac versions, select an email address, hold down Shift, and then choose Make Address Book Entry ([Cmd]-[Shift]-K).

   Eudora displays the New Nickname (Mac) or Make Address Book Entry (Windows) dialog box (**Figure 2**).

2. Enter a nickname, and if desired, check the "Put it on the recipient list" checkbox. (*See "Using the recipient list" in Chapter 2, "Creating Messages"*) In Eudora Pro, choose a file from the pop-up File menu. Click OK.

## To create individual nicknames (II)

1. Open the Address Book window (**Figure 3**) by choosing Address Book ([Cmd]-L/[Ctrl]-L) from the Special (Mac) or Tools (Windows) menu.

2. Click the New button to display the New Nickname dialog box.

3. Enter a nickname, and if desired, check the "Put it on the recipient list" checkbox. In Eudora Pro, choose a file from the pop-up File menu. Click OK.

4. In the Address(es) field, enter the nickname's email address. Optionally, check the Recipient List checkbox, and in the other fields, enter the person's real name, notes, and in Eudora Pro, postal address, phone number, and fax number. Choose Save from the File menu.

**Figure 1** To create an individual nickname for the sender of a message, open or select a message, then choose Make Address Book Entry from the Special menu.

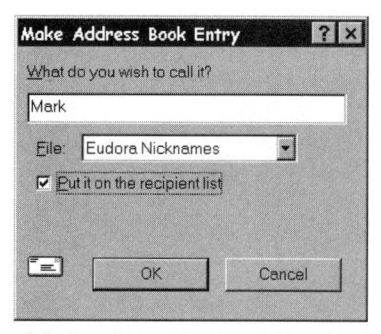

**Figure 2** Eudora displays the Make Address Book Entry (Windows) or New Nickname (Mac) dialog box. Enter a nickname, check the "Put it on the recipient list" checkbox if desired, choose a file in Eudora Pro, and click OK.

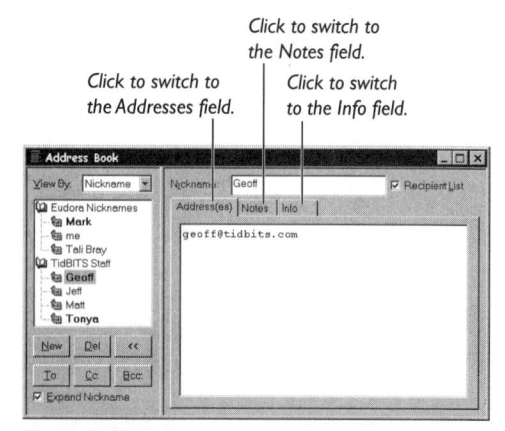

**Figure 3** Alternately, open the Address Book window, click the New button, enter a nickname in the Make Address Book Entry (Windows) or New Nickname (Mac) dialog box, then enter the email address in the Address(es) field.

# Working with the Address Book

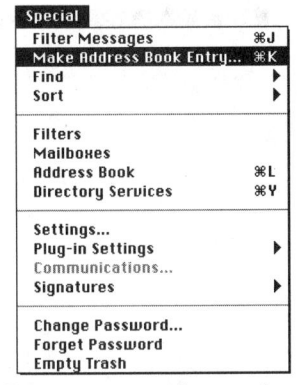

**Figure 4** To create a group nickname, select several messages, then choose Make Address Book Entry from the Special menu.

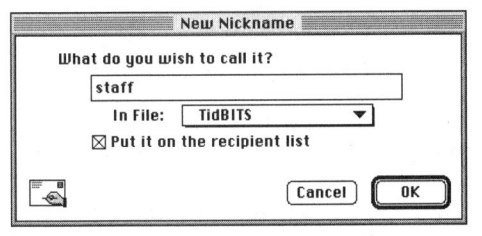

**Figure 5** Eudora displays the New Nickname (Mac) or Make Address Book Entry (Windows) dialog box. Enter a nickname, check the "Put it on the recipient list" checkbox if desired, choose a file in Eudora Pro, and then click OK.

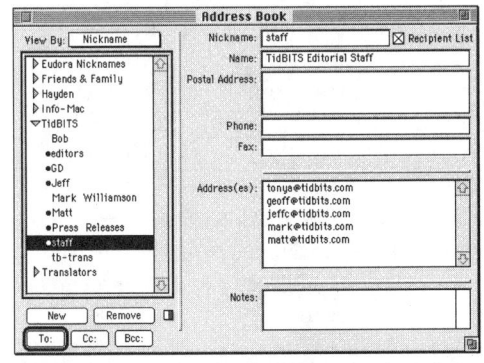

**Figure 6** Alternately, open the Address Book window, click the New button, enter a nickname in the New Nickname (Mac) or Make Address Book Entry (Windows) dialog box, then enter the email addresses in the Address(es) field.

## Creating group nicknames

Eudora also offers several ways to create nicknames for groups of people.

### To create group nicknames (I)

1. Select several messages, then choose Make Address Book Entry (Cmd-K/Ctrl-K) from the Special menu (**Figure 4**). This creates a group nickname for the senders of those messages.

   Or, in the Mac versions, select several addresses, hold down Shift, then choose Make Address Book Entry (Cmd-Shift-K).

   Eudora displays the New Nickname (Mac) or Make Address Book Entry (Windows) dialog box (**Figure 5**).

2. Enter a nickname, and if desired, check the "Put it on the recipient list" checkbox. (See "Using the recipient list" in Chapter 2, "Creating Messages") In Eudora Pro, choose a file from the pop-up File menu. Click OK.

### To create group nicknames (II)

1. Open the Address Book window by choosing Address Book (Cmd-L/Ctrl-L) from the Special (Mac) or Tools (Windows) menu (**Figure 6**).

2. Click the New button to display the New Nickname dialog box.

3. Enter a nickname, and if desired, check the "Put it on the recipient list" checkbox. In Eudora Pro, choose a file from the pop-up File menu. Click OK.

4. In the Address(es) field, enter the nickname's email addresses, separating them with commas or returns. Optionally, check the Recipient List checkbox, and in the other fields, enter a name for the group, any notes, and in Eudora Pro, a postal address, phone number, and fax number. Choose Save from the File menu.

# Nickname tips

A few tips may make creating and using nicknames easier.

## ✔ Tips

- You can't use spaces in nicknames, but you can use underscores (Eudora defaults to replacing spaces with underscores), hyphens, or most any other character.

- To simulate a space in your nicknames, hold down Option (Mac) or Control (Windows) and press the Spacebar. Remember that you'll have to type Option-Spacebar or Control-Spacebar to enter the nickname correctly.

- It's a good idea to make groups from other nicknames. That way, for instance, if you have a Family group nickname, and your sister changes her email address, you can change her individual nickname and have that change automatically reflected in the Family group nickname.

- Eudora knows about a special nickname called "me." If you create it and fill it in with your personal information, Eudora uses that information to determine who you are to satisfy the Include yourself checkbox in the Replying settings panel (**Figure 7**). In addition, Eudora uses the me nickname to determine if you're the sender of a message that you're redirecting (and if so, it adds your signature to the message).

- In the Windows versions of Eudora, you can right-click a nickname or the nickname list in the Address Book window to display a pop-up menu that duplicates some of the controls in the Address Book window.

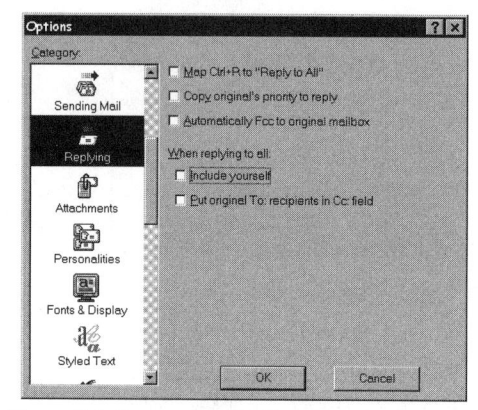

**Figure 7** Eudora uses the "me" nickname to determine who you are for the sake of the Include yourself checkbox in the Replying settings panel.

### Eudora's hidden glossary

Many word processors have glossary features that let you set up shortcuts for commonly used pieces of boilerplate text. For instance, you might type *add* and have the word processor replace that with your full postal address.

Eudora doesn't claim to have this feature, but it does! You can enter any text you want as the address of a nickname. Then, in a message, type the nickname, hold down Option (Mac) or Shift (Windows) and choose Finish and Expand Address Book Entry ([Cmd]-[Option]-,/[Ctrl]-[Shift]-,) from the Edit menu. I always use the keyboard shortcuts, but you could also hold down Option (Mac) or Shift (Windows) and choose a nickname from the hierarchical Insert And Expand Recipient menu in the Edit menu.

Make sure that the "Domain to add to unqualified names" field in the Sending Mail settings panel is empty, or Eudora will add that domain to the first word of your glossary entry, as in *This@tidbits.com is a test*.

Working with the Address Book

*Click to collapse the Address Book window.*

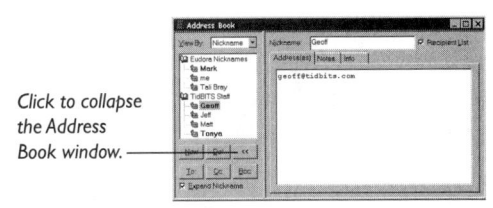

**Figure 8** To collapse the Address Book window, click the Collapse button.

*Click to expand the Address Book window.*

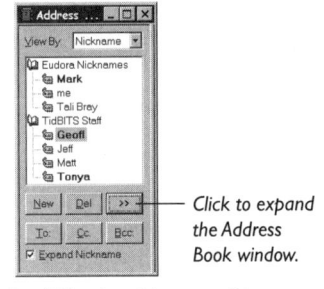

**Figure 9** Eudora then hides the nickname editing area.

*Click to expand the Address Book window.*

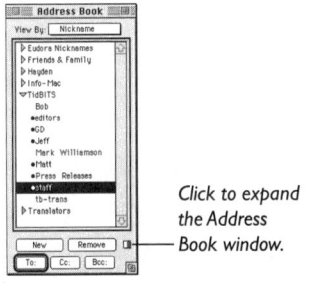

**Figure 10** To expand the Address Book window, click the Expand button (which is the same as the Collapse button in the Mac versions of Eudora).

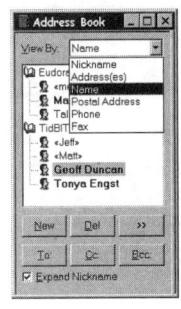

**Figure 11** To change the contents of the nickname list, choose one of the items from the View By pop-up menu. Here I've chosen Name instead of Nickname.

# Using the Address Book window

The Address Book window offers features that ease working with nicknames.

## To collapse and expand the Address Book window

1. To collapse the Address Book window and save screen space, click the Collapse button (**Figure 8**).

   Eudora hides the nickname editing area (**Figure 9**).

2. To expand the Address Book window (which is necessary to edit nicknames), click the Expand button, which is the same as the Collapse button in the Mac versions (**Figure 10**).

## To change the nickname list contents

1. To switch between Nickname, Address(es), Name, Postal Address, Phone, and Fax, choose the desired item from the View By pop-up menu (**Figure 11**).

   Eudora changes the nickname list to match the View By menu setting.

## ✔ Tips

- You can resize the nickname list pane by clicking and dragging the vertical line that separates it from the editing area.

- In the Mac version of Eudora Pro, to expand typed nicknames to their email addresses immediately, check the "Expand nicknames immediately" checkbox in the Sending Mail settings panel.

- In the Windows version of Eudora Pro, to expand typed nicknames to their email addresses immediately, check the Expand Nickname checkbox in the Address Book window.

137

# Adding nicknames to messages

If you're working in the Address Book window already, or if you want to send a message to a lot of different people, you can address a message directly from within the Address Book window. And, of course, you can always just type a nickname in the To, Cc, or Bcc fields of a message.

## To add nicknames to a message

1. Open the Address Book window by choosing Address Book ([Cmd]-L/[Ctrl]-L) from the Special (Mac) or Tools (Windows) menu.

2. Select one or more nicknames and click the To, Cc, or Bcc button (**Figure 12**).

   Eudora creates a new message if necessary and inserts the nicknames in the field corresponding to the button you clicked.

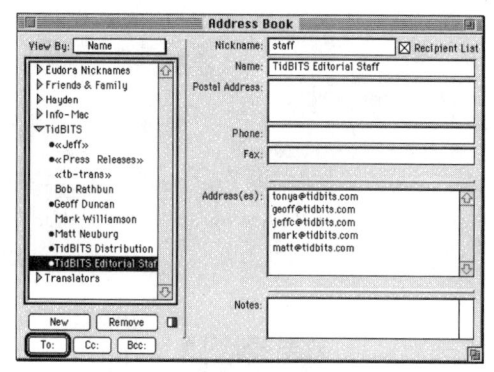

**Figure 12** To insert one or more selected nicknames in the To, Cc, or Bcc fields of an outgoing message, click the To, Cc, or Bcc button.

## ✔ Tips

- You can drag nicknames out of the Address Book window in the Mac versions of Eudora, but you get all the information in the nickname, not the nickname itself.

- To keep the Address Book window in the front after adding a nickname to a message, hold down Shift when you click the To, Cc, or Bcc button. This is handy if you want to add more nicknames to the message.

- In the Mac version of Eudora Pro, to expand a nickname immediately even if Eudora is set not to do so, hold down Option when you click the To, Cc, or Bcc button.

- Combine the two previous tips by holding down Shift-Option when clicking the To, Cc, or Bcc button.

### Adding nicknames to an existing outgoing message

Eudora generally creates a new message if you click the To, Cc, or Bcc button in the Address Book window. However, if you're working on an outgoing message, you can add nicknames to that message as well. Make sure the outgoing message window is in the front, then open the Address Book window, select nicknames, and click the To, Cc, or Bcc button to add the selected nicknames to the existing outgoing message. If any other window is in front when you open the Address Book window and click the To, Cc, or Bcc button, Eudora will create a new message instead of adding the nicknames to your existing outgoing message.

## Working with the Address Book

### EUDORA PRO ONLY!

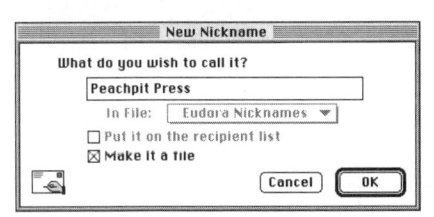

**Figure 13** To create a nicknames file, click the New button in the Address Book window and, in the New Nickname dialog box, check the "Make it a file" checkbox, and then click OK.

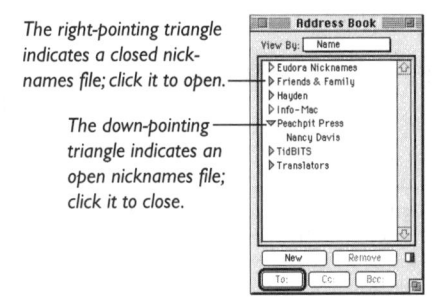

*The right-pointing triangle indicates a closed nicknames file; click it to open.*

*The down-pointing triangle indicates an open nicknames file; click it to close.*

**Figure 14** To expand and collapse nicknames files in the Mac version of Eudora Pro, click the triangles next to the nicknames file names.

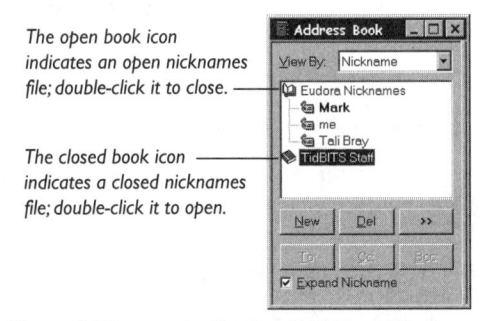

*The open book icon indicates an open nicknames file; double-click it to close.*

*The closed book icon indicates a closed nicknames file; double-click it to open.*

**Figure 15** To expand and collapse nicknames files in the Windows version of Eudora Pro, double-click the book icons next to the nicknames file names.

### Nicknames files

Eudora Pro stores nicknames files (which are just specially formatted text files) in the Nicknames Folder inside the Eudora Folder.

## Multiple nicknames files

Eudora Pro enables you to create multiple nicknames files for better categorization of your nickname collection.

### To create a new nicknames file

1. In the Address Book window, click the New button to bring up the New Nickname dialog box.

2. Enter a name for your nicknames file, and check the "Make it a file" checkbox (**Figure 13**). Click OK.

   Eudora creates a new nicknames file.

### To expand and collapse nicknames files

1. In the Mac version, to expand a nicknames file in the Address Book window, click the triangle to its left so that it points down. To collapse the file, click the triangle so it points right (**Figure 14**).

   In the Windows version, to expand a nicknames file in the Address Book window, double-click the closed book icon to its left. The book then opens; double-click it to collapse the file (**Figure 15**).

### To move nicknames between files

1. Click the nickname you want to move to select it.

2. Drag the nickname within the nickname list into another nicknames file.

### ✔ Tips

- It's easier to move nicknames between nicknames files if you collapse the intervening nicknames files.

- The Mac version of Eudora Pro always sorts nicknames files alphabetically; the Windows version sorts by creation order.

Chapter 9

# Finding nicknames

After you've created a number of nicknames, you might have trouble finding any given one. Luckily, Eudora provides some assistance in this area.

### To find a nickname (I)

1. Open the Address Book window by choosing Address Book (`Cmd`-L/`Ctrl`-L) from the Special (Mac) or Tools (Windows) menu.

2. Type the first few letters of the nickname you want to find.

    Eudora scrolls the list to the first nickname whose first few letters match what you typed (**Figure 16**).

### To find a nickname (II—Mac)

1. Open the Address Book window by choosing Address Book (`Cmd`-L) from the Special menu.

2. Open the Find window by choosing Find (`Cmd`-F) from the hierarchical Find menu in the Special menu.

3. Enter the search term in the Find field and click the Find button (**Figure 17**).

    Eudora finds the first nickname whose information matches the search term and selects it (**Figure 18**).

### ✔ Tip

- In the Mac versions of Eudora, you can use the Find window to find information in any of the Address Book's fields.

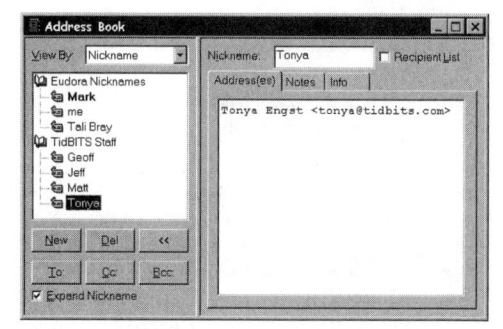

**Figure 16** To find a nickname in the Address Book window quickly, type the first few characters of the nickname. Here, I've typed "to" and Eudora has selected Tonya properly.

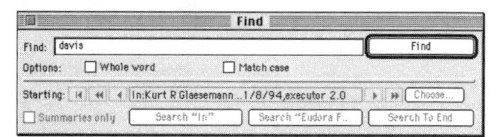

**Figure 17** In the Mac versions of Eudora, you can also use the Find window to find nicknames. Just open the Address Book window, then the Find window, enter your search term (any piece of information that might be stored in the address book), and click Find.

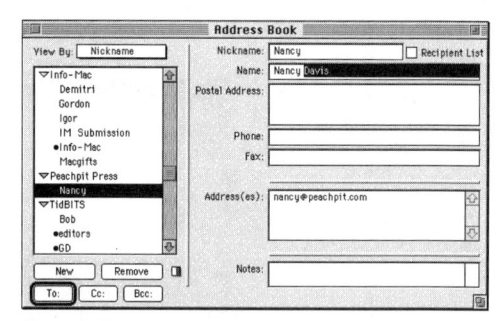

**Figure 18** Eudora then selects the nickname whose information matches your search term. Here, I've searched for "davis" to find the nickname for Nancy Davis, my extremely nice editor at Peachpit Press.

Working with the Address Book

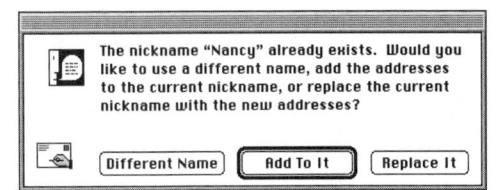

**Figure 19** If you try to create a nickname with the same name as an existing nickname, Eudora asks if you want to create a nickname with a different name, add the email address or addresses to the existing nickname, or replace it.

## Modifying nicknames

Eventually you'll want to modify one or more of your nicknames.

### To modify a nickname (I)

1. Open the Address Book window by choosing Address Book (Cmd-L/Ctrl-L) from the Special (Mac) or Tools (Windows) menu. Make sure the Address Book window is expanded to display the nickname editing fields. (*See "Using the Address Book window" in this chapter*)

2. Select the nickname you wish to modify.

3. Make the desired changes, then choose Save from the File menu.

### To modify a nickname (II)

1. First, open or select a message, then choose Make Address Book Entry (Cmd-K/Ctrl-K) from the Special menu to create a nickname based on the sender's email address.

   Or, in the Mac versions, select an email address, hold down Shift, and then choose Make Address Book Entry (Cmd-Shift-K).

   Eudora displays the New Nickname (Mac) or Make Address Book Entry (Windows) dialog box with a suggested nickname.

2. Enter an existing nickname and click OK. In Eudora Pro, choose the file containing the existing nickname.

   Eudora displays the Duplicate Nickname dialog box (**Figure 19**).

3. Click Different Name to create a new nickname, Add To It to add the address to the existing nickname, or Replace It to replace the old address with the new one.

### Nickname conflicts

In Eudora Pro, different nicknames files can contain different, but identically named nicknames. When in doubt, Eudora Pro uses the one that's highest in the nickname list. I recommend avoiding this situation entirely by never creating identically named nicknames. Otherwise you risk sending a message to the wrong person, which can be tremendously embarrassing.

# Managing your recipient list

You can modify a nickname's inclusion on your recipient list menus. I recommend that you maintain your recipient list to ensure that it stays short and useful.

## To add a nickname to the recipient list

1. Open the Address Book window by choosing Address Book (Cmd-L/Ctrl-L) from the Special (Mac) or Tools (Windows) menu. Make sure the Address Book window is expanded to display the nickname editing fields.

2. Select the nickname you wish to add to your recipient list.

3. Check the Recipient List checkbox (**Figure 20**), then choose Save from the File menu.

## To delete a nickname from the recipient list

1. Open the Address Book window by choosing Address Book (Cmd-L/Ctrl-L) from the Special (Mac) or Tools (Windows) menu. Make sure the Address Book window is expanded to display the nickname editing fields.

2. Select the nickname you wish to delete from your recipient list.

3. Uncheck the Recipient List checkbox, then choose Save from the File menu.

## ✔ Tip

- The recipient list appears in the hierarchical Insert Recipient menu in the Edit menu and the hierarchical New Message To, Forward To, and Redirect To menus in the Message menu.

Check the Recipient List checkbox to place the nickname on your recipient list.

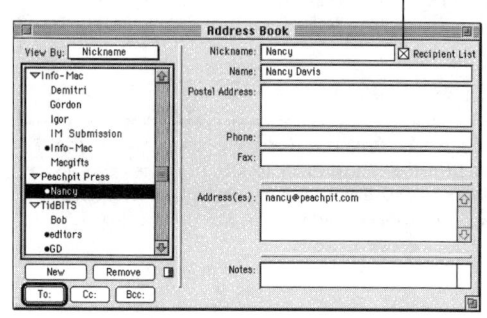

**Figure 20** To add a nickname to your recipient list, check the Recipient List checkbox in the Address Book window. To remove it from the recipient list, uncheck the Recipient List checkbox.

### Recipient list hints

It's awkward to look at one of the hierarchical menus that contains the recipient list to determine who's in it. Luckily, you can see who's in the recipient list at a glance in the Address Book window.

In the Mac versions of Eudora, nicknames in the recipient list have bullets (•) next to their names. The Windows versions show nicknames in the recipient list in bold. If you look at screenshots of the Address Book window in this chapter, you can see which nicknames I've put on my recipient list.

## Working with the Address Book

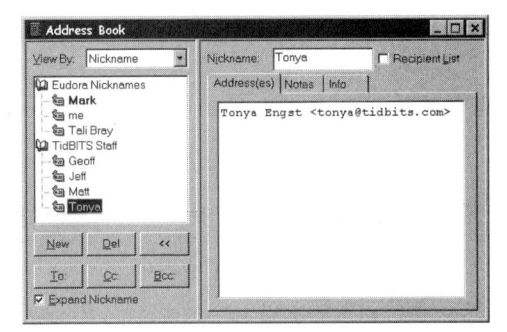

**Figure 21** To delete a nickname, select it and click the Del (Windows) or Remove (Mac) button.

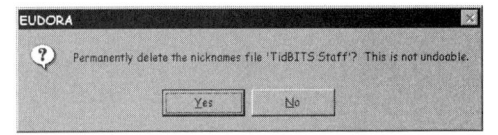

**Figure 22** When you try to delete a nicknames file, Eudora asks to make sure you know what you're doing, since doing so also deletes all nicknames in the file.

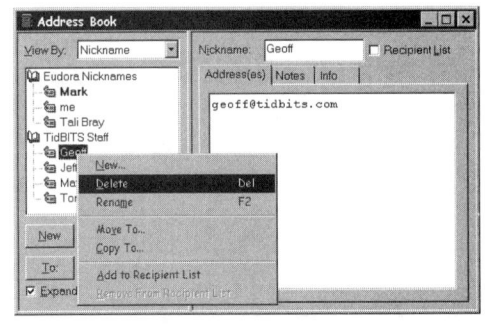

**Figure 23** In the Windows versions of Eudora, you can also right-click a nickname or a nicknames file and choose Delete from the pop-up menu to delete the nickname or nicknames file.

## Deleting nicknames

Don't keep nicknames for people with whom you're unlikely to correspond again—it's worth deleting them to keep your address book clean and up-to-date.

### To delete nicknames

1. Open the Address Book window by choosing Address Book ([Cmd]-L/[Ctrl]-L) from the Special (Mac) or Tools (Windows) menu.

2. Select the nickname or nicknames you wish to delete.

3. Click the Remove (Mac) or Del (Windows) button (**Figure 21**). Choose Save from the File menu.

### ✔ Tips

- To delete a nicknames file and all the nicknames it contains, select it and click the Remove (Mac) or Del (Windows) button. Eudora asks to make sure you know what you're doing (**Figure 22**), then deletes the entire file.

- In the Windows versions of Eudora, you can also select one or more nicknames and press the Forward Delete key to delete them.

- In the Windows versions of Eudora, you can also right-click an address book entry and choose Delete from the pop-up menu (**Figure 23**) to delete it.

143

# Working with the Toolbar

# 10

Eudora offers several different interfaces to satisfy different ways of working. You can choose menu items with the mouse, use keyboard shortcuts, or click buttons on toolbars (I assume you know how to click a button on a toolbar, so I don't provide steps for that).

I use keyboard shortcuts when possible, and when they aren't available, I turn to menus. I'm not a toolbar fan because the graphics often aren't clear and the buttons are usually too small.

I don't use Eudora's toolbar that often. If you find that it works well for you, great, but remember that there's nothing on the toolbar that's not available from menus as well. Also, note that this chapter covers the main toolbar, not the formatting toolbar available within message windows in Eudora Pro. (*See Chapter 3, "Writing Messages" for additional information on the formatting toolbar*)

The various versions of Eudora offer different toolbar functionality. The Windows version of Eudora Light has a static toolbar, and the Mac version of Eudora Light lacks a toolbar entirely. Both versions of Eudora Pro feature customizable toolbars, but the methods you use to customize them differ.

So, if you're a toolbar fan, read on for the neat things you can do with Eudora's toolbar!

# Turning the toolbar on and off

Eudora turns the toolbar on by default, but you can turn it off and back on manually, too.

## To turn the toolbar on

1. From the Special menu choose Settings (Mac) or from the Tools menu choose Options (Windows) to bring up the Settings/Options dialog box.

2. Scroll down in the list of settings panels and click either Toolbar (Mac) or Fonts & Display (Windows) (**Figure 1**).

3. Check the Show toolbar checkbox and click OK to turn the toolbar on.

## To turn the toolbar off

1. From the Special menu choose Settings (Mac) or from the Tools menu choose Options (Windows) to bring up the Settings/Options dialog box.

2. Scroll down in the list of settings panels and click either Toolbar (Mac) (**Figure 2**) or Fonts & Display (Windows).

3. Uncheck the Show toolbar checkbox and click OK to turn the toolbar off.

## ✔ Tips

- In the Windows versions of Eudora, right-click the toolbar or the status bar to bring up a pop-up menu (**Figure 3**) that enables you to show or hide the Mailboxes window, the toolbar, and the status bar.

- If neither the toolbar nor the status bar is showing in the Windows versions of Eudora, the only way to turn the toolbar and status bar back on is through the Fonts & Display settings panel in the Options dialog box.

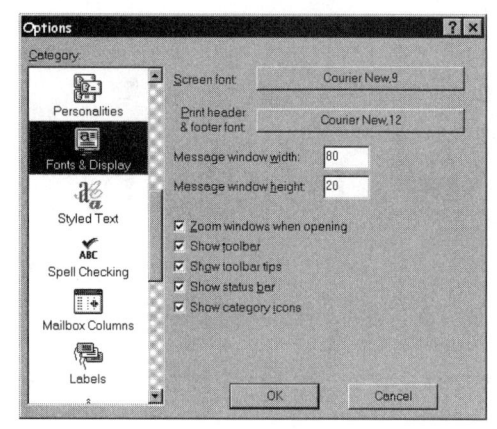

**Figure 1** To turn the toolbar on, open the Settings/Options dialog box, click Fonts & Display (Windows) or Toolbar (Mac), and check the Show toolbar checkbox.

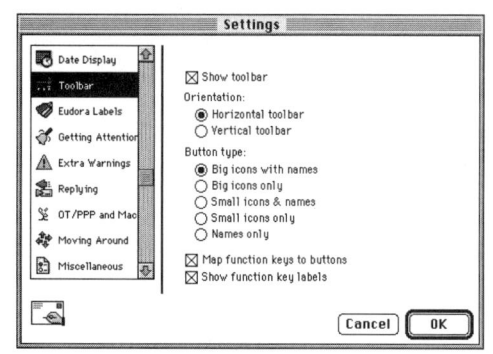

**Figure 2** To turn the toolbar off, open the Settings/Options dialog box, click Toolbar (Mac) or Fonts & Display (Windows), and uncheck the Show toolbar checkbox.

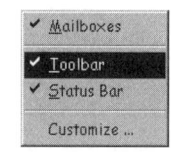

**Figure 3** Alternately, in the Windows versions, right click the toolbar or status bar, then choose Toolbar to turn the toolbar on or off.

# Toolbar settings

You have a number of options for how the toolbar displays, all available from the Toolbar settings panel (Mac) (**Figure 4**) or the Fonts & Display settings panel (Windows) (**Figure 5**) of the Settings/Options dialog box.

## Toolbar settings (Mac)

- The Orientation radio buttons determine whether the toolbar displays horizontally or vertically.

- The Button type radio buttons control how the buttons display. Experiment with different settings to see which you prefer—the specifics will depend on your monitor size, eyesight, hand-eye coordination, and working habits.

- The "Map function keys to buttons" checkbox controls whether you can press one of the function keys at the top of the keyboard instead of clicking a toolbar button.

- The "Show function key labels" checkbox controls whether function key labels appear with their associated buttons.

## Toolbar settings (Windows)

- The Show toolbar tips checkbox controls whether Eudora displays a small help note when you move the cursor over a toolbar button.

- The Show status bar checkbox controls whether Eudora displays a status bar at the bottom of the screen that contains more information than the toolbar tips about the toolbar buttons.

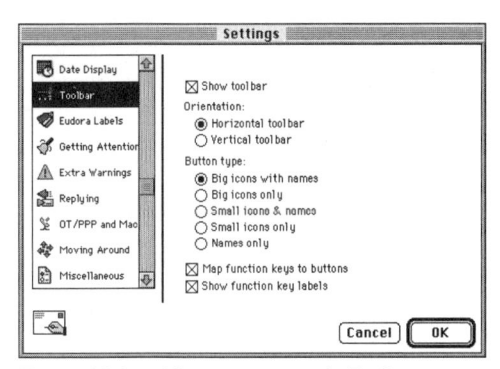

**Figure 4** Select different settings in the Toolbar settings panel to control how the Mac version of Eudora Pro displays the toolbar.

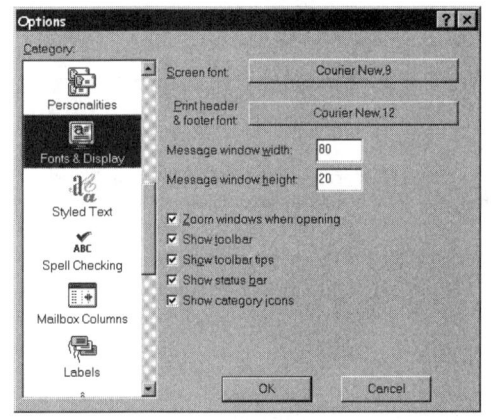

**Figure 5** Select different settings in the Fonts & Display settings panel to control how the Windows versions of Eudora display the toolbar.

Chapter 10

# Default toolbar functions

Although the button names in the Mac version of Eudora Pro (**Figure 6**) and toolbar tips in the Windows versions of Eudora (**Figure 7**) explain what each button does, here's a quick overview of the default functions of the toolbar buttons.

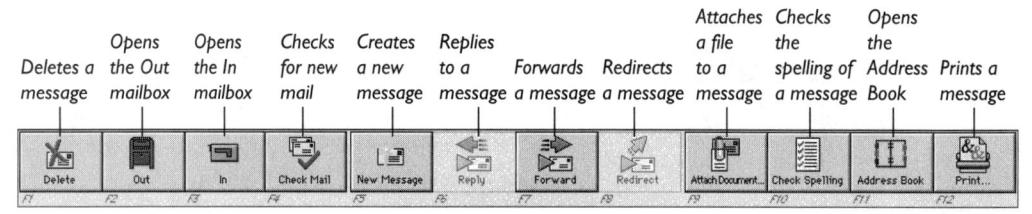

**Figure 6** Here are the default buttons on the toolbar in the Mac version of Eudora Pro. Note that Reply and Redirect are disabled because I had a new outgoing message window open when I took this screenshot. Toolbar buttons are active only if they make sense for the current situation.

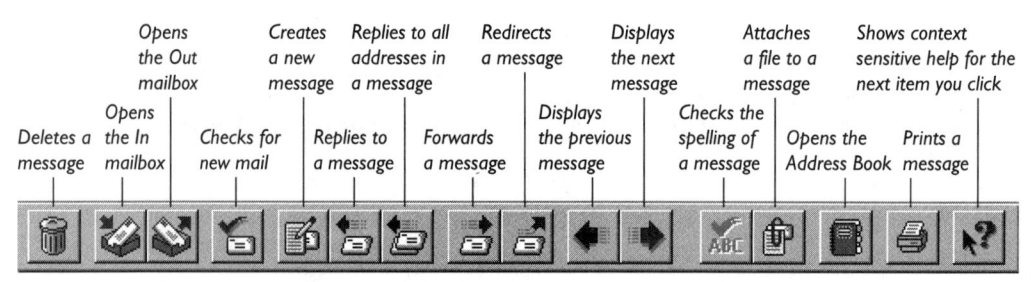

**Figure 7** Here are the default toolbar buttons in the Windows versions of Eudora. Note that Check Spelling is disabled because I had a mailbox window open when I took this screenshot. Toolbar buttons are active only if they make sense for the current situation.

# Adding a button to the toolbar

**EUDORA PRO ONLY! MACINTOSH ONLY!**

In Eudora Pro, you can customize the toolbar by adding buttons for functions that aren't represented on the toolbar by default.

## To add a button to the toolbar (Mac)

1. Hold down Command and click between any two buttons on the toolbar to insert a blank button at that point (**Figure 8**).

    Eudora displays the Toolbar Button Creation dialog box (**Figure 9**), which asks you to choose a menu item or press a keyboard shortcut. To back out, click Remove Button.

2. Choose any menu item or press a keyboard shortcut.

    Eudora assigns that function to the button, names it, and gives it an icon (**Figure 10**).

## ✔ Tips

- When you're holding down Command and have the cursor positioned between two buttons on the toolbar, the cursor changes to a line with two arrows pointing out on either side to indicate you can click to insert a blank button.

- To add a button that opens a specific mailbox, you can either create a button normally, choosing the mailbox from the Mailbox menu, or you can drag the mailbox from the Mailboxes window to the toolbar.

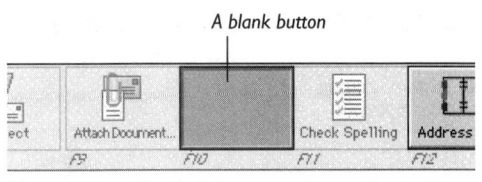

**Figure 8** To add a blank button to the toolbar, hold down Command and click between two existing buttons on the toolbar.

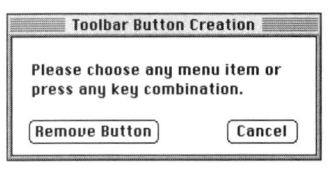

**Figure 9** Eudora presents the Toolbar Button Creation dialog box. Choose a menu item or press a keyboard shortcut to assign that function to the button. If you made a mistake, click Remove Button.

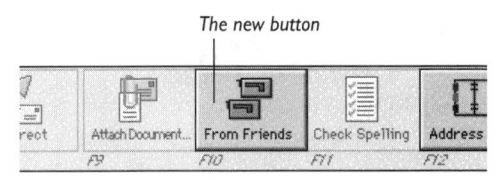

**Figure 10** Here, I've chosen my From Friends mailbox from the Mailbox menu. Clicking the From Friends button on the toolbar will now open the From Friends mailbox.

# Adding a button to the toolbar

**EUDORA PRO ONLY! WINDOWS ONLY!**

In Eudora Pro, you can customize the toolbar by adding buttons for functions that aren't represented on the toolbar by default.

## To add a button to the toolbar

1. Right-click the toolbar to bring up a pop-up menu (**Figure 11**), and choose Customize.

    Eudora displays the Customize Toolbar dialog box (**Figure 12**).

2. Select a category in the Categories list (they mostly parallel the menu items), then select a button in the Buttons area to view a description in the Description area.

3. Drag a button from the Buttons area to the desired spot on the toolbar (**Figure 13**).

4. If Eudora needs additional information (such as which mailbox to open, or to which recipient to redirect a message), it displays an explanatory dialog box (**Figure 14**), then a menu from which you choose the desired item (**Figure 15**).

## ✔ Tip

- Double-clicking a button in the Buttons area executes that function. This even works with the Exit button, which promptly quits the program, much to my amusement.

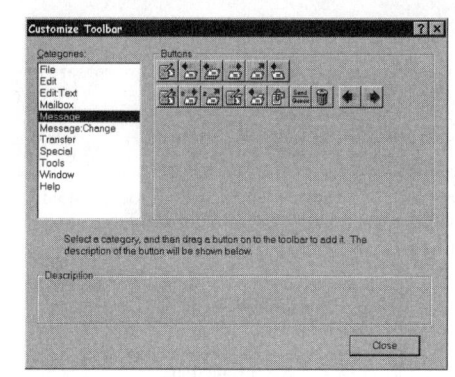

**Figure 12** Eudora Pro displays the Customize Toolbar dialog box. Select a category in the Categories list and click a button in the Buttons area to see a description of it in the Description area. Then, drag the button to the desired location on the toolbar to add it.

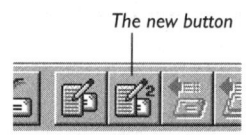

**Figure 13** The new button (in this case one that creates a new message addressed to Tonya) appears in the toolbar where you dropped it.

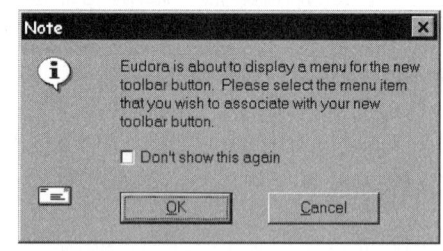

**Figure 14** If necessary, Eudora Pro prompts you to choose an item from a menu that it displays after this dialog box.

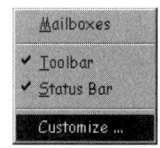

**Figure 11** To add a button to the toolbar, right-click the toolbar to bring up a pop-up menu, then choose Customize.

**Figure 15** Choose the desired item from the menu that Eudora Pro displays if a button needs customization.

**EUDORA PRO ONLY!**

## Button ideas

Don't be constrained by the obvious commands that appear on most toolbars, like Save, Print, and Quit. There are many items that you could add to your Eudora Pro toolbar that you might not have considered initially. Anything that you do regularly is a candidate for a toolbar button.

### Button ideas

- Make a button that creates a new message addressed to your most frequent correspondent. You could do the same thing for Forward and Redirect.

- Make a button that creates a new message using your most common pieces of stationery. Consider also a button that replies with stationery.

- Make a button that transfers messages to a specific mailbox, especially if the mailbox is several levels down in the Transfer menu.

- For easy categorization, make a button that changes the labels of messages.

- Make buttons for the formatting commands you use, so you don't have to display the formatting toolbar in every outgoing message window.

## Moving toolbar buttons

If you use the toolbar, you should customize it exactly the way you want it, which includes moving buttons around.

### To move a button (Mac)

1. Hold down Command and drag a button either between any two other buttons or to either end of the toolbar (**Figure 16**).

   When you Command-drag the button between two other buttons, the cursor changes to a line with two arrows pointing out on either side to indicate that it's okay to drop the button in that location.

### To move a button (Windows—I)

1. Hold down Alt and drag a button in the toolbar to the desired location.

### To move a button (Windows—II)

1. Right-click the toolbar to bring up a pop-up menu, and choose Customize.

   Eudora displays the Customize Toolbar dialog box.

2. Click a button in the toolbar and drag it to the desired location.

**EUDORA PRO ONLY!**

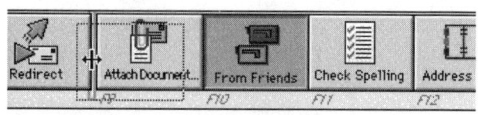

**Figure 16** To move a toolbar button in the Mac version of Eudora Pro, hold down Command and drag the button to the new location. In the Windows version of Eudora Pro, hold down Alt and drag the button to the new location.

## Deleting toolbar buttons

You'll undoubtedly find some of the default toolbar buttons superfluous, and you may want to remove some of those you create as projects finish or life changes.

### To delete a button (Mac—I)

1. Hold down Command and drag a button to the Trash in the Finder.

### To delete a button (Mac—II)

1. Hold down Command and click a button on the toolbar.

   Eudora displays the Toolbar Button Creation dialog box (**Figure 17**).

2. Click Remove Button.

### To delete a button (Windows—I)

1. Hold down Alt and drag a button off the toolbar.

### To delete a button (Windows—II)

1. Right-click the toolbar to bring up a pop-up menu, and choose Customize.

   Eudora displays the Customize Toolbar dialog box.

2. Drag a button off the toolbar.

### ✔ Tip

- In the Mac version, make sure the Trash in the Finder isn't obscured by a window before you start dragging a button to the Trash.

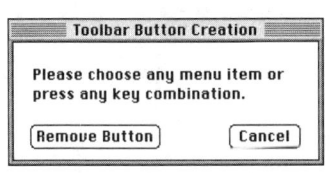

**Figure 17** To delete a button from the toolbar in the Mac version of Eudora Pro, hold down Command, click the desired button, and then, in the Toolbar Button Creation dialog box, click Remove Button.

## Changing button functions

What if you just want to change the function of a button on the toolbar? You can, of course, just remove one button and replace it with another, but the Mac version of Eudora Pro provides an easier method.

### To change a button function

1. Hold down Command and click a button on the toolbar (**Figure 18**).

    Eudora displays the Toolbar Button Creation dialog box (**Figure 19**), which asks you to choose a menu item or press a keyboard shortcut. (To back out, click Cancel.)

2. Choose any menu item or press a keyboard shortcut.

    Eudora assigns that function to the button, along with a new name and icon, replacing the previous icon, name, and function (**Figure 20**).

**EUDORA PRO ONLY! MACINTOSH ONLY!**

**Figure 18** To change the function of a button, hold down Command and click the button.

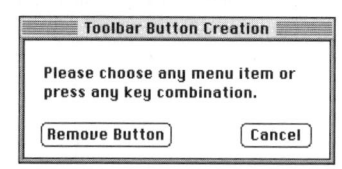

**Figure 19** Eudora presents the Toolbar Button Creation dialog box. Choose a menu item or press a keyboard shortcut to assign that function to the button.

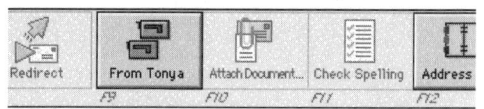

**Figure 20** Eudora then changes the button's function and name (and icon, if necessary) to reflect your change. Here, I've changed the button that opens the From Friends mailbox to one that opens the From Tonya mailbox.

# Using Directory Services

# 11

## INTRODUCTION TO DIRECTORY SERVICES

A problem with email is that it can be difficult to find someone's email address if you only know that person's name.

Eudora supports two older methods of looking up information about people. Called Ph and Finger, these Internet services are handy, but by no means universal. In this chapter, I show you how to use both Ph and Finger from within Eudora.

Let me state up front that there is no centralized Internet directory. You cannot reliably look up someone's email address if you know only that person's name. Some Web sites attempt to provide such functionality, but even they are extremely limited.

In addition, you must keep in mind that neither Ph nor Finger will do you any good unless the person you're looking for is at an organization that runs a Ph or Finger server. There is no way of knowing if that's true for any given person. Academic institutions are more likely to run Ph servers than commercial Internet service providers, and smaller (and older) Internet service providers are more likely to run Finger services than large or new Internet service providers.

Eudora provides a number of neat features if you do want to use Ph or Finger—let's see what you can do.

### What are Ph and Finger?

You can best think of Ph (pronounced as two separate letters) as an electronic version of an organization-specific telephone book. Ph servers contain contact information about only the people who work at a particular business, university, or institution.

Finger works like Ph but uses even older technology. Finger servers also tend not to be as comprehensive as Ph servers.

You use both Ph and Finger to look up information (telephone numbers, email addresses, or office numbers) about people, just as you might use a telephone book specific to that person's organization.

# Setting up Ph and Finger

The tricky part of starting, particularly with Ph, is that you can't find any Ph servers unless you already know a Ph server to ask. You don't have to set up a Finger server, but since you're likely to query the same Finger server most of the time (probably the one your Internet service provider runs, if it runs one), entering a Finger server makes queries easier.

## To define Ph and Finger servers

1.  From the Special menu (Mac) or Tools menu (Windows), choose Settings (Mac) or Options (Windows).

    Eudora opens the Settings/Options dialog box.

2.  Click Hosts in the left-hand column to display the Hosts settings panel (**Figure 1**).

3.  In the Ph field, enter **ns.uiuc.edu**

4.  In the Finger field, enter **halcyon.com**

5.  Click the OK button to save your changes.

## ✔ Tips

- If you leave the Finger field blank, Eudora uses your SMTP server as your Finger server, which might or might not work.

- If you leave the Ph field blank, the Mac versions of Eudora default to the Ph server at *ns.uiuc.edu*.

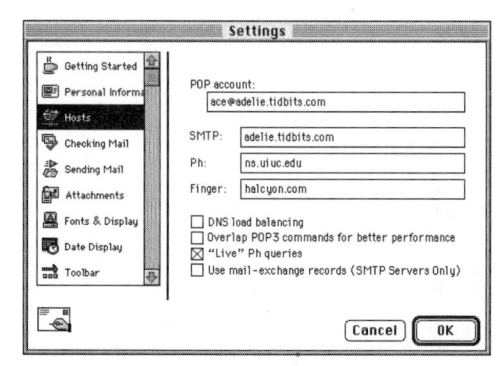

**Figure 1** To set up your default Ph and Finger servers, choose Settings (Mac) or Options (Windows) from the Special menu (Mac) or Tools menu (Windows), click Hosts in the left-hand column, then enter the names of your Ph and Finger servers in the appropriate fields.

### Entering your own servers

In this book, I use the University of Illinois at Urbana-Champaign's Ph server and my Internet service provider's (Northwest Nexus) Finger server because I need something here to explain Ph and Finger.

However, unless you regularly want to look up people who study or work at UIUC or people who get their Internet connections from Northwest Nexus, I recommend you change these settings.

It's best to set your Ph server to an organization where you're likely to want to look up people.

It's generally best to set your Finger server to be the machine you're most likely to use for fingering people. For me, that's Northwest Nexus. Try entering the domain part of your email address (like *halcyon.com*) and if that fails, ask your Internet service provider if they run a Finger server or know of a good one to use.

## Selecting another Ph server

As large as the University of Illinois is, I don't expect you will want to look up only people there. You can easily use other Ph servers.

### To select another Ph server

1. From the Special menu (Mac) or Tools menu (Windows), choose Directory Services ([Cmd]-Y/[Ctrl]-Y).

   Eudora opens the Directory Services window.

2. In the Mac versions of Eudora, click the globe button, and in the Windows versions of Eudora, click the Server button.

   Eudora asks the UIUC Ph server for the list of all the Ph servers that it knows about, and displays them in the bottom pane (**Figure 2**).

   Note that a Ph URL appears next to each organization name—like other URLs, it's blue and underlined.

3. Scroll through the list, and when you see a Ph server you want to query, double-click its URL.

   Eudora changes the server field to the new Ph server (**Figure 3**).

   You can now search the new Ph server for people at that organization. (See "Searching a Ph server" on the next page)

### ✔ Tips

- The Windows versions of Eudora keep track of all the Ph servers you've visited in the Server pop-up menu (**Figure 4**). Choose any server from that menu for quick access.

- In the Mac versions of Eudora, you can switch back to your main Ph server and search for other servers by holding down Option and clicking the globe button.

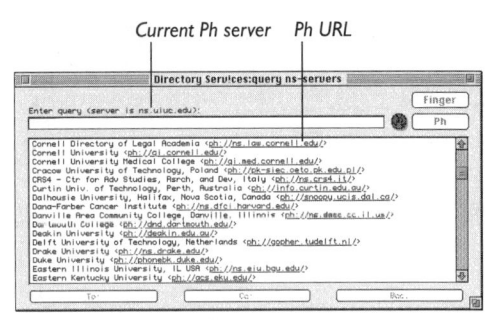

**Figure 2** To select a Ph server other than your default Ph server, choose Directory Services from the Special menu (Mac) or Tools menu (Windows), then click the globe button (Mac) or Server button (Windows). After Eudora retrieves the list of Ph servers and displays it in the lower pane, double-click the desired Ph URL to use that server.

*Note that the server became qi.cornell.edu, after I clicked the Ph URL for that server in Figure 2.*

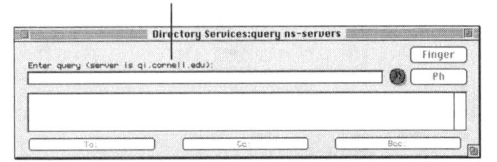

**Figure 3** After you double-click a Ph server URL, Eudora switches to using that new server.

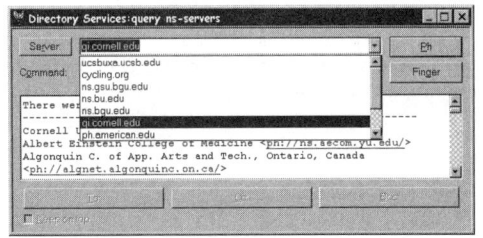

**Figure 4** The Windows versions of Eudora track all the Ph servers you've used. To select a previously used Ph server, choose it from the Server pop-up menu.

Chapter 11

# Searching a Ph server

Once you've selected the appropriate Ph server, the next task is to perform a search in that server.

## To search a Ph server

1. Open the Directory Services window by choosing Directory Services (Cmd-Y/Ctrl-Y) from the Special menu (Mac) or Tools menu (Windows).

2. In the Enter query field (Mac) or Command field (Windows), type the name of the person you want to find and click the Ph button.

   Eudora queries the current Ph server and returns the listings for people who match your search request (**Figure 5**).

## ✔ Tips

- In the Mac versions of Eudora, select a word or two, then hold down Shift and choose Directory Services (Cmd-Y) from the Special menu to insert the selected text in the Enter query field.

- In the Mac versions of Eudora, if you check the "Live" Ph queries checkbox in the Hosts settings panel (**Figure 6**), Eudora makes Ph queries automatically if you type something in the Enter query field and pause. It also looks up inserted text (from the previous tip) immediately.

- In the Windows versions of Eudora, check the Keep on top checkbox to keep the Directory Services window on top of any other Eudora windows.

- Try not to search for common first names because you'll get way too many people in the results listing.

- I generally search on last name, although if I'm positive of my spelling, I'll search on first and last name.

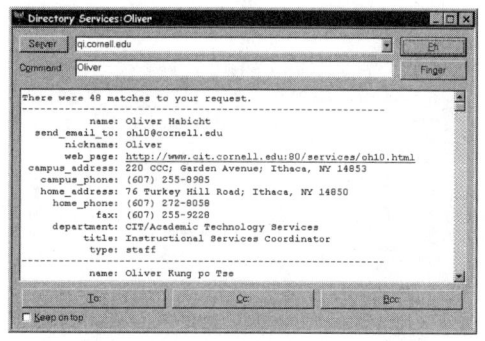

**Figure 5** To search for someone using Ph, open the Directory Services window by choosing Directory Services from the Tools menu (Windows) or Special menu (Mac). Then enter the name of the person you want to find (in this case, my friend Oliver) and click the Ph button.

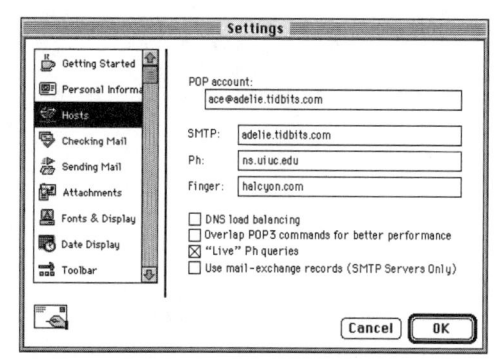

**Figure 6** Note that I've checked the "Live" Ph queries checkbox so Ph queries happen automatically without me having to click the Ph button. Instead, I just pause after typing the search terms.

## Using the results of a Ph search

Ph results usually fall into what my high school math teacher called the "look, see" method. You look at the results, and you see what you need. However, Eudora adds several useful features.

### To send email from a Ph search (Eudora Pro only)

1. Do a Ph search, then select some text in one or more of the results (**Figure 7**).

2. Click the To (or press Return/Enter), Cc, or Bcc button to create a new outgoing message addressed to the person or people whose entries you selected.

### To make a nickname from a Ph search

1. Do a Ph search, and select some text in one or more of the results.

2. Choose Make Address Book Entry ([Cmd]-K/[Ctrl]-K) from the Special menu (**Figure 8**).
   Eudora displays the New Nickname dialog box (Mac) or Make Address Book Entry dialog box (Windows) (**Figure 9**).

3. Enter a nickname for the person or people, select a file if you're using Eudora Pro, and check the "Put it on the recipient list" checkbox if you want the nickname on your recipient list. Click the OK button when you're done. (*See Chapter 9, "Working with the Address Book"*)

### ✔ Tip

- If you have an outgoing message window active, clicking the To, Cc, or Bcc button adds that person to the appropriate header line rather than creating a new message addressed to that person.

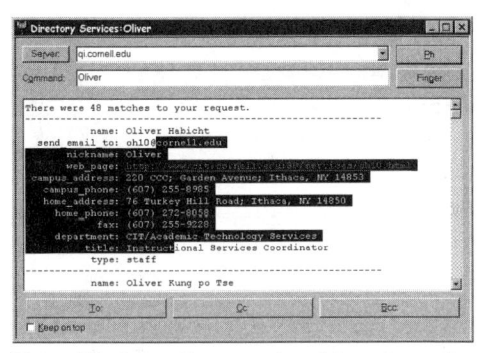

**Figure 7** In Eudora Pro, to send email from the results of a Ph search, select some text in one or more of the results, then click the To, Cc, or Bcc button.

**Figure 8** To make a nickname from the results of a Ph search, select some text in one or more of the results, as I did in Figure 7, then choose Make Address Book Entry from the Special menu.

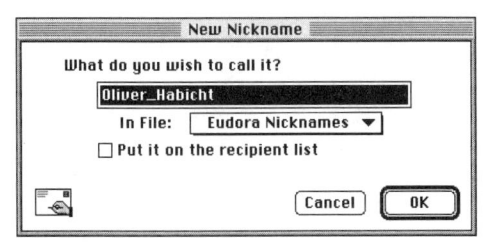

**Figure 9** Eudora then prompts you for the name of the nickname. Change the default nickname if you wish, choose a file if you're using Eudora Pro, then click the OK button to create the nickname. If desired, check the "Put it on the recipient list" checkbox.

# Searching a Finger server

Searching a Finger server is different than searching a Ph server.

### To search your default Finger server

1. Open the Directory Services window by choosing Directory Services ([Cmd]-Y/[Ctrl]-Y) from the Special menu (Mac) or Tools menu (Windows).

2. In the Enter query field (Mac) or Command field (Windows), type the name or username (the part of an email address before the @) of the person you want to find, then click the Finger button.

   Eudora queries your default Finger server and returns the listings for people who match your search request (**Figure 10**).

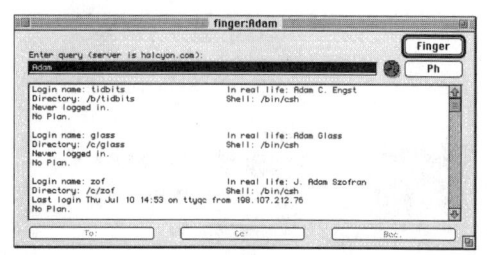

**Figure 10** To search for someone using your default Finger server, open the Directory Services window by choosing Directory Services from the Special menu (Mac) or Tools menu (Windows). Then enter the name of the person you want to find (in this case, me, at another of my email accounts) and click the Finger button.

### To search another Finger server

1. Open the Directory Services window by choosing Directory Services ([Cmd]-Y/[Ctrl]-Y) from the Special menu (Mac) or Tools menu (Windows).

2. In the Enter query field (Mac) or Command field (Windows), type the name or email username of the person you want to find, followed by an @ character and the domain name of the Finger server you want to query, and then click the Finger button.

   Eudora queries the specified Finger server and returns the listings for people who match your search request (**Figure 11**).

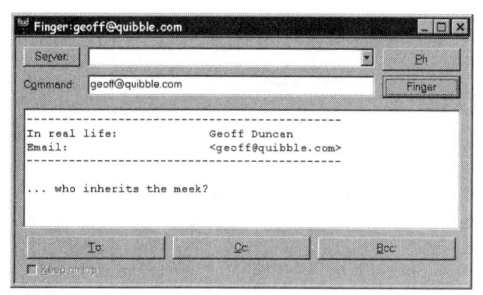

**Figure 11** To search for someone using another Finger server, open the Directory Services window by choosing Directory Services from the Tools menu (Windows) or Special menu (Mac). Then enter the name of the person you want to find (in this case, my friend Geoff), followed by an @ character and the domain name of the Finger server, and then click the Finger button.

### ✔ Tip

- Although both are always visible, Eudora makes either the Ph or the Finger button the default (pressing Return/Enter is the same as clicking a default button) based on the last type of search you performed.

---

### Finding Finger servers

Unfortunately, there is no directory of Finger servers, as there is with Ph. The only way to figure out if an organization or Internet service provider runs a Finger server is to try to use it or to ask.

## Online directories on the Web

Ph and Finger are relatively elderly Internet technologies, and in fact, a number of Web sites have sprung up that help you find people's email addresses. They're by no means perfect either, but if you have Web access, they're worth trying. There may be other online Web directories as well, but these are the main ones that I've used.

### Online Web directories

- Bigfoot
  http://www.bigfoot.com/
- Four11 Directory Services
  http://www.four11.com/
- InfoSpace
  http://www.infospace.com/
- Internet Address Finder
  http://www.iaf.net/
- WhoWhere?
  http://www.whowhere.com/

### Integrating Web directories with Eudora

Unfortunately, there's no guaranteed method of communication between the online Web directories and Eudora other than copy and paste.

However, in some versions of the main Web browsers (mainly Microsoft Internet Explorer), clicking a mailto link (a link that's an email address—the Web directories often display these) can automatically create a new outgoing message in Eudora and address it.

The Windows versions of Eudora have a checkbox called "Intercept Netscape mailto URLs" in the Miscellaneous settings panel. When that's checked, clicking a mailto link in Netscape Navigator or Netscape Communicator creates a new message in Eudora rather than in Netscape Mail or Netscape Messenger (the built-in email programs in different versions of Netscape).

To set the Mac versions of Eudora to intercept Netscape mailto URLs, read and follow the instructions on the Eudora as Netscape's Mailto Helper Web page at *http://www.amherst.edu/~atstarr/eudora/eudorawithnetscape.html*.

# WORKING WITH SETTINGS/OPTIONS | 12

## Getting more help

If you're confused about a setting in Eudora's Settings/Options dialog box, Eudora itself can often provide additional information.

In the Mac versions of Eudora, choose Show Balloons from the Guide menu (which looks like a question mark), then point at the setting in question to display a help balloon.

In the Windows versions of Eudora, click the question mark button in the dialog box's title bar, then click the setting in question to display context-sensitive help.

## ❗ Important settings

Eudora has far too many settings for me to document them all, and frankly, some of them aren't at all interesting. Look for the above exclamation point graphic next to especially interesting or important settings—the exclamation point will repeat next to the explanatory text for those settings.

By now I'm sure you have the sense that Eudora is a deep program. Recognizing that everyone works differently, Eudora's designers have provided multiple ways for you to use almost every part of the program.

Nowhere is this more evident than in Eudora's Settings (Mac) or Options (Windows) dialog box, where you control many of Eudora's settings. In fact, Eudora provides so much flexibility that the Settings/Options dialog box can seem overwhelming. Don't worry though, because apart from the few settings we modified back in Chapter 1, "Eudora Basics," the defaults are fine for most situations.

This chapter differs from most of the others in this book. Those chapters teach you how to perform specific tasks, but there aren't many tasks to perform in the Settings/Options dialog box. Instead, on each page, I discuss a specific settings panel, calling out interesting or especially useful settings.

Some of Eudora's settings panels are rather technical and esoteric, and others aren't standard (particularly in the Mac versions, to which you can add settings panels by dropping special files in your Eudora Folder). I won't cover those, but rest assured that I will cover the most important and useful settings panels.

*INTRODUCTION TO EUDORA'S SETTINGS*

# Getting Started

The Getting Started settings panel (**Figure 1** and **Figure 2**) is the first and most important settings panel in Eudora. In it, you provide the bare minimum information Eudora needs to send and receive messages.

## Settings

- The Real name field holds your real name. If you want to be cute, of course, you can enter anything you like here. I always recommend that people use their names.

- The POP account field holds your POP account, which looks like an email address. In fact, it is your email username, followed by an @ character, and the name of your POP server. Note that your POP account may not be the same as your return address.

    You get your POP account from your Internet service provider or network administrator—don't bother guessing.

- The Return address field holds your email address. If your return address is the same as your POP account, you may leave the Return address field blank.

- The Connection method options control how Eudora connects to send and receive email. In almost all cases, TCP/IP (Mac) or Winsock (Windows) is the correct choice. Eudora has the capability to dial a modem itself if you select Communications Toolbox (Mac) or Shell account access (Windows), but few people use those options any more.

- Check the Offline (no connections) checkbox if you aren't connected to the Internet temporarily (because you're using a laptop on the road, say) and want to prevent Eudora from checking for messages automatically.

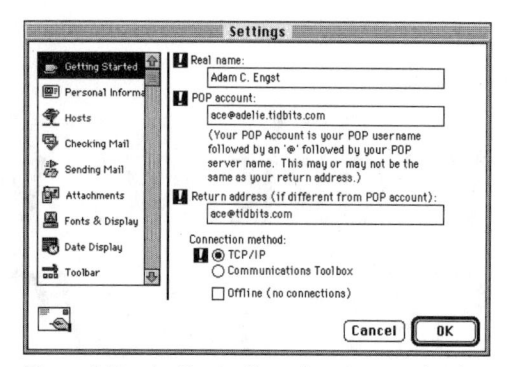

**Figure 1** Use the Getting Started settings panel in the Mac versions of Eudora to enter the basic information necessary to use Eudora.

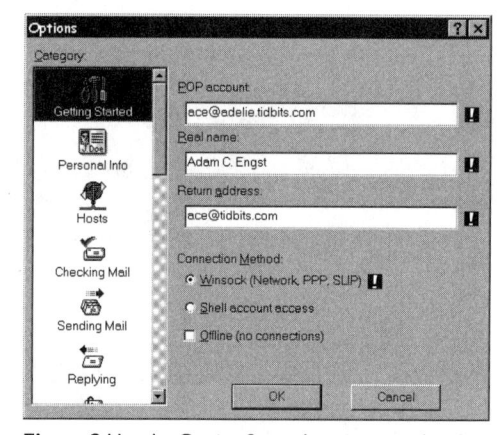

**Figure 2** Use the Getting Started settings panel in the Windows versions of Eudora to enter the basic information necessary to use Eudora.

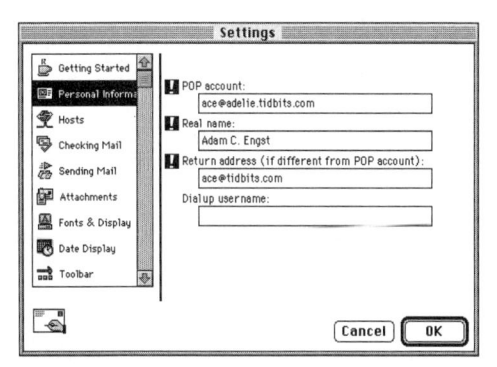

**Figure 3** Use the Personal Information settings panel in the Mac versions of Eudora to enter information about yourself. Much of the information is shared with other settings panels.

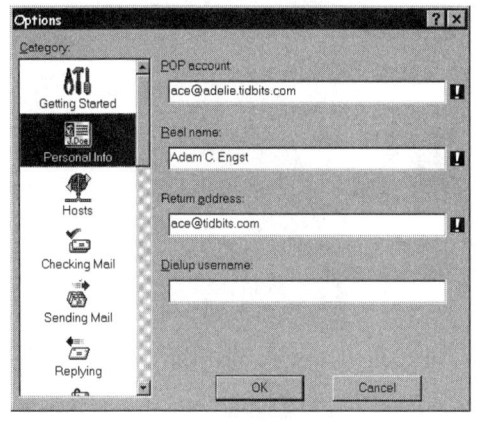

**Figure 4** Use the Personal Info settings panel in the Windows versions of Eudora to enter information about yourself. Much of the information is shared with other settings panels.

# Personal Information

The Personal Information settings panel (**Figure 3** and **Figure 4**) picks up most of its information from the Getting Started settings panel. Eudora's settings panels often share information because users often aren't sure where to look for any specific setting and it may logically fit in multiple settings panels.

## Settings

- The POP account, Real name, and Return address fields match the fields in the Getting Started settings panel covered on the previous page. Information entered in the Getting Started settings panel is shared by the Personal Information settings panel, and vice versa. So, if you want to change these settings, you can do it here, in the Getting Started Settings panel, or in any settings panel that shares the same fields.

- The Dialup username field can be left blank unless you use the Communications Toolbox (Mac) or Shell account access (Windows) and have Eudora connect to the Internet directly via a modem. Most people should ignore the Dialup username field.

# Hosts

The Hosts settings panel (**Figure 5** and **Figure 6**) holds the names of various Internet servers that Eudora talks to for different reasons. Eudora picks up some Hosts panel settings from either the Getting Started or Personal Information settings panel.

## Settings

- The POP account field holds your POP account (shared by the Getting Started, Personal Information, and Checking Mail settings panels).

- The SMTP server field holds the name of the server to which Eudora sends outgoing messages. If you leave it blank, Eudora sends messages to the machine that runs the POP server. Since many computers that run POP servers also run SMTP servers, this technique works much of the time.

  You must ask your Internet service provider or network administrator if you should fill in the SMTP server field, and if so, what to enter there.

- The Ph and Finger fields hold the names of your default Ph and Finger servers. (*See Chapter 11, "Using Directory Services"*)

- The Mac versions of Eudora offer several additional checkboxes, none of which offer necessary functionality.

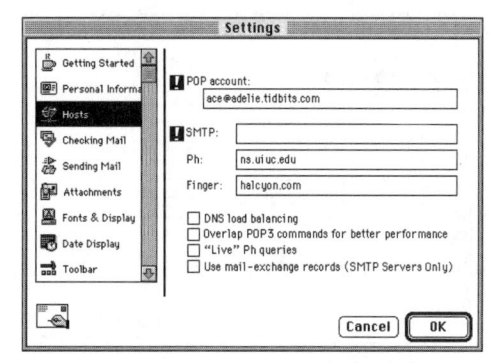

**Figure 5** Use the Hosts settings panel in the Mac versions of Eudora to enter the names of the various Internet servers Eudora talks to.

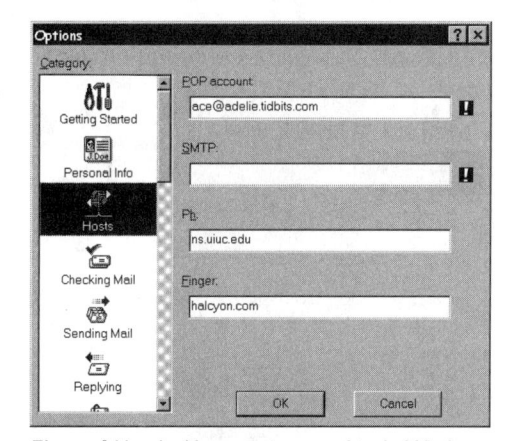

**Figure 6** Use the Hosts settings panel in the Windows versions of Eudora to enter the names of the various Internet servers Eudora talks to.

# Checking Mail

The Checking Mail settings panel (**Figure 7** and **Figure 8**) provides numerous options that let you customize how Eudora checks mail. (*See Chapter 4, "Sending and Receiving Messages"*)

## Settings

- The POP account field holds your POP account (shared by the Getting Started, Personal Information, and Hosts settings panels).

- The "Check for mail every X minutes" section controls if and how often Eudora automatically checks for mail.

- The "Skip messages over X K" checkbox and field control whether Eudora downloads messages over a specified size.

- The Leave mail on server sections and the "Delete from server when emptied from Trash" checkbox offer options for storing messages on the server and deleting them after a specified number of days.

- The "Send on check" checkbox controls whether Eudora sends outgoing messages when you check for new incoming messages. I recommend you check it.

- The Save password checkbox controls whether Eudora remembers your password or asks for it every time you check for new incoming messages. I recommend you check it.

- The Authentication radio buttons control how Eudora proves to your POP server that you are who you say you are. Leave Passwords selected unless your Internet service provider or network administrator tells you to select a different radio button.

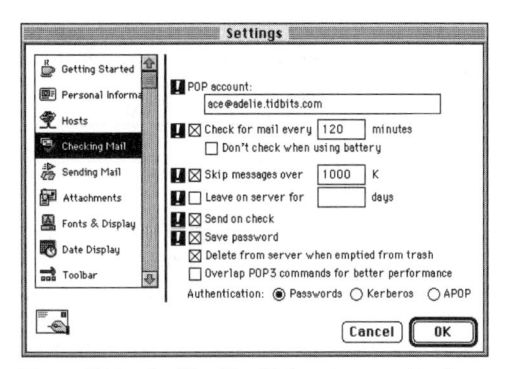

**Figure 7** Use the Checking Mail settings panel in the Mac versions of Eudora to customize how Eudora checks for mail.

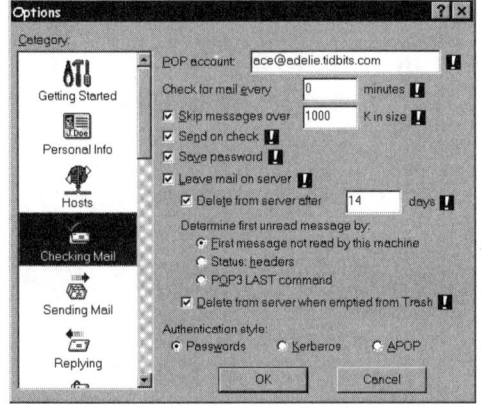

**Figure 8** Use the Checking Mail settings panel in the Windows versions of Eudora to customize how Eudora checks for mail.

# Sending Mail

The Sending Mail settings panel (**Figure 9** and **Figure 10**) enables you to customize how Eudora sends messages. (*See Chapter 4, "Sending and Receiving Messages"*)

## Settings

- The Return address and SMTP server fields match the fields with the same names in the Getting Started, Personal Information, and Hosts settings panels.

- The Immediate send checkbox controls whether Eudora sends messages immediately or queues them. I strongly recommend you uncheck this checkbox so Eudora queues messages.

- The "Send on check" checkbox is duplicated from the Checking Mail settings panel. Leave it checked.

- In the Mac versions, the Fix curly quotes checkbox tells Eudora to translate characters like curly quotes into more common characters like straight quotes for accurate transmission. Leave it checked.

- In Eudora Pro, all new messages can use a specific piece of stationery.

- In the Mac version of Eudora Pro, check the Expand nicknames immediately checkbox to replace nicknames with their associated email addresses.

  The Windows version puts this checkbox in the Miscellaneous settings panel.

- The message content checkboxes and menus: Word wrap, May use quoted-printable, Tabs in body of message (Windows), Keep copies of outgoing mail, and Signature set defaults for the outgoing message toolbar menus and buttons. I recommend using the defaults. (*See Chapter 3, "Writing Messages"*)

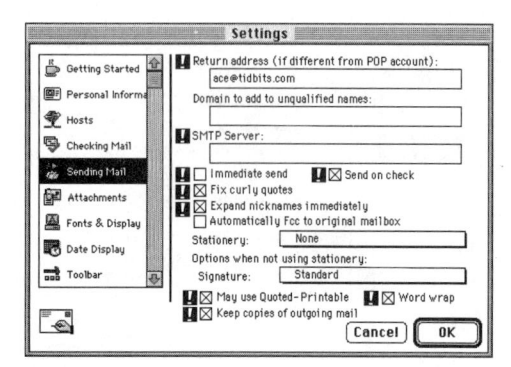

**Figure 9** Use the Sending Mail settings panel in the Mac versions of Eudora to customize how Eudora sends messages.

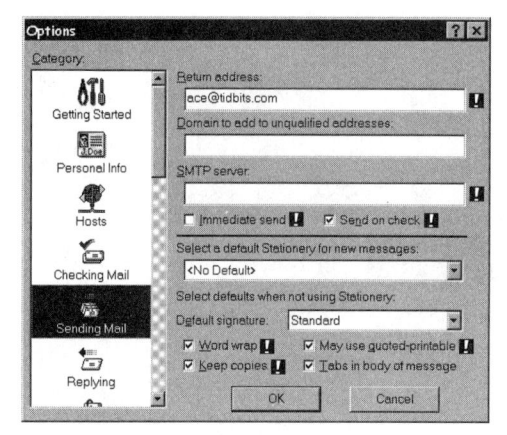

**Figure 10** Use the Sending Mail settings panel in the Windows versions of Eudora to customize how Eudora sends messages.

# Working with Settings/Options

## Attachments

The Attachments settings panel (**Figure 11** and **Figure 12**) lets you set Eudora's default encoding format for outgoing attachments and where incoming attachments should be stored. (*See Chapter 3, "Writing Messages"*)

## Settings

- The Encoding method radio buttons set the default encoding format for outgoing attachments. In general, leave the Mac versions of Eudora set to AppleDouble and leave the Windows versions set to MIME.

- In the Mac versions, the "Always include Macintosh information" makes Eudora send file type and creator information with the attachment. Leave it checked.

- In the Mac version of Eudora Pro, the "Receive MIME digests as attachments" checkbox makes Eudora treat a MIME digest (from a mailing list) as an attachment that you can open to get a mailbox of all messages in the digest.

- The Attachment Folder/directory button enables you to select an alternate location for received attachments. It defaults to the Attachments (Mac) or Attach (Windows) folder in your Eudora Folder.

- In the Mac versions, the "Trash attachments with messages" checkbox makes Eudora move attachment files to the Finder's Trash when you move a message to the Trash mailbox.

    In the Windows versions, the "Delete attachments when emptying Trash" checkbox deletes attachment files when you empty the Trash mailbox.

- In the Mac versions, the "TEXT files belong to" button lets you set which application opens text file attachments.

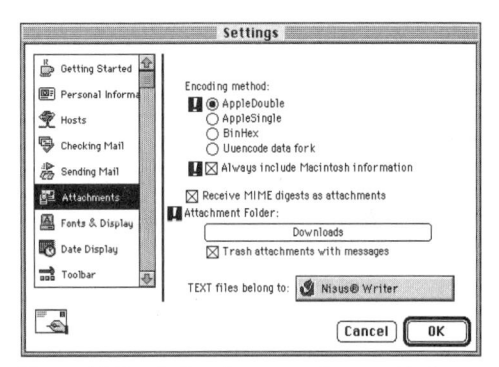

**Figure 11** Use the Attachments settings panel in the Mac versions of Eudora to set Eudora's default encoding format for outgoing attachments and location for incoming attachments.

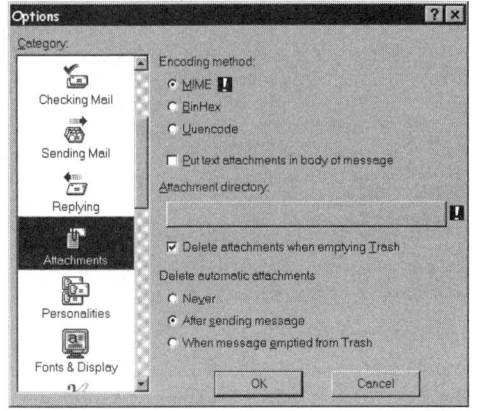

**Figure 12** Use the Attachments settings panel in the Windows versions of Eudora to set Eudora's default encoding format for outgoing attachments and location for incoming attachments. The Attachment directory button is blank because Eudora uses the Attach folder by default.

# Fonts & Display

The Fonts & Display settings panel (**Figure 13** and **Figure 14**) controls Eudora's interface.

## Settings

- The Screen and Print font and size controls (a menu and field in the Mac versions; a button that opens a Font dialog box in the Windows versions) enable you to set the font and size used for viewing messages.

- The Mac versions of Eudora enable you to pick the text and background colors from a color wheel. I still like black and white.

- The Message window width and Message window height fields enable you to set the size of message windows in characters (width) and lines (height).

- The "Zoom windows when opening" checkbox zooms windows to display as much content as possible.

- In the Mac versions of Eudora, the "Waste cycles drawing trendy 3D junk" checkbox toggles between a 3D and 2D interface.

- In the Mac version of Eudora Pro, the "Display graphics attachments inline" checkbox enables display of graphics in message bodies.

- In the Windows versions, the Show toolbar, Show toolbar tips, and Show status bar checkboxes control the main toolbar options. In the Mac version of Eudora Pro, the Show formatting toolbar checkbox toggles the formatting toolbar in outgoing message windows (the Toolbar settings panel handles the main toolbar options).

- In the Windows versions, the Show category icons checkbox controls whether the settings panels list at the left of the Options dialog box has icons.

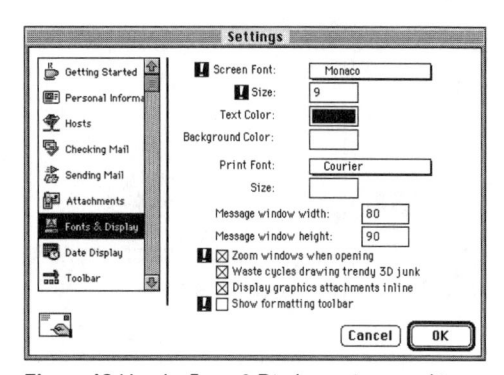

**Figure 13** Use the Fonts & Display settings panel in the Mac versions of Eudora to customize how Eudora displays text and windows.

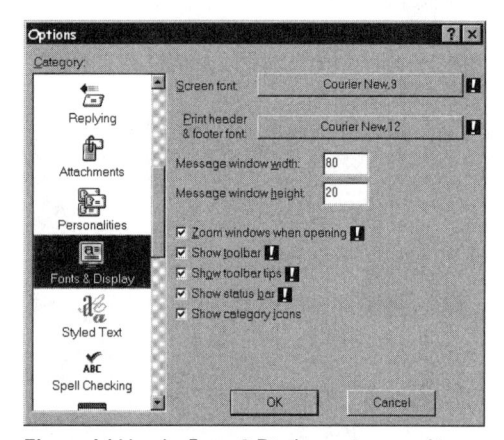

**Figure 14** Use the Fonts & Display settings panel in the Windows versions of Eudora to customize how Eudora displays text and windows, along with toolbars.

## Toolbar

**EUDORA PRO ONLY!**
**MACINTOSH ONLY!**

The Toolbar settings panel (**Figure 15**) controls the display of the main toolbar in the Mac version of Eudora Pro. (*See Chapter 10, Working with the Toolbar"*)

### Settings

- The Show toolbar checkbox controls whether the toolbar displays.

- The Orientation radio buttons control whether the toolbar displays horizontally or vertically.

- The Button type radio buttons control how the buttons display. I recommend starting with icons and names, and working your way down to only icons if you need the screen space. It can be hard to remember what functions map to specific icons without the names.

- The "Map function keys to buttons" checkbox assigns the function keys at the top of your keyboard to different buttons.

- The "Show function key labels" checkbox displays labels indicating which function keys map to which buttons. If you use the function keys, I recommend leaving this checkbox checked.

### ✔ Tip

- The Windows versions of Eudora have toolbars as well, but their controls are located in the Fonts & Display settings panel rather than in a separate Toolbar settings panel.

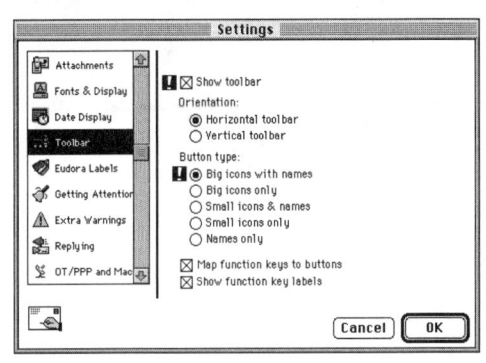

**Figure 15** Use the Toolbar settings panel in the Mac version of Eudora Pro to control the display of the main toolbar.

## Eudora Labels/Labels

**EUDORA PRO ONLY!**

The Eudora Labels (Mac) or Labels (Windows) settings panel (**Figure 16** and **Figure 17**) enables you to name and color labels.

### Settings

- To name any label, replace the text in the label name field with your desired name.

- To change the color of a label, click the color button to the left of the label name field, then select a color from the color picker.

### ✔ Tip

- The Mac version of Eudora Pro provides eight labels, but those are in addition to the seven standard Macintosh labels set in the Labels control panel (available from the Control Panels folder in the Apple menu).

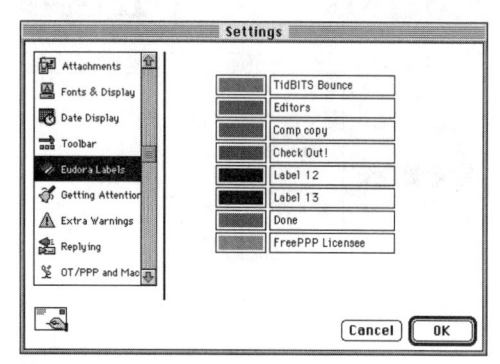

**Figure 16** Use the Eudora Labels settings panel in the Mac version of Eudora Pro to create and modify labels beyond the basic seven provided by the Finder's Labels control panel.

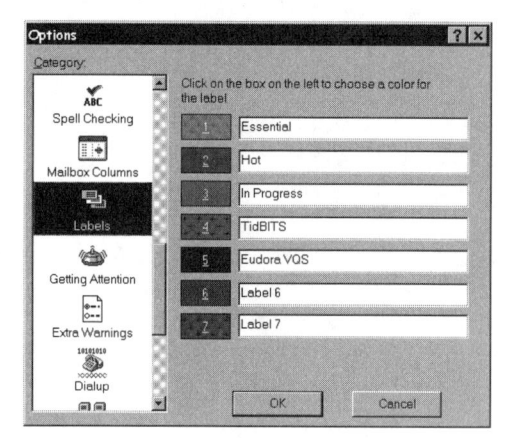

**Figure 17** Use the Labels settings panel in the Windows version of Eudora Pro to create and modify labels.

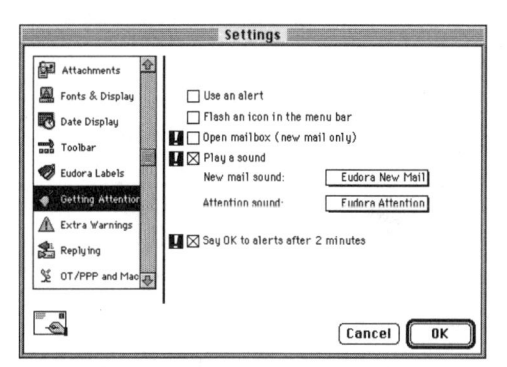

**Figure 18** Use the Getting Attention settings panel in the Mac versions of Eudora to control how Eudora alerts you to new messages and other interesting events.

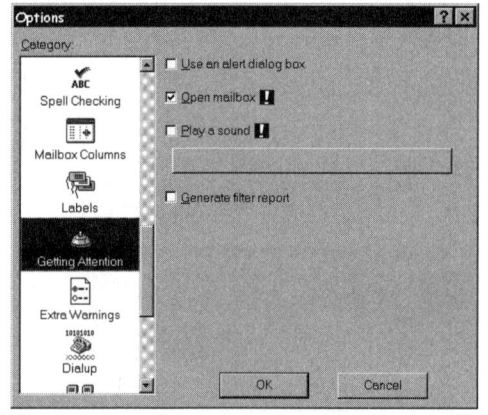

**Figure 19** Use the Getting Attention settings panel in the Windows versions of Eudora to control how Eudora alerts you to new messages and other interesting events.

# Getting Attention

The Getting Attention settings panel (**Figure 18** and **Figure 19**) controls how Eudora alerts you to new messages and other events of note.

## Settings

- The Use an alert checkbox makes Eudora pop up an alert dialog box when you have new mail. I find it a pain.

- The "Flash an icon in the menu bar" (Mac) checkbox makes Eudora flash an icon to alert you to new mail.

- The Open mailbox checkbox tells Eudora to open mailboxes that contain new messages after checking for new mail. I often do this instead with filters so I can control which mailing list mailbox windows open.

- The Play a sound checkbox and menu (Mac) or button (Windows) enables you to set Eudora to play a specified sound when you receive new mail or when Eudora needs your attention (Mac).

- In the Mac versions of Eudora, check the "Say OK to alerts after 2 minutes" checkbox to dismiss Eudora's alert dialog boxes after two minutes automatically.

   The Windows versions of Eudora have the same setting, but it's located in the Miscellaneous settings panel.

- In the Windows versions of Eudora, check the Generate filter report checkbox to see a report of where Eudora has filtered messages after processing them.

   The Mac versions of Eudora have the same setting, but it's located in the Miscellaneous settings panel.

# Extra Warnings

The Extra Warnings setting panel (**Figure 20** and **Figure 21**) lets you manipulate Eudora's "nag factor." I enjoy setting Eudora to warn me only about what I consider important events, rather than mere niggling details. Most of these settings are obvious, so I focus on a few that I think are important. I've used Mac checkbox names here, but the Windows checkbox names are extremely similar.

## Settings

- I check "Try to queue a message with styled text" because I only occasionally want to send styled text. The warning gives me a chance to remove the styles. *(See Chapter 3, "Writing Messages")*

- I check "Try to quit with messages queued to be sent" because I don't want to quit Eudora and forget to send messages that are waiting to go out. *(See Chapter 4, "Sending and Receiving Messages")*

- I check "Try to send a message whose size is more than X K" because it can take a long time to send a large message and I may not want to wait for the message to go out at that moment. *(See Chapter 4, "Sending and Receiving Messages")*

- I check "Empty the Trash mailbox" because I don't want to lose all the messages in there accidentally. I delete messages from my Trash mailbox manually. *(See Chapter 6, "Working with Mailboxes")*

- I check "Try something that requires too much memory" (Mac) because it provides a chance to avoid an unnecessary crash.

- I check "Start Eudora and it's not the default mailer" (Windows) because other email programs occasionally try to make themselves the default email program for Windows, and I hate that.

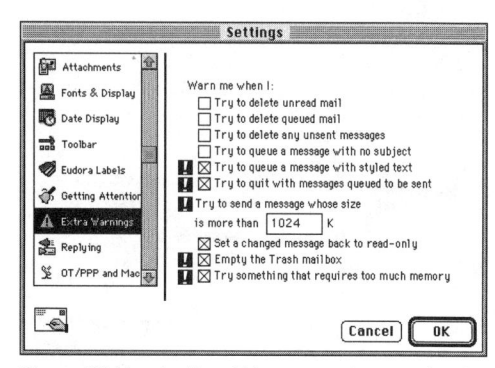

**Figure 20** Use the Extra Warnings settings panel in the Mac versions of Eudora to fine-tune how often Eudora nags you.

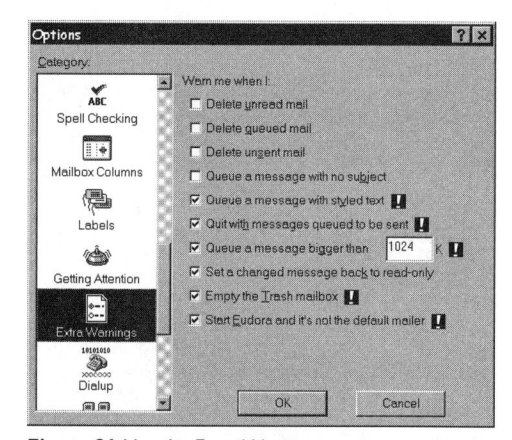

**Figure 21** Use the Extra Warnings settings panel in the Windows versions of Eudora to fine-tune how often Eudora nags you.

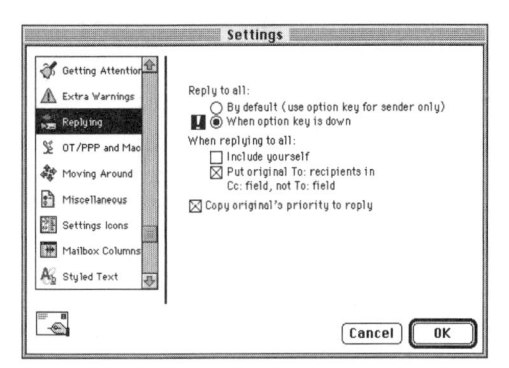

**Figure 22** Use the Replying settings panel in the Mac versions of Eudora to control how Eudora replies to incoming messages.

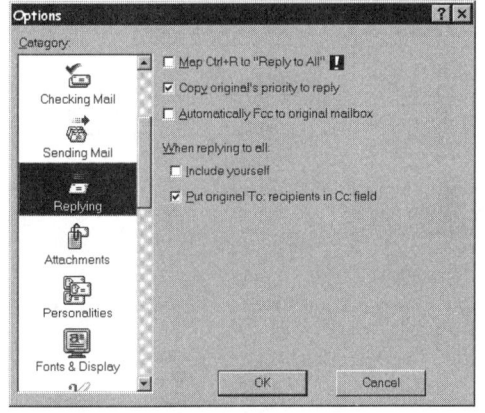

**Figure 23** Use the Replying settings panel in the Windows versions of Eudora to control how Eudora replies to incoming messages.

# Replying

The Replying settings panel (**Figure 22** and **Figure 23**) enables you to control how Eudora replies to incoming messages.

## Settings

- In the Mac versions of Eudora, the Reply to all radio buttons control whether Reply to all is the default action or requires that Option be held down. I strongly recommend you select the "When option key is down" radio button to make it more difficult to send replies to multiple people, which can prove embarrassing. Similarly, in the Windows versions of Eudora, leave unchecked the "Map Ctrl+R to Reply to All" checkbox. (*See Chapter 2, "Creating Messages"*)

- The "When replying to all" checkboxes control whether you're included in a reply to all and where the original recipients' addresses go in the message header. Frankly, neither option matters much, but I usually uncheck Include yourself.

- The "Copy original's priority to reply" checkbox assigns the priority setting of the original message to your outgoing reply message. It simply ensures that if someone thinks a message deserves a specific priority, the reply to that message shares the same priority level.

- In the Windows version of Eudora Pro, the "Automatically Fcc to original mailbox" checkbox puts a copy of each reply in the same mailbox that contains the original message. The same checkbox appears in the Mac version of Eudora Pro in the Sending Mail settings panel. I've never seen the utility of it, personally.

# OT/PPP and MacSLIP / Advanced Network

The OT/PPP and MacSLIP (Mac) (**Figure 24**) and Advanced Network (Windows) (**Figure 25**) settings panels simplify connecting if you have a dial-up connection to the Internet. The OT/PPP and MacSLIP settings panel is only of use if your Mac connects to the Internet using Apple's Open Transport PPP or Hyde Park Software's MacSLIP. The Advanced Network settings panel's connection options require that you've installed the dial-up networking services in Windows 95.

## Settings

- In the Mac versions of Eudora, the "Don't make automatic checks when MacSLIP or OT/PPP is not already connected" checkbox prevents Eudora from checking mail automatically unless you're already connected to the Internet. This prevents Eudora from dialing your modem and connecting automatically.

- In the Mac versions of Eudora, the "Disconnect MacSLIP or OT/PPP if Eudora connected it" checkbox makes Eudora hang up the modem after checking for new mail only if an automatic mail check caused OT/PPP or MacSLIP to connect to the Internet. I recommend you check this checkbox if you use OT/PPP or MacSLIP and have Eudora check mail periodically.

- In the Windows versions of Eudora, the "Automatically dial & hangup this connection" checkbox enables Eudora to connect to the Internet automatically to send and receive mail. Choose your Internet service provider from the Entry pop-up menu and enter your username in the Username field. Check the Save password checkbox if you don't want to enter your password for every connection.

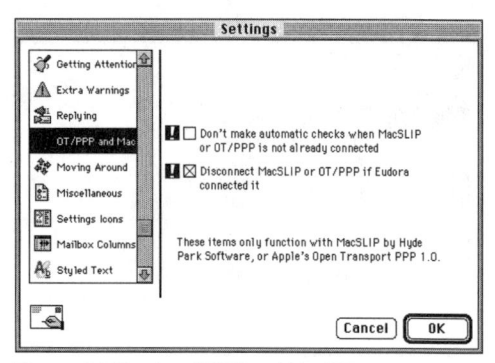

**Figure 24** Use the OT/PPP and MacSLIP settings panel in the Mac versions of Eudora to control how Eudora makes and breaks connections if you use OT/PPP or MacSLIP to connect to the Internet.

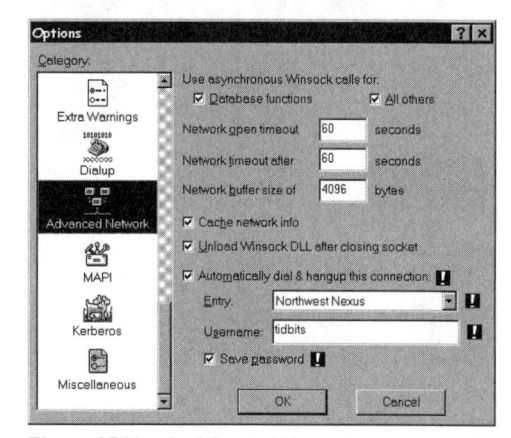

**Figure 25** Use the Advanced Network settings panel in the Windows versions of Eudora to control how Eudora makes and breaks Internet connections if you're using a dial-up connection to the Internet.

## Moving Around

**MACINTOSH ONLY!**

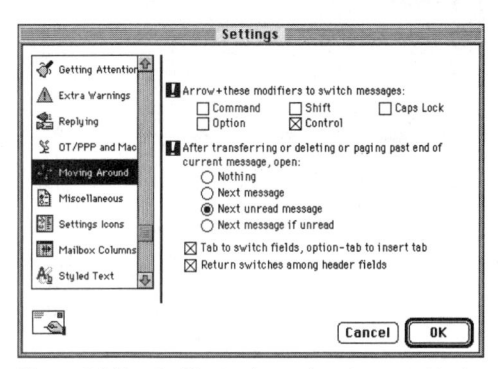

**Figure 26** Use the Moving Around settings panel in the Mac versions of Eudora to determine how you navigate between messages in Eudora.

The Moving Around settings panel (**Figure 26**) enables you to set how you navigate between messages in Eudora.

### Settings

- The "Arrow + these modifiers to switch messages" checkboxes enable you to pick which, if any, modifier keys work in conjunction with the arrow keys to switch between messages.

- The "After transferring or deleting or paging past end of current message, open" radio buttons enable you to decide what Eudora should open after you move past a message. I usually select Next unread message.

- The "Tab to switch fields, option-tab to insert tab" checkbox controls whether pressing Tab inserts a tab or moves the insertion point between header fields. I don't use tabs in messages much, so I always leave this checkbox checked.

- The "Return switches among header fields" checkbox enables you to decide if pressing Return in the header of a message should insert a Return character or move the insertion point to the next header field. Since there's seldom any reason to insert a Return character in the header fields, I always leave this checkbox checked.

### ✔ Tip

- The Windows version of Eudora lacks a Moving Around settings panel but provides much of the same functionality in the Miscellaneous settings panel.

# Miscellaneous

The Miscellaneous settings panel (**Figure 27** and **Figure 28**) contains, as you might expect, a hodgepodge of unrelated settings. I call out only those that I think are important below. Note that the Windows versions of Eudora include a number of important settings that appear elsewhere in the Mac versions' settings panels—I've marked them with exclamation point graphics, but I won't discuss them again.

## Settings

- I leave the "Close messages with mailbox" checkbox unchecked because I like message windows to remain open when their mailboxes close.

- I leave the "Empty Trash on Quit" checkbox unchecked because I prefer to keep messages in my Trash mailbox for a while. (*See Chapter 6, "Working with Mailboxes"*)

- I check the "Turbo redirect by default" checkbox because it speeds up the process of redirecting messages.

- In the Windows versions of Eudora, I check the "Automatically open next message" checkbox because I find it makes reading mail go faster.

- In the Windows versions of Eudora, I check the "Allow drag and drop transfers" checkbox. That's what the mouse is for, after all!

- In the Windows versions of Eudora, I check the "Intercept Netscape mailto URLs" checkbox because I want to use Eudora for all my messages, even if I'm using Netscape Navigator or Communicator to browse the Web.

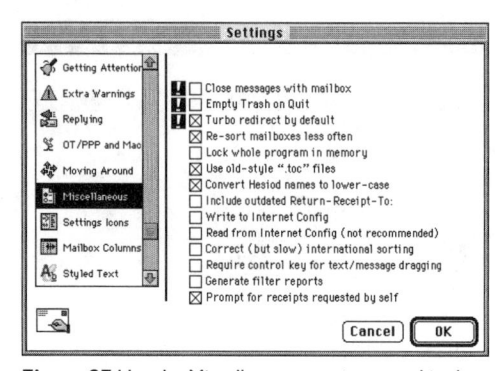

**Figure 27** Use the Miscellaneous settings panel in the Mac versions of Eudora to control a wide variety of unrelated settings.

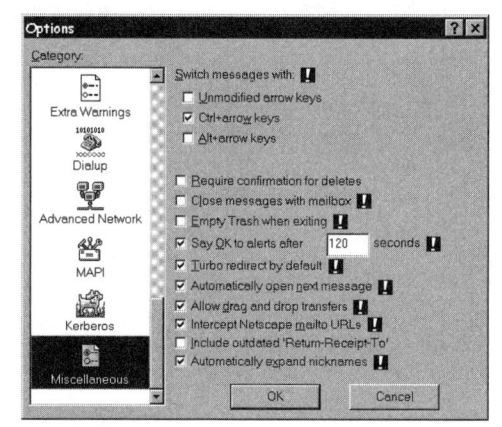

**Figure 28** Use the Miscellaneous settings panel in the Windows versions of Eudora to control a wide variety of unrelated settings.

## Settings Icons

The Settings Icons settings panel (**Figure 29**) enables you to pick the display style of the scrolling list in the Settings dialog box.

### Settings

- The Icon sizes radio buttons let you pick whether Eudora should display the settings panel list with big icons with names, big icons only, small icons with names, or names only. I prefer small icons with names, because there are too many settings panels to scroll through easily with big icons showing.

### ✔ Tip

- The Windows version of Eudora lacks a Settings Icons settings panel but provides a Show category icons checkbox in the Fonts & Display settings panel. Checking that checkbox displays icons for each settings panel, rather than just the name.

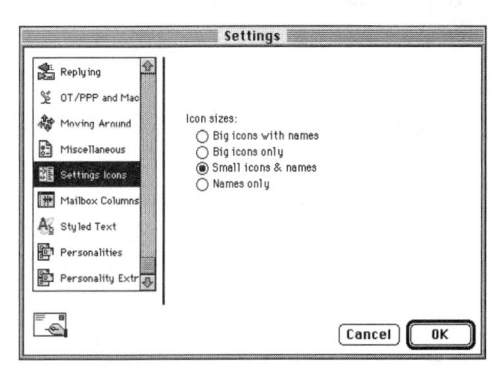

**Figure 29** Use the Settings Icons settings panel in the Mac versions of Eudora to pick the display style of the scrolling list in the Settings dialog box.

# Mailbox Columns

The Mailbox Columns settings panel (**Figure 30** and **Figure 31**) enables you to pick which columns should display in mailbox windows. Since I have large monitors, I leave all columns showing, but if you're tight for space, you might want to turn some off.

## Settings

- The Show columns checkboxes determine which columns will display in mailbox windows. Check a checkbox to display that column.

- In the Mac versions of Eudora, you can uncheck the Draw separator lines checkbox to prevent Eudora from drawing separator lines between message summaries and mailbox columns. Personally, I like them.

## ✔ Tip

- Eudora Pro provides two additional columns beyond those offered by Eudora Light: Label and Server status.

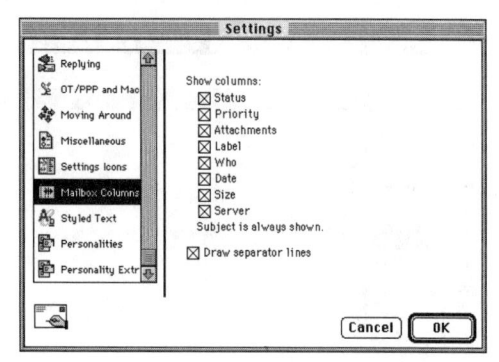

**Figure 30** Use the Mailbox Columns settings panel in the Mac versions of Eudora to determine which columns display in mailbox windows.

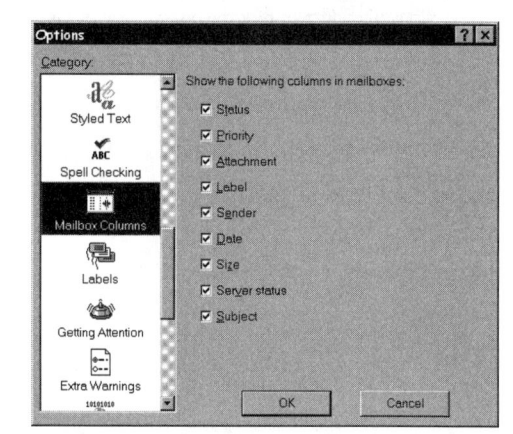

**Figure 31** Use the Mailbox Columns settings panel in the Windows versions of Eudora to determine which columns display in mailbox windows.

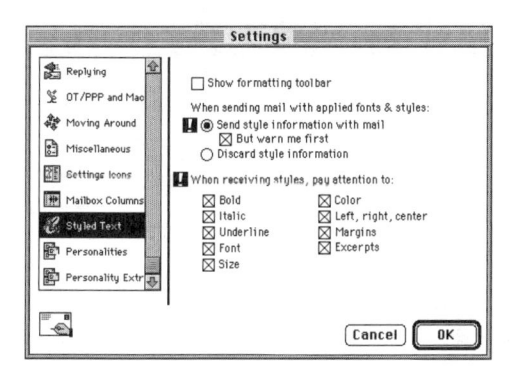

**Figure 32** Use the Styled Text settings panel in the Mac versions of Eudora to control how Eudora displays incoming messages containing styled text and, in Eudora Pro, whether to send outgoing messages with styled text.

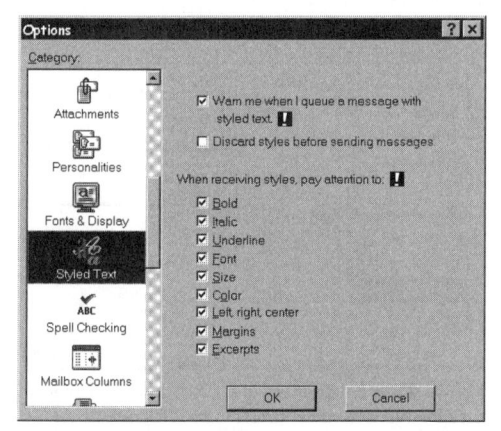

**Figure 33** Use the Styled Text settings panel in the Windows versions of Eudora to control how Eudora displays incoming messages containing styled text and, in Eudora Pro, whether to send outgoing messages with styled text.

# Styled Text

The Styled Text settings panel (**Figure 32** and **Figure 33**) controls how Eudora displays received messages containing styled text. In addition, in Eudora Pro, the Styled Text settings panel enables you to decide whether to send messages with styled text.

## Settings

- In the Mac version of Eudora Pro, you can check the Show formatting toolbar checkbox to display the formatting toolbar in outgoing message windows.

- The controls for sending messages with styled text enable you to either send the styles or discard the style information in outgoing messages. I let Eudora Pro send styled messages but set it to prompt me first, so I can decide on a per-message basis if I actually want to send styles.

- The "When receiving styles, pay attention to" checkboxes determine which styles Eudora displays in message windows. Check a checkbox to display that style if it's present in an incoming message. I leave all of these checked, just in case someone sends a heavily styled message.

# Personalities and Personality Extras

The Personalities and Personality Extras (Mac) settings panels (**Figure 34**, **Figure 35**, and **Figure 36**) enable you to create, modify, and delete personalities. Personalities are usually used to manage email on multiple accounts, but more generically, they are collections of settings that apply to outgoing messages.

## Settings

- To switch between personalities, choose one from the pop-up Personality menu.

- To create a new personality, click the New button. Then fill in all desired fields in the Personality and Personality Extras (Mac) settings panels.

- To remove a personality, choose it from the pop-up Personality menu, then click the Remove button.

## ✔ Tips

- The settings in the Personalities and Personality Extras (Mac) settings panels duplicate many of those we've already looked at in this chapter. Flip back for information on specific fields and checkboxes.

- Personalities are especially useful if you have multiple email accounts. You can create a personality for each account and have Eudora Pro check each account regularly. In addition, when creating messages, you can decide which personality a message should be from. (*See Chapter 3, "Writing Messages"*)

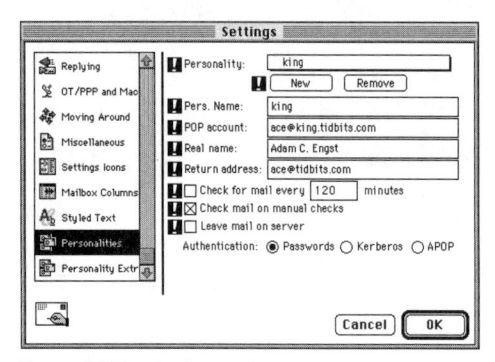

**Figure 34** Use the Personalities settings panel in the Mac versions of Eudora to enter basic information for alternate personalities.

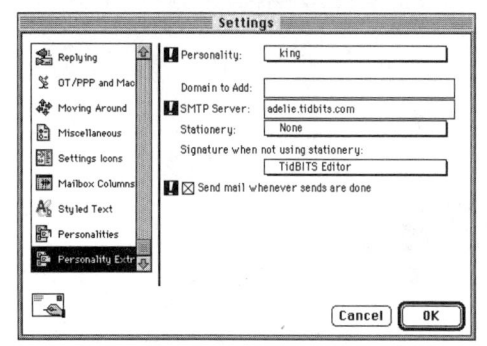

**Figure 35** Use the Personality Extras settings panel in the Mac versions of Eudora to customize additional settings for alternate personalities.

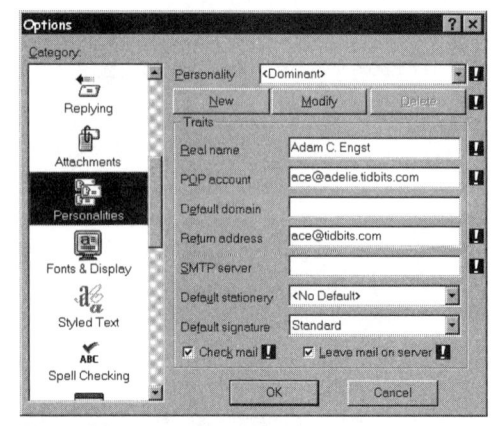

**Figure 36** Use the Personalities settings panel in the Windows versions of Eudora to enter basic information for alternate personalities.

## Spell Checking

**EUDORA PRO ONLY!**
**WINDOWS ONLY!**

The Spell Checking settings panel (**Figure 37**) enables you to control precisely how Eudora Pro checks the spelling of message text. You can also change most of these settings by clicking the Options button in the Check Spelling dialog box. (*See Chapter 3, "Writing Messages"*)

Most of the options in the Spell Checking settings panel are obvious; I call out only the interesting ones below.

### Settings

- I check the Ignore original text checkbox because it's too time-consuming to check other people's writing when replying to their messages.

- If you're truly concerned about your spelling, check the "Check when message queued/sent" checkbox to check every message before it goes out.

### ✔ Tip

- The Mac version of Eudora Pro has no equivalent Spell Checking settings panel, but you can set similar preferences by choosing Preferences from the File menu when the spell checking window is open.

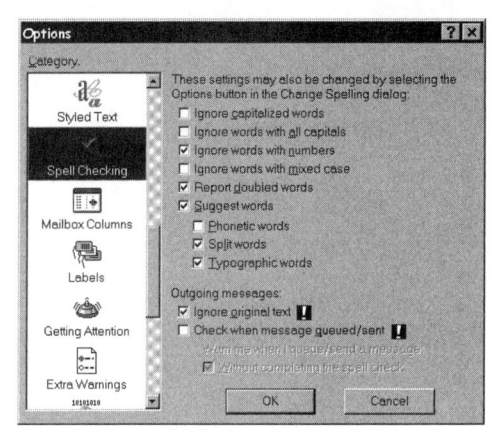

**Figure 37** Use the Spell Checking settings panel in the Windows version of Eudora Pro to control how Eudora Pro checks the spelling of message text.

# INDEX

## A

about
  the address book   133
  attachments   53
  filters   111
  message plug-ins   38
  Ph and Finger servers   155
  signatures   49
  the toolbar   145
activating filters   117
adding toolbar buttons   149
address book   133–143
  adding names to messages   138
  addressing messages
    from alternate email   33
    to multiple recipients   32
    to recipient list   25
  introducing the   133
  multiple nicknames files   139
  nicknames
    adding to recipient list   142
    creating   134, 135
    deleting   142, 143
    finding   140
    modifying   141
    tips for   136
  toolbar button for   148
  using the Address Book window   137
Address Book window
  collapsing and expanding the   137
  creating nicknames   134, 135
  keeping in front   138

aliases (Macintosh)
  configuring Eudora for multiple people   8
  creating   6
  for mailboxes   107
America Online attachments   56
AppleSingle encoding format (Macintosh)   56
AppleDouble encoding format (Macintosh)   56
archiving messages   108
attachments
  about   53
  changing format for   57
  copying (Macintosh)   88
  deleting   89, 167
  moving   88
  opening   87
  selecting formats for   56
  text files as   36
  via dialog boxes   54
  via drag and drop   55
  with voice recordings   59
Attachments settings panel   169

## B

BinHex encoding format   56
Blah button   81
boilerplate messages   27–29
boring headers   81
buttons
  adding toolbar   149

185

## Index

buttons (continued)
   changing functions of   154
   deleting on toolbar   153
   ideas for toolbar   151
   moving on toolbars   152
   for outgoing message toolbar   58
   toolbar, illustrated   148

## C

case plug-ins   38
Change Queueing dialog box   63, 64
changing
   message labels   77
   message personality   79
   message priority   76
   message status   78
   message text   80
Check Mail   66, 71
Check Mail Specially   71
Check Spelling dialog box (Windows)   40
Checking Mail settings panel   7, 167
checking messages
   incoming   66, 67
   for PowerBook users   67
   retrieving messages by size   70
   for spelling   39–41
Clear Formatting button   48
closing mailbox folders   102
Compact Mailboxes (Windows)   106
compacting mailboxes   106
configuring Eudora   7–10
conflicts with nicknames   141
Contains pop-up menu   115
contextual help   12
Copy and Unwrap   37
copying attachment files (Macintosh)   88
creating
   aliases (Macintosh)   6
   buttons to open mailboxes   149, 150
   clippings files   90
   filters   112
   group nicknames   135
   mailbox folders   100, 101
   mailboxes   97, 99
   messages   17–19
   multiple nickname files   139

creating (continued)
   nicknames for individuals   134, 159
   pane interface (Windows)   83
   shortcuts (Windows)   6
   stationery messages   27–28
   To and Subject lines   18
   and using signatures   50
custom signatures   51
Customize Toolbar dialog box
   (Windows)   150

## D

decoding plug-ins   38
defaults
   for attachment formatting   57
   Reply to All   21
   for sorting messages   96
   for toolbar buttons   148
Delete attachments when emptying Trash
   checkbox   89, 167
Delete from server after X days checkbox   69
Delete Mailbox button (Macintosh)   105
deleting
   attachments   89, 167
   buttons on toolbar   153
   filters   122
   mailbox folders   105
   messages   69, 70, 71, 85
   nicknames   142, 143
dial-up connection settings   176
directory services   155–161
   about Ph and Finger   155
   online directories on the Web   161
   searching
      a Finger server   160
      for names on a Ph server   158
   selecting Ph servers   157
   setting up Ph and Finger servers   156
   using search results from Ph server   159
disk space
   compacting mailboxes   106
   recovering by emptying Trash
      mailbox   109
Don't Send radio button   65
Don't transfer, just create mailbox checkbox
   (Windows)   100

# Index

downloading Eudora   3
drag and drop attachments   55
dragging messages to another mailbox   98

## E

editing
   signatures   52
   text   37
email. *See* messages
email glossary   14–16
encoding
   formats for   56
   plug-in for   38
Encoding format menu   57
encrypting and decrypting messages   60
etiquette for redirecting messages   23
Eudora
   address book   133–143
   configuring   7–10
   controlling interface for   170
   creating messages   17–19
   directory services   155–161
   filters   111–122
   getting software   3
   getting started   1–16
   glossary feature   136
   hardware and software
      requirements   2, 11
   installing
     for Macintosh   4
     for Windows   5
   launching and quitting   6
   mailboxes   93–109
   newsgroups and Web sites for   13
   printing windows from   91
   settings and options for   163–183
   toolbar   145–154
   *See also* Eudora Pro; messages
Eudora 1.3.1   2
Eudora Labels settings panel
   (Macintosh)   172
Eudora Light   3
Eudora Pro
   adding button to toolbar   149, 150
   adjusting font sizes, styles, and
     color   44–46

Eudora Pro (*continued*)
   changing
     button functions   154
     fonts for   43
     indents   48
   choosing a personality   33
   configuring for multiple accounts   10
   creating
     multiple nicknames files   139
     and replying with stationery
       messages   27–29
   deleting buttons on toolbar   153
   Eudora Labels settings panel
     (Macintosh)   172
   formatting messages   42
   getting software for   3
   ideas for buttons on toolbar   151
   justifying   47
   removing sorting from (Macintosh)   96
   special mail transfer options   71
   spell checking   39–41
   Spell Checking settings panel
     (Windows)   183
   Toolbar settings panel (Macintosh)   171
   *See also* Eudora
expanding and collapsing the Address Book
   window   137
Extra Warnings settings panel   174

## F

Fetch button   70
files
   attaching   54, 55
   attachments as text   36
   copying attachment (Macintosh)   88
   creating clippings   90
   nicknames   139
   table of contents   106
filters   111–122
   activating   117
   creating   112
   deleting   122
   examining header lines with   114
   finding (Macintosh)   119
   introducing   111
   modifying   120

filters (continued)
    reordering   121
    selecting
        actions for   116
        messages to filter   113
    setting search parameters for   115
    suggestions for using   118
Find dialog box
    for Macintosh   124
    for Windows   125
finding
    filters (Macintosh)   119
    nicknames   140
    text   123–131
        in a mailbox folder (Macintosh)   127
        in a mailbox (Macintosh)   126
        in a message   124, 125
        in message summaries   130
        in multiple mailboxes
            Macintosh   128
            Windows   129
    searching for names on a Ph server   158
    stopping a search   128, 129, 131
    tips and tricks for searching   131
    *See also* starting point
Finger servers
    searching   160
    setting up   156
fonts
    adding styles to   44
    adjusting sizes of   46
    changing   43
    changing colors of   45
Fonts & Display settings panel   146, 147, 170
formatting toolbar   48
forwarding messages   22
From line   19
function keys (Macintosh)   171

## G

Getting Attention settings panel   173
getting started   1–16
    configuring
        Eudora   7, 8, 9
        Eudora Pro for multiple accounts   10
    email glossary   14–16

getting started (continued)
    Eudora newsgroups and Web sites   13
    getting software for Eudora Light and
        Eudora Pro   3
    hardware and software requirements   2
    installing Eudora
        for Macintosh   4
        for Windows   5
    launching and quitting Eudora   6
    online help   12
    RAM requirements (Macintosh)   11
Getting Started settings panel   7, 164
glossary   14–16
glossary feature   136
Group Subjects (Macintosh)   95
Guess Paragraphs checkbox   90

## H

hanging indents   48
hard returns   37
headers
    examining with filters   114
    for forwarded messages   22
    including when saving messages   90
    options for retrieving   71
    revealing   81
help
    online   12
    for settings and options   163
    Web sites for   13
Hosts settings panel   166

## I

Include Headers checkbox   90
indents   48
installer
    for Macintosh   4
    for Windows   5
ISPs (Internet Service Providers), preventing
    disconnects from   67

## K

Keep Copies button   58

# Index

keyboard shortcuts
   for glossary feature   136
   for Mail Transfer Options dialog box   71
   for selecting messages   74
   for sending queued messages   62
   *See pull-out keyboard shortcuts page*

## L

Labels settings panel (Windows)   172
launching Eudora   6
Leave mail on server checkbox   69
leaving messages on the server   69

## M

Macintosh
   adding button to toolbar   149
   aliased mailboxes and mailbox folders   107
   changing button functions   154
   checking messages for PowerBook users   67
   configuring Eudora for two people   8
   copying attachment files   88
   creating
      aliases for users   6, 8
      clippings files   90
   encoding formats for   56
   finding
      information in Address Book   140
      text in mailbox folders   127
      text in multiple mailboxes   128
   Getting Started settings panel   164
   hardware and software requirements for   2
   installing Eudora for   4
   launching Eudora from   6
   message plug-ins for   38
   modifying filters   120
   Moving Around settings panel   177
   Nuke   85
   Personal Information settings panel   165
   RAM requirements for   11
   removing sorting from Eudora Pro   96
   replying to part of a message   20
   resetting the starting point   131
   searching for names on a Ph server   158

Macintosh (*continued*)
   selecting color for text   170
   setting toolbar options in   170, 171
   Settings Icons settings panel   179
   spell checking   39, 41
   switching back to previous Ph server   157
   toggling balloon help on and off   12
   unwrapping quoted text   37
Macintosh Info button   58
Mail Transfer Options dialog box   71
Mailbox Columns settings panel   180
mailbox folders
   creating
      in Mailboxes window   101
      from menus   100
   deleting   105
   finding text in (Macintosh)   127
   opening and closing   102
   renaming   103
   reorganizing   104
Mailbox menu   97
mailboxes   93–109
   aliases (Macintosh)   107
   archiving messages   108
   compacting   106
   creating   97
      buttons to open   149, 150
      during a message transfer   99
      mailbox folders   100, 101
   deleting   105
   finding text in (Macintosh)   126
   opening   94
   renaming   103
   reorganizing   104
   searching for text in multiple
      Macintosh   128, 131
      Windows   129
   sorting messages in   95, 96
   transferring messages into   98
   Trash   109
   *See also* mailbox folders
Make Address Book Entry   134, 135
Make Address Book Entry dialog box (Windows)   134
Make it a folder checkbox   100, 101
"me" nickname   136
message labels   77

# Index

Message Options dialog box   33
message plug-ins   38
message priorities   77
messages   17–71
  about
    attachments   53
    message plug-ins   38
  adding nicknames to   138
  archiving   108
  changing
    incoming message text   80
    message labels   77
    message personality   79
    message priority   76
    message status   78
  choosing a personality   33
  creating   17–19
  deleting
    attachments   89, 167
    messages   85
  finding text in
    Macintosh   124
    Windows   125
  forwarding   22
  indicators for unread   94
  moving attachments   88
  navigating
    between   83
    within   82
  opening
    attachments   87
    messages   75
  printing   91
  redirecting   23
  replying
    to messages   19–21
    with stationery messages   27–29
  resending   24
  revealing headers   81
  saving messages   90
  selecting   74
  sending and receiving   61–71
    checking for incoming messages   66, 67
    deleting on the POP server   69
    at later date or time   64
    leaving messages on the server   68, 69
    messages left on the POP server   68

messages, sending and receiving (continued)
    preventing messages from being sent   65
    retrieving and deleting messages by size   70
    sending messages immediately   53, 63
    sending messages later   64
    sending queued messages   62
    special mail transfer options   71
  sorting in mailboxes   95
  transferring to mailboxes   86, 98
  using the recipient list   25
  using Turbo Redirect   26
  visiting URLs from   84
  writing
    addressing   32
    adjusting font colors, sizes, and styles   44–46
    attaching files   54, 55
    changing fonts for   43
    changing indents   48
    changing justification of   47
    editing text   37
    encrypting with PGP plug-in   60
    entering a subject   34
    entering text   36
    formatting text for   42
    outgoing message toolbar buttons   58
    outgoing message toolbar menus   57
    PureVoice plug-in   59
    selecting attachment formats   56
    spell checking   39–41
    text selection and navigation   35
    using signatures   49–52
  *See also* attachments; queued messages; quoted messages
messages summaries   130
MIME encoding format   56
Miscellaneous settings panel   178
modifying
  filters   120
  nicknames   141
mouse   35
moving
  attachments   88
  buttons on toolbars   152
  nicknames between files   139

Moving Around settings panel
    (Macintosh)   177
multiple accounts
    configuring Eudora for   10
    sending mail to   18
multiple nicknames files   139

## N

navigating
    between messages   83
    through text   35
    within messages   82
New Mailbox dialog box   97, 99
New Message   18
New Nickname dialog box
    (Macintosh)   134, 135
newsgroups and Web sites   13
nickname list   137
nicknames
    adding
        to messages   138
        to recipient list   142
    conflicts with   141
    creating
        from a Ph search   159
        group   135
        for individuals   134
    deleting   142, 143
    dragging to address lines   32
    finding   140
    modifying   141
    tips for creating and using   136
nicknames files   139
Nicknames Folder   139
Nuke (Macintosh)   85

## O

online resources
    help   12
    Web directories   161
Open mailbox checkbox   94
Open Next Message button (Windows)   83
Open Previous Message button
    (Windows)   83

opening
    attachments   87
    mailbox folders   102
    mailboxes   94
    messages   75
Options dialog box (Windows). *See*
    Settings/Options dialog box
OT/PPP and MacSLIP/Advanced Network
    settings panels   176
Out mailbox   26
outgoing message toolbar menus   57

## P

Paste As Quotation   36
Personal Information settings panel   165
personalities
    choosing   33
    selecting   71
    sending mail to   18
    setting up in Macintosh   10
Personalities settings panel   10, 182
Personality Extras settings panel   182
PGP (Pretty Good Privacy) plug-in   60
Ph servers
    searching for names on   158
    selecting   157
    setting up and choosing   156
    using search results from   159
plug-ins
    message   38
    PGP   60
    PureVoice   59
POP account
    in Checking Mail settings panel   167
    entering   7
    in Getting Started settings panel   164
    in Hosts settings panel   166
    in Personal Information settings
        panel   165
POP server
    leaving or retrieving mail on   69
    messages left on   68
preventing
    disconnects from ISPs   67
    messages from being sent   65
Print dialog box   91

# Index

printing messages   91
Priority menu   57
Progress dialog box
   retrieving messages from SMTP server and   62
   sending queued messages and   62
   stopping a search in the   129
purchasing Eudora Pro   3
PureVoice plug-in   59

## Q

Qualcomm Web site   12
question mark button (Windows)   163
queued messages
   changing queueing for postponed messages   64
   preventing messages from being sent   65
   sending   62, 63
   warnings for   174
quitting Eudora   6
quoted messages
   in forwarded mail   22
   pasting in text   36
   replying with selections of (Macintosh)   20
Quoted-Printable button   58

## R

RAM requirements (Macintosh)   11
Real name field
   in Getting Started settings panel   164
   in Personal Information settings panel   165
receiving messages. See sending and receiving messages
recipient list
   adding nicknames to   142
   addressing messages to   25
recipients
   addressing messages to multiple   32
   replying to all   21
   using list of   25
Redirect To menu (Windows)   26
redirecting messages   23
   Turbo Redirect   26
reminders   64

removing sorting from Eudora Pro   96
renaming mailbox folders   103
reordering filters   121
reorganizing mailbox folders   104
Reply   19
Reply Quoting Selection (Macintosh)   20
Reply to All   21
replying
   to all recipients   21
   to messages   19
   to part of a message (Macintosh)   20
   setting options for   175
Replying settings panel   175
resending messages   24
retrieving messages by size   70
Return address field
   in Getting Started settings panel   164
   in Personal Information settings panel   165
   in Sending Mail settings panel   168
Return Receipt button (toolbar)   58
revealing headers   81
Right Now radio button   63
Rot13 Text plug-in (Macintosh)   38

## S

Save As   27
saving messages   18, 19, 90
Screen and Print font and size controls   170
searching text. See finding text
security   60
selecting
   actions for filters   116
   messages   74
   messages to filter   113
   words and paragraphs   35
Send Again   24
Send on check checkbox   67
Send Queued Messages   62
Sender column   130
sending and receiving messages   61–71
   checking incoming messages   66, 67
   leaving messages on the server   69
   messages left on the POP server   68
   preventing messages from being sent   65

# Index

sending and receiving messages (continued)
    retrieving and deleting messages by size  70
    sending
        messages later  64
        messages now  53, 63
        queued messages  62
    special mail transfer options  71
Sending Mail settings panel  7, 168
settings and options  163–183
    Attachments settings panel  169
    Checking Mail settings panel  167
    Eudora Labels/Labels settings panel  172
    Extra Warnings settings panel  174
    Fonts & Display settings panel  170
    Getting Attention settings panel  173
    Getting Started settings panel  164
    Hosts settings panel  166
    Mailbox Columns settings panel  180
    Miscellaneous settings panel  178
    Moving Around settings panel (Macintosh)  177
    OT/PPP and MacSLIP/Advanced Network settings panels  176
    Personal Information settings panel  165
    Personalities and Personality Extras settings panels  182
    Replying settings panel  175
    Sending Mail settings panel  168
    Settings Icons settings panel (Macintosh)  179
    Spell Checking settings panel (Windows)  183
    Styled Text settings panel  181
    Toolbar
        Macintosh  147, 171
        Windows  147, 170
Settings dialog box (Macintosh). *See* Settings/Options dialog box
Settings Icons settings panel (Macintosh)  179
Settings/Options dialog box
    checking for mail periodically  67
    Delete attachments when emptying Trash checkbox (Windows)  89, 167
    Delete from server after X days checkbox  69

Settings/Options dialog box (continued)
    Getting Started settings panel  7, 164
    Leave mail on server checkbox  69
    Open mailbox checkbox  94
    replying to all recipients  21
    Screen and Print font and size controls  170
    Send on check checkbox  67
    Show toolbar checkbox  146
    Trash attachments with messages checkbox (Macintosh)  89
    Word wrap option  168
    *See also* settings and options
shortcut keys. *See* keyboard shortcuts
shortcuts (Windows)
    creating Eudora  6
    for multiple users  9
Show toolbar checkbox  146
signatures
    about  49
    creating and using  50
    custom  51
    editing  52
    selecting  57
Signatures menu  51, 57
Skip messages over X K checkbox  70
SMTP server
    as default Finger server  156
    entering information for  7, 166, 168
    setting for Eudora Pro  10
software for Eudora Light and Eudora Pro  3
Sort  95, 96
sorting messages
    in mailboxes  95
    methods for  96
spaces
    converting to tabs  38
    in nicknames  136
spam filters  118
special mail transfer options  71
spell checking  39–41
    for Macintosh  39
    options for  41
    toolbar button for  148
    for Windows  40
Spell Checking settings panel (Windows)  183

starting point
  with multiple mailboxes (Macintosh)   128
  resetting before retrying searches (Macintosh)   131
  setting for searches (Macintosh)   126
stationery messages   27–29
styled text   174
Styled Text settings panel   181
Subject line
  creating messages and   18
  entering a   34
  replying to messages and   19
Summaries only checkbox   130
switching between messages   83

## T

table of contents files   106
tabs
  converting to spaces   38
  options for in body of message   58, 168
Tabs in Body button   58
text
  editing   37
  entering   36
  formatting   42
  justifying   47
  pasting quotations in   36
  removing styled   174
  selecting and navigating through   35
  selecting color for (Macintosh)   170
  tips and tricks for finding   131
  wrapping and unwrapping   37
  *See also* finding text; fonts
Text as Attachment button   58
text files   36
To line
  creating messages and   18
  replying to messages and   19
toolbar   145–154
  buttons
    adding   149, 150
    changing functions for   154
    default   148
    deleting   153
    ideas for   151

toolbar, buttons (*continued*)
    moving   152
    introducing the   145
  menus for outgoing message   57
  settings   147
    for Macintosh   170, 171
    for Windows   170
  turning on and off   146
Toolbar Button Creation dialog box   149, 153
Toolbar settings panel (Macintosh)   146, 147, 171
Transfer menu   98
transferring messages to mailboxes   86, 98
Trash attachments with messages checkbox (Macintosh)   89
Trash mailbox   109
Turbo Redirect   26
Turbo Redirect To menu (Macintosh)   26
turning toolbar on and off   146

## U

unread message indicator   94
Unwrap Selection   37
URLs
  in messages   84
  selecting Ph server   157
using filters   118
Uuencode encoding format   56

## V

VCR buttons (Macintosh)   126, 131
voice messages   59

## W

warnings   174
Web sites
  downloading Eudora from   3
  for Eudora help   13
  online directories   161
  Qualcomm   12
Whole word checkbox (Macintosh)   119

# Index

Windows
    adding button to toolbar   150
    changing preferences for spell
        checking   41
    choosing stationery for messages in   28
    compacting mailboxes   106
    configuring Eudora for two people   9
    creating
        mailbox without transferring
            messages   100
        pane interface   83
    deleting attachments   89, 167
    encoding formats for   56
    Getting Started settings panel   164
    hardware and software requirements for   2
    installing Eudora for   5
    launching Eudora from   6
    message plug-ins for   38
    moving attachments for   88
    Personal Info settings panel   165
    reorganizing mailboxes and mailbox
        folders   104
    searching for text in multiple
        mailboxes   129
    selecting previously used Ph servers
        from   157
    setting toolbar options in   170
    spell checking   40

Word Services window (Macintosh)   39
Word Wrap button   58
Word wrap option   168
Wrap Selection   37
wrapping and unwrapping text   37, 38
writing messages   31–60
    addressing   32
    adjusting font colors, sizes, and
        styles   44–46
    attaching files   54, 55
    buttons for outgoing message toolbar   58
    changing
        fonts for   43
        indents   48
        justification of   47
    editing text   37
    encrypting with PGP plug-in   60
    entering
        a subject   34
        text   36
    formatting text for   42
    menus for outgoing message toolbar   57
    PureVoice plug-in   59
    selecting attachment formats   56
    spell checking   39–41
    text selection and navigation   35
    using signatures   49–52

# Mac keyboard shortcuts

Eudora has numerous keyboard shortcuts, listed below. However, you access many other less common functions by holding down Option or Shift and choosing a menu item or clicking a button. Choose Shortcuts from the Guide menu to see a list of them. Shortcuts unique to Eudora Pro are shaded.

## Macintosh standard shortcuts

|  |  |
|---|---|
| Cmd-. | Stop current action |
| Cmd-O | Open |
| Cmd-P | Print |
| Cmd-Shift-P | Print Selection |
| Cmd-Q | Quit |
| Cmd-S | Save |
| Cmd-Option-S | Save All |
| Cmd-W | Close |
| Cmd-Option-W | Close All |
| Cmd-Z | Undo |

## Copying and pasting shortcuts

|  |  |
|---|---|
| Cmd-A | Select All |
| Cmd-C | Copy |
| Cmd-Option-C | Copy & Unwrap |
| Cmd-Shift-C | Copy Without Styles |
| Cmd-Option-Shift-C | Copy Without Styles & Unwrap |
| Cmd-V | Paste |
| Cmd-Shift-V | Paste Without Styles |
| Cmd-' | Paste As Quotation |
| Cmd-X | Cut |

## Finding and searching shortcuts

|  |  |
|---|---|
| Cmd-F | Opens Find window |
| Cmd-G | Find Again |
| Cmd-= | Enter Selection (in Find window) |
| Cmd-; | Search Again |

## Text formatting shortcuts

|  |  |
|---|---|
| Cmd-B | Make selected text bold |
| Cmd-I | Make selected text italic |
| Cmd-T | Make selected text plain |
| Cmd-U | Make selected text underlined |

## Message shortcuts

|  |  |
|---|---|
| Cmd-D | Delete |
| Cmd-E | Send or Queue current message |
| Cmd-Option-E | Change Queueing |
| Cmd-N | New Message |
| Cmd-R | Reply |
| Cmd-Shift-R | Reply Quoting Selection |

## Sending and receiving shortcuts

|  |  |
|---|---|
| Cmd-- | Send Queued Messages |
| Cmd-Option-- | Send Messages Specially |
| Cmd-M | Check Mail |
| Cmd-Option-M | Check Mail Specially |

## Mailbox shortcuts

|  |  |
|---|---|
| Cmd-0 | Open the Out mailbox |
| Cmd-1 | Open the In mailbox |

## Address Book shortcuts

|  |  |
|---|---|
| Cmd-, | Finish Address Book Entry |
| Cmd-Option-, | Finish & Expand Address Book Entry |
| Cmd-K | Make Address Book Entry |
| Cmd-Shift-K | Make Address Book Entry from selection |
| Cmd-L | Open Address Book window |

## Miscellaneous shortcuts

|  |  |
|---|---|
| Cmd-6 | Check Spelling |
| Cmd-\ | Send to Back (a window) |
| Cmd-H | Attach Document |
| Cmd-J | Filter Messages |
| Cmd-Y | Open Directory Services window |

# Keyboard Shortcuts

## Windows keyboard shortcuts

Eudora has numerous keyboard shortcuts, listed below. However, you access many other less common functions by holding down Shift and choosing a menu item or clicking a button. For more information, choose Topics from the Help menu, then double-click Modifiers or Shortcuts in the Reference section. Shortcuts unique to Eudora Pro are shaded.

### Windows standard shortcuts

| | |
|---|---|
| Ctrl-O | Open Text File |
| Ctrl-P | Print |
| Ctrl-Q | Quit |
| Ctrl-S | Save |
| Ctrl-Shift-S | Save All |
| Ctrl-W | Close |
| Ctrl-Shift-W | Close All |
| Ctrl-Z | Undo |

### Copying and pasting shortcuts

| | |
|---|---|
| Ctrl-A | Select All |
| Ctrl-C | Copy |
| Ctrl-Shift-C | Copy & Unwrap |
| Ctrl-V | Paste |
| Ctrl-Shift-V | Paste Without Styles |
| Ctrl-' | Paste As Quotation |
| Ctrl-Shift-' | Paste As Quotation Without Styles |
| Ctrl-X | Cut |

### Sending and receiving shortcuts

| | |
|---|---|
| Ctrl-M | Check Mail |
| Ctrl-Shift-M | Check Mail Specially |
| Ctrl-T | Send Queued Messages |
| Ctrl-Shift-T | Send Messages Specially |

### Mailbox shortcuts

| | |
|---|---|
| Ctrl-0 | Open the Out mailbox |
| Ctrl-1 | Open the In mailbox |

### Finding shortcuts

| | |
|---|---|
| Ctrl-F | Opens Find window |
| F3 / Ctrl-G | Find Again |
| Alt-F3 / Ctrl-= | Enter Selection (in Find window) |
| Ctrl-; | Find Next Message |

### Message shortcuts

| | |
|---|---|
| Ctrl-D | Delete |
| Ctrl-E | Send or Queue current message |
| Ctrl-Shift-E | Change Queueing |
| Ctrl-N | New Message |
| Ctrl-Shift-N | Message Options for new messages |
| Ctrl-R | Reply |
| Ctrl-Shift-R | Message Options for replies |

### Text formatting shortcuts

| | |
|---|---|
| Ctrl-B | Make selected text bold |
| Ctrl-I | Make selected text italic |
| Ctrl-U | Make selected text underlined |

### Window management shortcuts

| | |
|---|---|
| Shift-F4 | Tile Horizontal |
| Shift-F5 | Cascade |
| Ctrl-F6 | Send to Back |

### Address Book shortcuts

| | |
|---|---|
| Ctrl-, | Finish Address Book Entry |
| Ctrl-Shift-, | Finish & Expand Address Book Entry |
| Ctrl-K | Make Address Book Entry |
| Ctrl-L | Open Address Book window |

### Miscellaneous shortcuts

| | |
|---|---|
| Ctrl-6 | Check Spelling |
| Ctrl-H | Attach Document |
| Ctrl-J | Filter Messages |
| Ctrl-Y | Open Directory Services window |

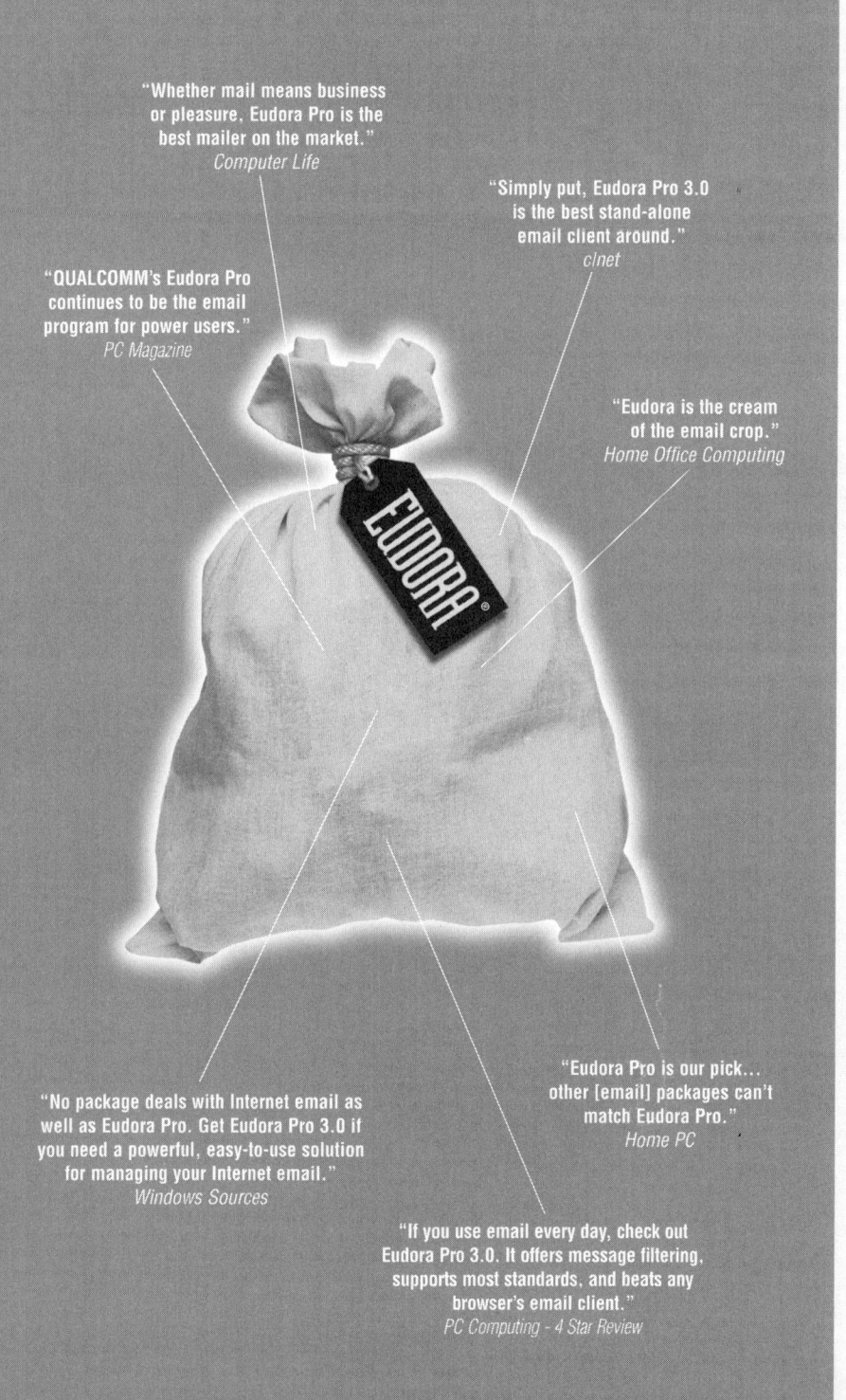

# The email that gets fan mail.

Critics and fans rarely agree. And when critics start acting like fans, it's time to take notice. The top technology critics are echoing the praises of Eudora Pro's 18 million dedicated users.

## $10 Discount
off the MSRP directly from QUALCOMM Inc.

Now readers of this book can become Eudora fans, too. We're offering Eudora Pro version 3.0 for $10.00 off of the MSRP. To receive this discount mail this page to **Eudora Sales – Peachpit, 6455 Lusk Blvd., San Diego, CA 92121-2779** with your Visa/Mastercard number and expiration date. Include your ship to address, phone number and email address. If you wish to pay by check, please call 1-800-2-EUDORA for tax and shipping costs.

"Whether mail means business or pleasure, Eudora Pro is the best mailer on the market."
*Computer Life*

"Simply put, Eudora Pro 3.0 is the best stand-alone email client around."
*cInet*

"QUALCOMM's Eudora Pro continues to be the email program for power users."
*PC Magazine*

"Eudora is the cream of the email crop."
*Home Office Computing*

"No package deals with Internet email as well as Eudora Pro. Get Eudora Pro 3.0 if you need a powerful, easy-to-use solution for managing your Internet email."
*Windows Sources*

"Eudora Pro is our pick... other [email] packages can't match Eudora Pro."
*Home PC*

"If you use email every day, check out Eudora Pro 3.0. It offers message filtering, supports most standards, and beats any browser's email client."
*PC Computing - 4 Star Review*

**QUALCOMM**

**EUDORA**